IMAGES
of America

ALLENTOWN FAIRGROUNDS

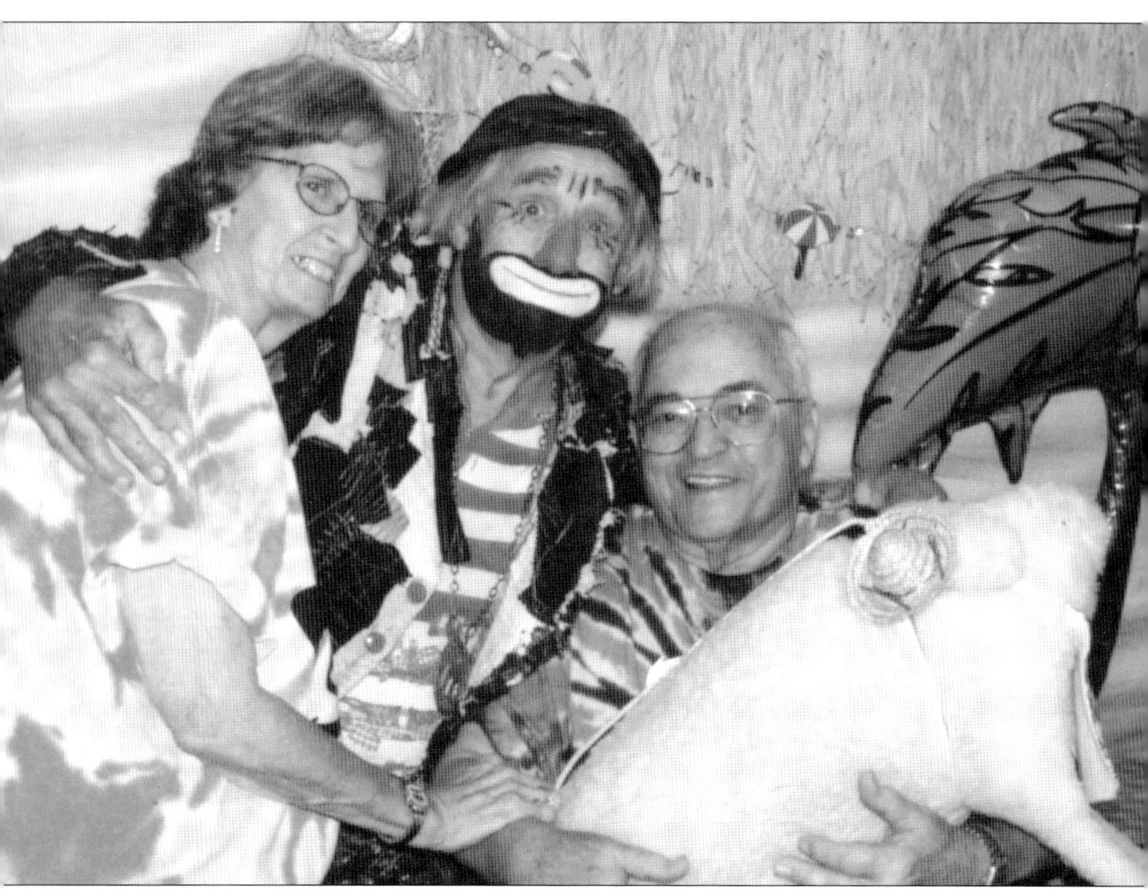

For nearly 40 years, Dapper Dan the clown strolled the midway, generating laughs from visitors of all ages. With his rubber chicken, Cosmos, and his "pet" pig on wheels named Porkchop, Dan poses here with Harriet and Donald Hawk. The Hawks worked at their family's concession stand, Danner's. (Courtesy of the Danner family.)

On the Cover: This is the last harness race ever held at the fairgrounds on July 4, 1976, for America's bicentennial celebration. Harness racing began in 1853 at the previous fairgrounds, making it a priority to build the half-mile track at the new fairgrounds when the land was purchased in 1889. (Courtesy of Lehigh County Agricultural Society.)

IMAGES
of America

Allentown Fairgrounds

Kelly Ann Butterbaugh

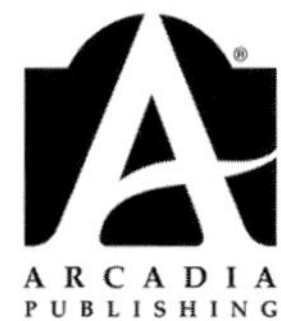
ARCADIA
PUBLISHING

ISBN 978-1-4671-6257-9

Published by Arcadia Publishing
Charleston, South Carolina

Printed in the United States of America

Library of Congress Control Number: 2025930308

For all general information, please contact Arcadia Publishing:
Telephone 843-853-2070
Fax 843-853-0044
E-mail sales@arcadiapublishing.com

Visit us on the Internet at www.arcadiapublishing.com

As always, to my husband and to my son. You are my everything.

Contents

ACKNOWLEDGMENTS

Without the work of the Lehigh County Agricultural Society (LCAS), there would be no fair and, ultimately, no book about the fair. The society's work over the last 173 years is the reason we have the Great Allentown Fair and the generations of memories that it has created. Thanks to everyone who keeps the fair running year after year, and thanks to everyone who preserved the memories of it in boxes of photographs in their attics and in the fair office. Unless otherwise noted, all images appearing in this book were provided by the LCAS.

Thank you to the LCAS for asking me to write this book and for all the photographs and information shared with me. Thank you also to all of the people who donated their time, photographs, and knowledge to this book: David Bausch, Bonnie Brosious, Robert Burns, Jessica Ciecwisz, Beverly Gruber, Brad Greenawalt, Gary Iacocca, Doris Koenig, Karl Mohr, Michelle Ritter, Sterling Ritter, Mark Sorrentino, Cheryl Urmy, Kelly Weisner, and Brian Wetzel. A special thank you goes to Daryl Urmy for his idea to write this book and for all of his help tracking down photographs and information along the way.

A special thank you goes to my husband, Robert, and my son, Christopher, for their love and help during this and every one of my projects. Thanks for encouraging me to do what I love. Never did I imagine that when I was a child petting cows and entering my handicrafts at the Allentown Fair, I would be honored with the opportunity to write a book about it.

A final thank you to my editors at Arcadia, Caroline Vickerson and Erin Vosgien, for their assistance with photograph selection and answering the most random of questions along the way.

INTRODUCTION

"Let's go to the fair!" Just the mention of a fair invokes a sense of nostalgia mixed with excitement. Our minds begin to unlock memories of prizes won on the midway, ice cream dripping on our hands, and blue rosette ribbons on homemade pies. Thoughts of Ferris wheels, concerts, and cotton candy excite our senses. This is what a fair means to generations of people in towns all across America, and these are the memories that the Great Allentown Fair has created for generations of people since 1852.

A glance at the executive board list of today's Lehigh County Agricultural Society shows names that have been there long before, reflecting children who followed in their parents' footsteps by taking similar executive positions. Other names there started as 4-H competitors at the fair and now organize those very competitions. Former marketing director for the Allentown Fair Bonnie Brosious is one of those names; her father, Edward Charles, was the fair's board chairman. When Brosious, who worked for the fair for 37 years, describes the Great Allentown Fair, she compares it to a person's entire life. People who grew up going to the Allentown Fair first saw it from a stroller, and their first encounter was with the farm animals. Then, they graduated to the midway, Brosious describes. For many, the shows at the grandstand were the next step as they got older. Up until 1985, when it was converted to a nightclub, locals saw it as a rite of passage to enjoy a trip to the Bier Garten behind the Fairgrounds Hotel. Then, before they know it, they are the ones pushing the strollers through the animal pens at the fair. Indeed, this is how many who spent their lives at the fair remember it.

Even the fair "grew up" over the years. From its beginnings as the Lehigh County Agricultural Fair on rented land, the fair moved to its permanent home in 1853, where it became the Allentown Fair. It continued its growth and eventually moved on to today's larger property in 1889, when it was renamed the Great Allentown Fair. This new home, the Allentown Fairgrounds, became as important as the yearly event it hosts. The grandstand and Agri-Plex host events throughout the year, from concerts to trade shows, and two banks lease lots on the fairgrounds. The Allentown Farmer's Market opens weekly aside of the grandstand, and the original Fairgrounds Hotel still welcomes guests for a seafood dinner.

Since 1853, the fairgrounds have always been there to support the community that surrounds it. The original fairgrounds was used much like today's fairgrounds, hosting community celebrations and gatherings. When conflicts arose, both the old and new fairgrounds were donated to military use. The old fairgrounds was used by the military in 1862 when the Civil War cast a pall over the country. The fair was suspended that year, and seven companies of the 176th Pennsylvania Militia occupied the fairgrounds. The militia was then transferred to the Allentown train station, where it was shipped out for deployment. At the present fairgrounds, the need for military occupation arose again during World War I. From May 28, 1917, until April 10, 1919, the fairgrounds were occupied by the US Army Ambulance Corps and used as a medical training ground, cancelling both the 1917 and 1918 fairs. These disruptions, the only ones that ever canceled the fair, were only temporary as the fairgrounds were returned to their original condition and the fall fair returned as if it had never been missed.

As the Great Allentown Fair prepares to celebrate its 175th anniversary in 2027, it carries on with its traditions and accepts the need to change. While the early years of the fair were almost entirely agrarian, like the town around it, the fair shifted to include nonagricultural traditions as the community moved away from agriculture. There are still pens of farm animals at the fair, but the numbers are nowhere near the 1912 fair, when 462 heads of cattle were entered and housed at the neighboring Griesemer farm. So many sheep were entered that year that five men housed their herd in train cars on a siding at Liberty Street. By 1919, the largest number of birds was entered in the fair, requiring both poultry barns to house the 4,000 poultry birds and 1,200 pigeons exhibited. In 1920, horses were the prime draw to the fair, whether competing on the track or in the judging ring. But two decades later, automobiles lined the streets instead of horses with carriages, and the horse barns at the fair grew less and less crowded. The interest in harness racing, the main draw to the racetrack since the earliest days of the fair, started to wane in the 1950s when automobile racing took over the dirt track. Just when it seemed like automobile racing would take the title of king of the track, that too ended in 1968. Like the interests of the visitors, the fair has changed over the years.

Yet the Great Allentown Fair has been a constant for generations who have lived in and near Lehigh County. Talk to someone about the fair, and the same memories are shared: the antics of Candy Candido, the fair's goodwill ambassador and Disney voice actor; the crashes and wrecks of the annual demolition derby; and the taste of a cheesesteak and French fries with vinegar at the concessions stands. Ask if they have a favorite part of the fair and you will hear about Dapper Dan the clown who performed at the fair until he was 90 years old, or you will hear about the bingo games that found a way to operate around the gambling laws in Pennsylvania that threatened to close them down each year.

So loved is the fair that, as early as 1901, a day of the fair was designated as Children's Day. In 1906, teachers in Allentown were encouraged to bring their classes to the fair on the special day. On this special day in later years, schools closed so children could attend the fair in the afternoons. In 1916, children under 17 were not allowed in the fair due to the polio epidemic. This ban was put in place again in 1941, but this time, the ban caused quite an uproar. Signs posted read, "We miss the children at the Fair but we want to protect them from Polio." Allentown High School students went on strike as a result. Meanwhile, many youths tried to gain entrance to the fair by hiding in hay wagons and climbing the fences to get in. Extra guards were on duty to prevent their access.

There is indeed something special about the Great Allentown Fair. Maybe it is the blend of agriculture and thrill rides. Maybe it is the mix of talent shows and Grammy winners at the theaters. Maybe it is the criteria that placed the Great Allentown Fair on the nation's Top 50 Fairs list several times in its history. Whatever it is, it cemented the Allentown Fairgrounds into the community and the history of the county around it. More importantly, the Allentown Fairgrounds has found its way into people's memories of attending the fair just as their parents and grandparents had before them.

One

The Allentown Fairgrounds

When the newly formed Lehigh County Agricultural Society hosted its first fair in 1852, it was hosted on a five-acre plot of land in Allentown, east of Fourth Street between Union Street and Walnut Street. The success of that fair led the society to purchase 11 acres north of Liberty Street between Fifth and Sixth Streets for $3,085 in 1853. The grounds were not only used during fair week but also for year-round events such as political rallies, Independence Day celebrations, and other community activities. In 1882, an additional six acres was leased from Robert J. Yeager for $180 a year. With a small grandstand and a third-mile racetrack for harness racing, the fair ran there successfully for 36 years until it outgrew its home.

In 1888, the fair's executive committee resolved to purchase a bigger lot; the fair had grown to be "too great for its own good." The society sold its current lot and on April 4, 1889, for $19,310 purchased 37 acres from Solomon Griesemer, S.D. Lehr, and Catharine Newhart for the new fairgrounds. Structures from the old fairgrounds were moved to the new tract, and the old tract was divided into plots and sold. The priority at the new fairgrounds was to build the half-mile racetrack and grandstand. By 1897, the fair needed even more room on the west end for its agricultural equipment displays and livestock barns, so it purchased 14 more acres.

Buildings were added and razed over the years. Additional animal barns and exhibition halls were constructed in the early 1900s. The grandstand was replaced in 1911 with a larger structure. Fire destroyed five buildings: the western horse stables on September 21, 1900; the main exhibition hall on June 20, 1918; the Industrial Hall used as a farmers market on August 18, 1956; the Rural Youth Building on May 5, 1974; and the Ritz restaurant on June 14, 1998. Then, in 1956, plans were laid out to replace nearly all of the original buildings with more modern, fireproof structures. Only the poultry building, the grandstand, and the Ritz avoided demolition.

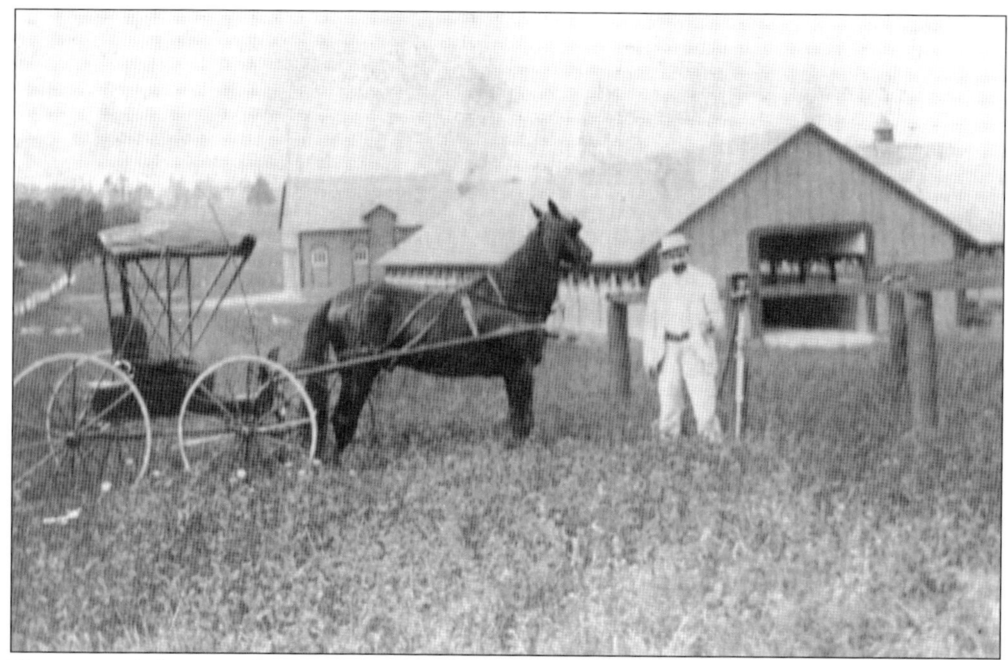

The original fairgrounds, known as the "old fairgrounds," hosted the fair from 1853 until 1888. These cattle buildings housed the animals brought for competition and stood along with Mechanics Hall, Floral Hall, a large exhibition hall, and other livestock shelters. When the new property was purchased, most of the structures at the fairgrounds were disassembled and rebuilt on the new property, including these barns.

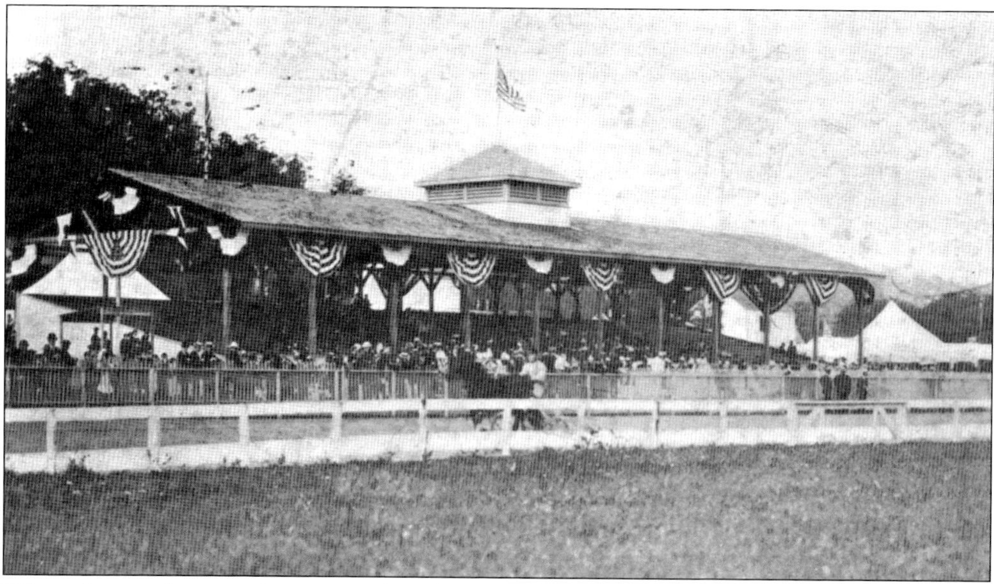

When the new fairgrounds were purchased in 1889, the priority was to erect a dirt racetrack and grandstand. This new grandstand could hold 2,500 spectators as they lined the fence to catch a close glimpse of the harness racing action. At times, the trees lining the track also served as viewing platforms for the dedicated fans. (Courtesy of David Bausch.)

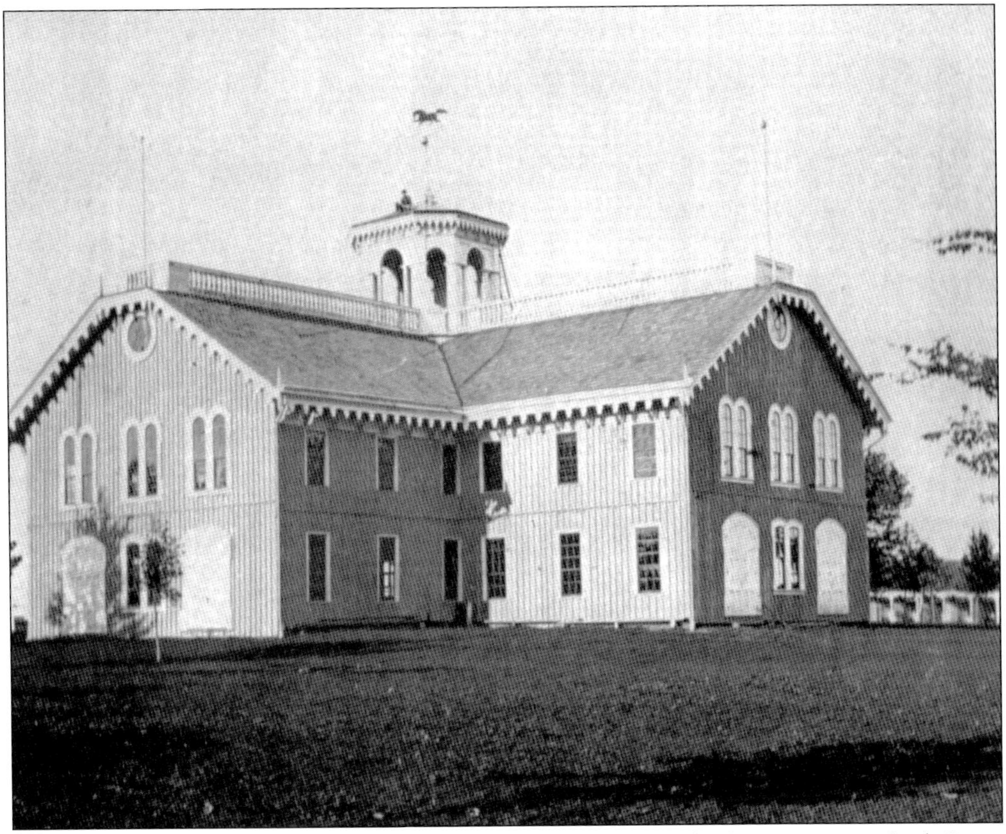

The main exhibition hall of the original fairgrounds was built at the fair entrance at Sixth Street and Liberty Street in 1853. Two side wings were added later to allow for more exhibition space, creating the cross-shaped building seen here. When LCAS moved to the new fairgrounds, this building was left behind. (Photograph by M.A. Kleckner; courtesy of LCAS.)

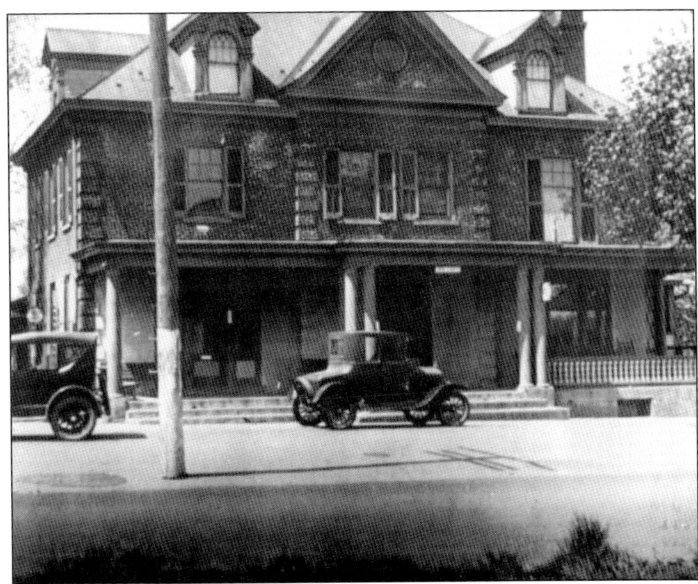

In 1889, the hotel at the corner of Seventeenth Street and Liberty Street was known as the Fairgrounds Hotel and was owned by LCAS. When this picture was taken in the 1920s, fairgoers knew the hotel more for the Bier Garten pavilions behind it and the drafts on tap during fair week. The hotel closed in 1969 and sat unused until the Germano family reopened it as a restaurant in 1982.

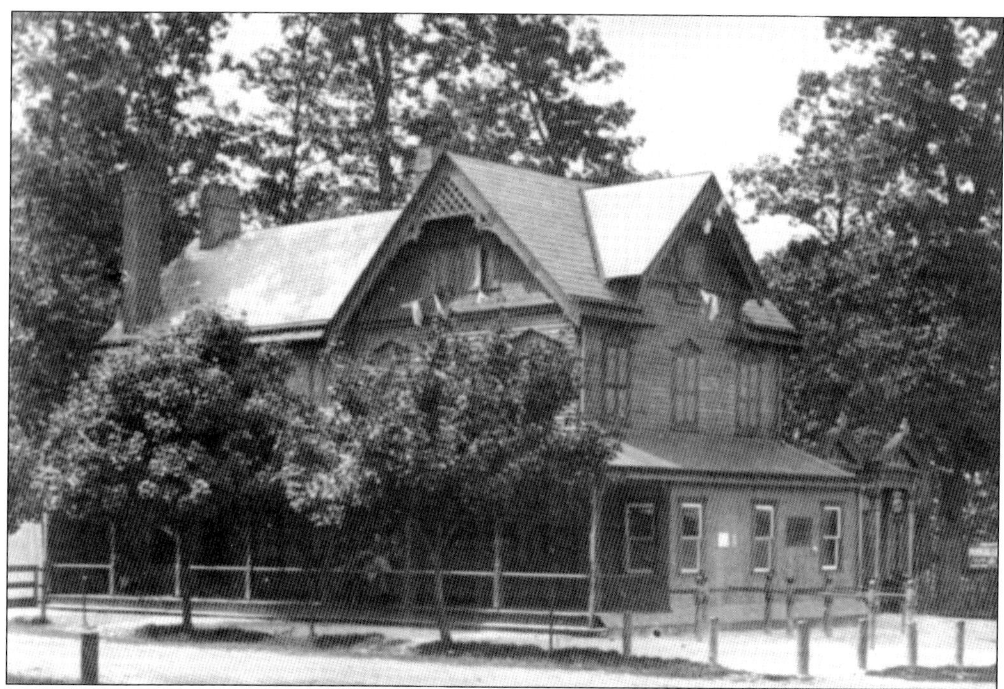

The original office for the fair officials was built on the corner of Seventeenth Street and Chew Street in 1889. The fair treasurer and clerks worked here while the grounds' overseer lived here year-round. The building was deemed an eyesore and torn down in 1952 when Allentown Hospital offered to pay for its demolition to make room for a parking lot.

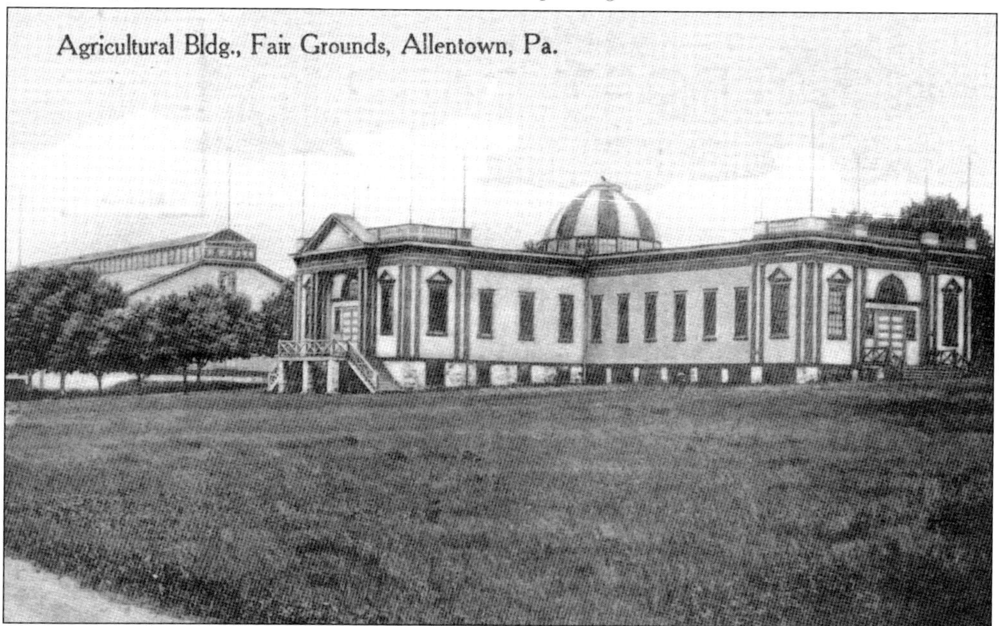

The original Horticultural Hall was a Roman cross shape with a domed center along Chew Street. Fruits and vegetables were displayed under the dome. This structure was torn down in 1957–1958 when the current Agricultural Hall was planned. One of the two poultry houses, built in 1899, can be seen in the background. (Courtesy of David Bausch.)

In 1902, the original Horticultural Hall exhibited 1,400 jellies, 1,350 jars of fruit preserves, 575 jars of dried fruit, and 413 bottles of wine. By the time this picture was taken in 1918, the preserves were replaced by the soldiers of Camp Crane. Steam-heat pipes can be seen leading to the building, so it could be used in the winter; these were added by the soldiers.

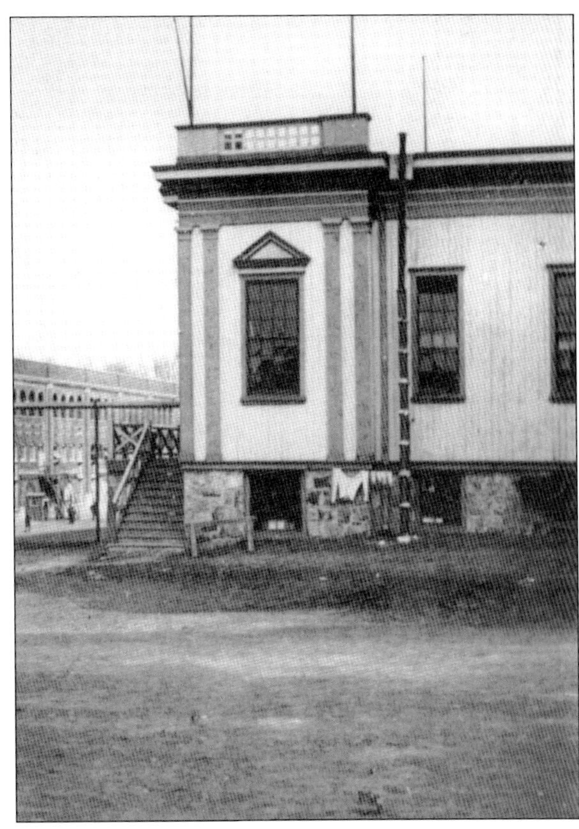

When the fair moved to its new location in 1889, these two buildings were brought from the old fairgrounds. Floral Hall, later named Horticultural Hall, is the octagonal Victorian building in front, and Mechanics Hall is in the background. During fair week, Floral Hall was filled with aromatic, flowering displays of every type. When the new Agricultural Hall was built, Floral Hall became a penny arcade before being razed in 1958.

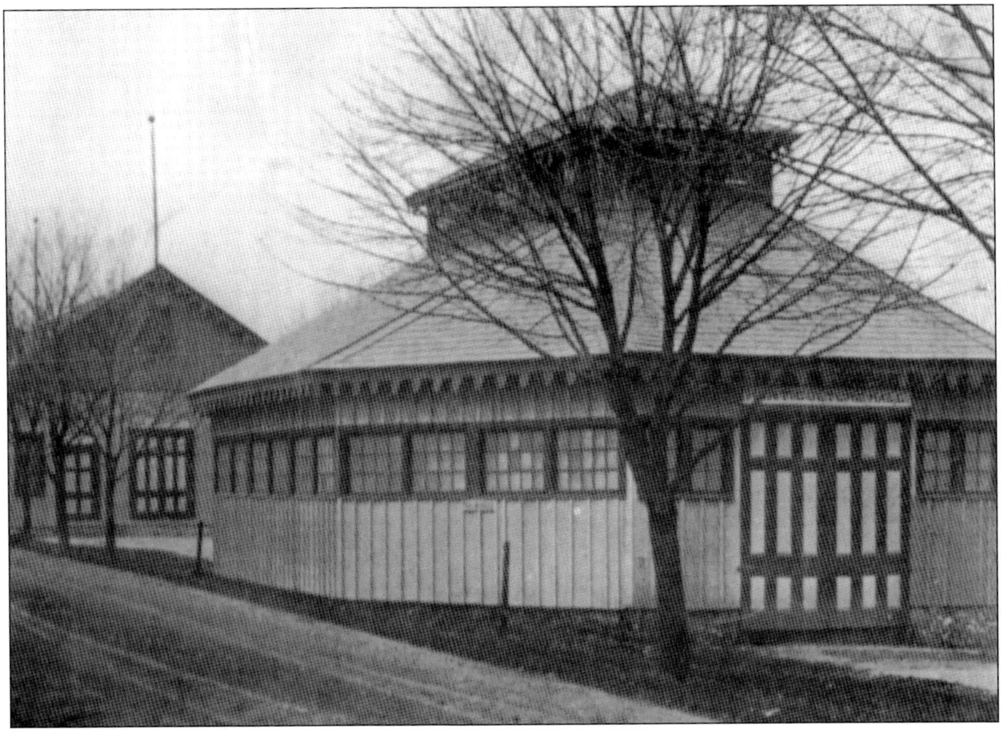

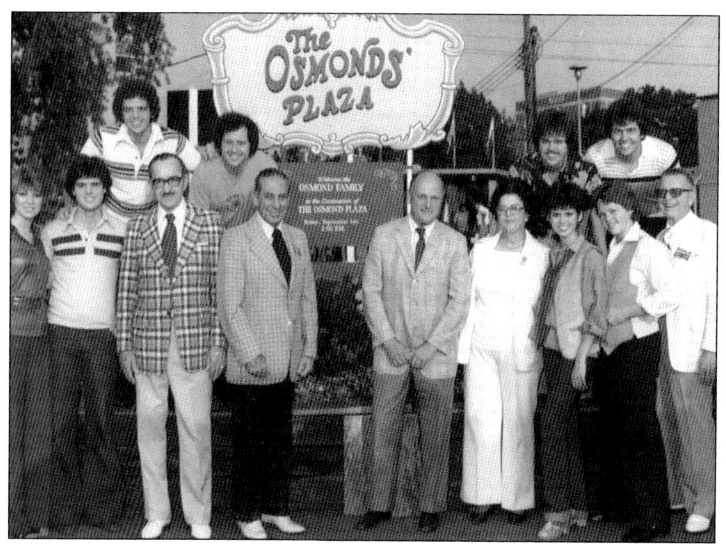

The Osmond family performed at the Allentown Fair more than any other act. In its honor, the main fairground's entrance at Seventeenth and Chew Streets was dedicated as Osmond Plaza in 1978. The family performed at the fair for a record eight years, spanning from 1963 to 1984. Seen here with some of the Osmond family on its dedication, the plaza sign was set up each year during fair week.

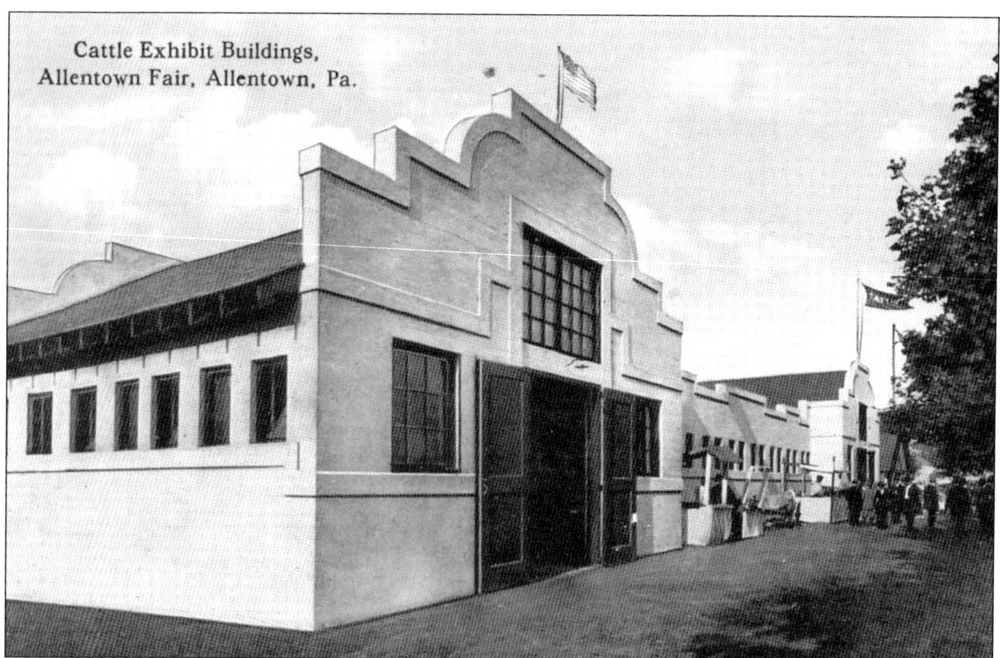

In 1909, these twin cement cattle buildings were constructed with an open-air paddock in the center. Sterling Ritter, former livestock superintendent, remembers farms each bringing 40 heads of cattle to the fair, quickly filling the barns. He also recalls two Holstein bulls that weighed 2,000 pounds each owned by Huber Miller. Miller gave each bull a beer to calm him before exhibition. (Courtesy of Kelly Ann Butterbaugh.)

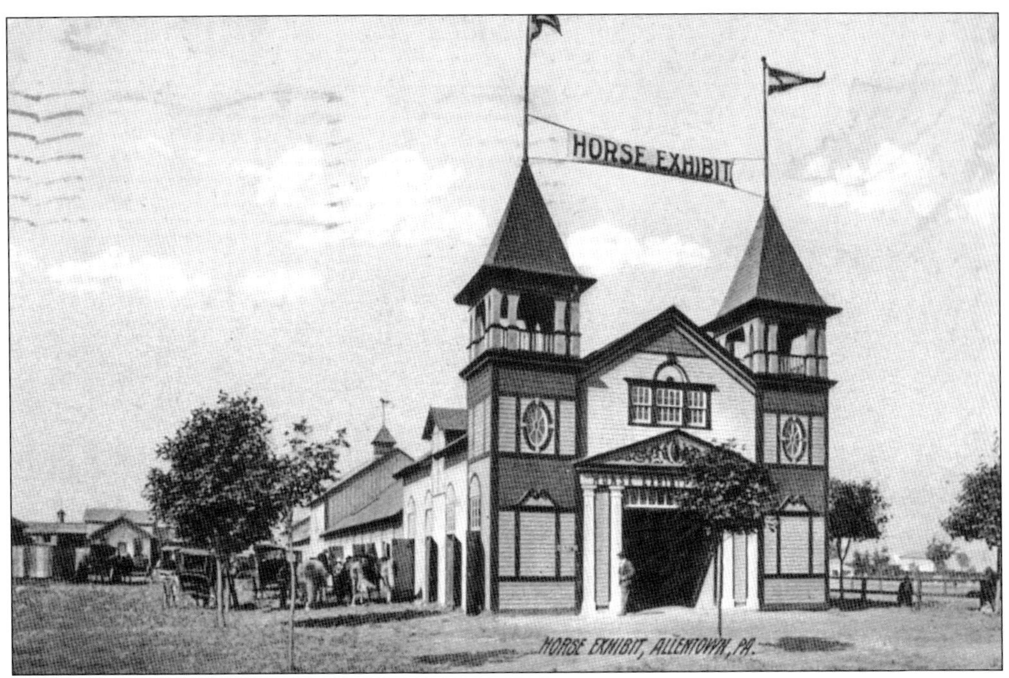

The Horse Exhibition Hall had 110 stalls; however, for the 1911 fair, 154 horses were entered. As a result, cattle sheds had to be used for the extra horses, and 50 more horses had to be turned away. In 1911, J. George Snyder of Allentown, one of the nation's most respected horse dealers and trainers, was responsible for managing the large Victorian-style hall. (Courtesy of Kelly Ann Butterbaugh.)

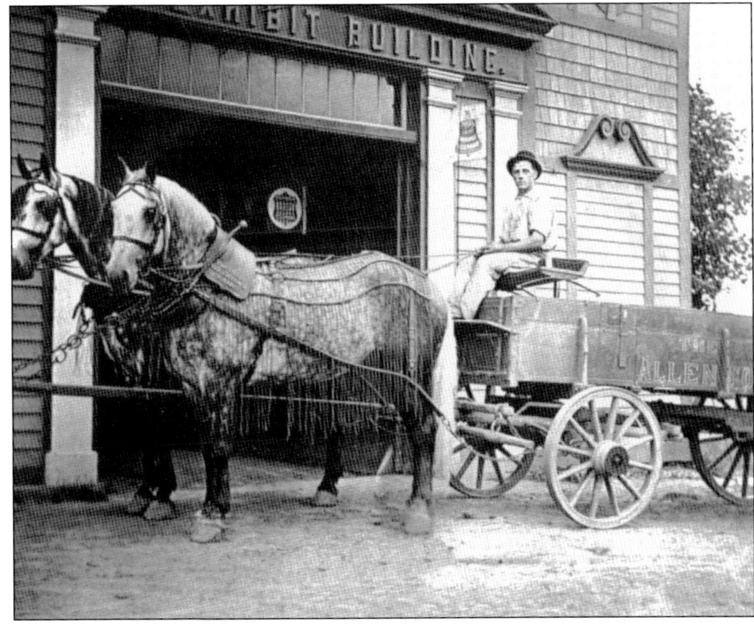

A driver and his team pose for a picture outside of the Horse Exhibition Hall around 1909. The wagon and harnesses display the name of the fair and were used for promotional purposes. Draft horses like these were entered in the fair as teams in the early 1900s. In 1912, W. John Merkle's Percherons were awarded the title of finest horse breed in an impressive year of entries.

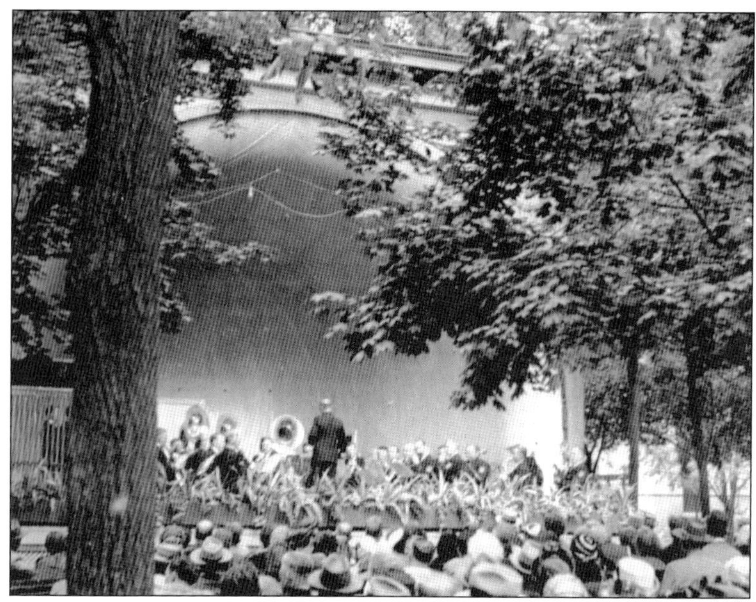

In 1892, members of the Allentown Band built a band shell at the fairgrounds in order to move away from the noises of the city. This band shell was located on the east side of the fairgrounds in the area known as "the Grove" because of its plentiful shade trees. Here also stood a fountain filled with rainbow trout that Col. Harry Trexler brought from his Cetronia dams.

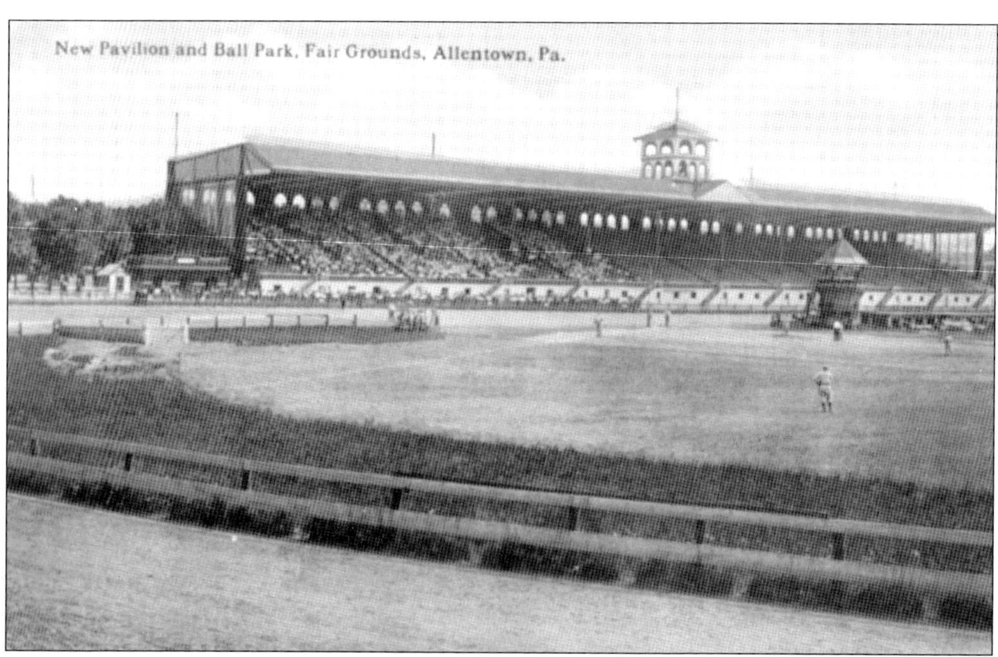

In the 1920s, a baseball diamond was constructed in the infield of the racetrack. The Philadelphia Athletics even played an exhibition game here; Ty Cobb was at center field and Eddie Collins played second base. Other local minor-league teams played at the field. Baseball was a popular pastime in Lehigh County during the first half of the 20th century, and most small towns had their own teams.

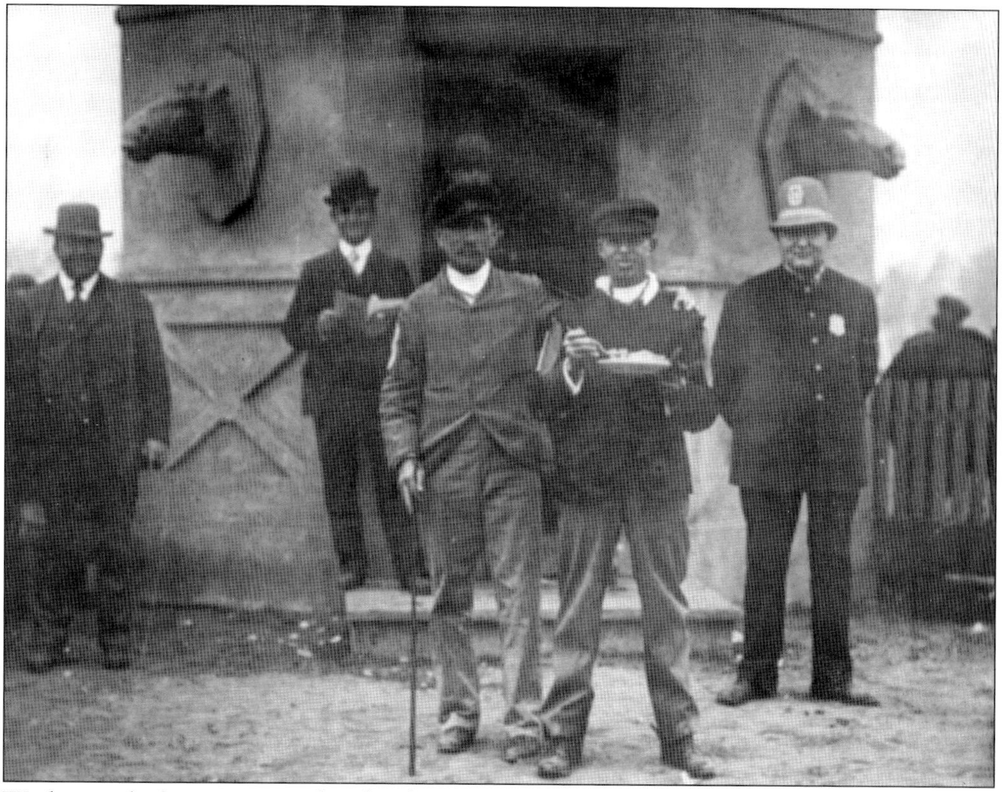

Workers at the harness races take a break to enjoy some of the fair's famous food. The Grove, just to the east of the track, was known for its many food vendors from the days of the first fair. Hot dogs were a most sought-after fare, as was the cotton candy craze of the 1920s. Oysters and oyster stew were popular choices, as were popped corn and candied apples.

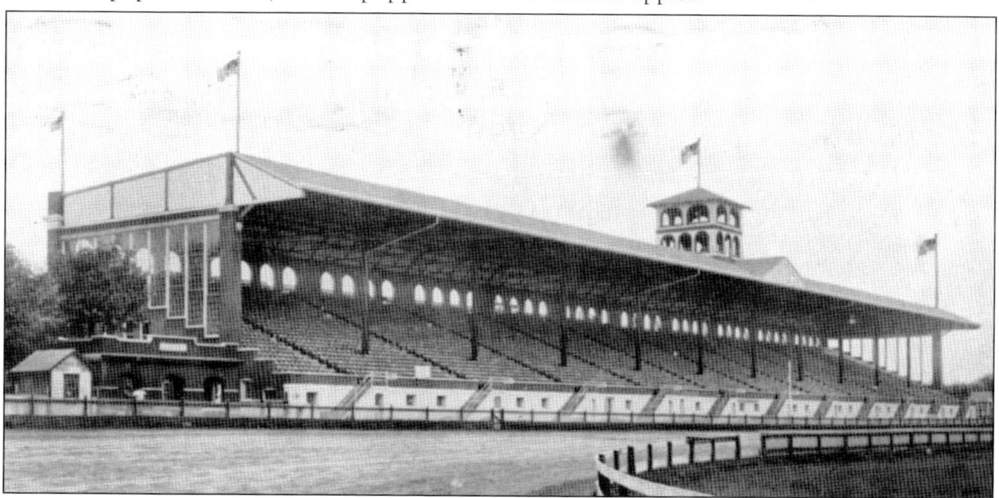

The current grandstand was built in 1911 to replace the original that had been constructed in 1889. With a total cost of $100,000, the new structure held 7,070 visitors. Designed by Robert S. Rathbun, built by Ochs Construction of Allentown, and framed with Bethlehem steel, the concrete structure had a large kitchen, offices, a telephone room, telegraph offices, a nursery, and even a holding cell for rowdy visitors.

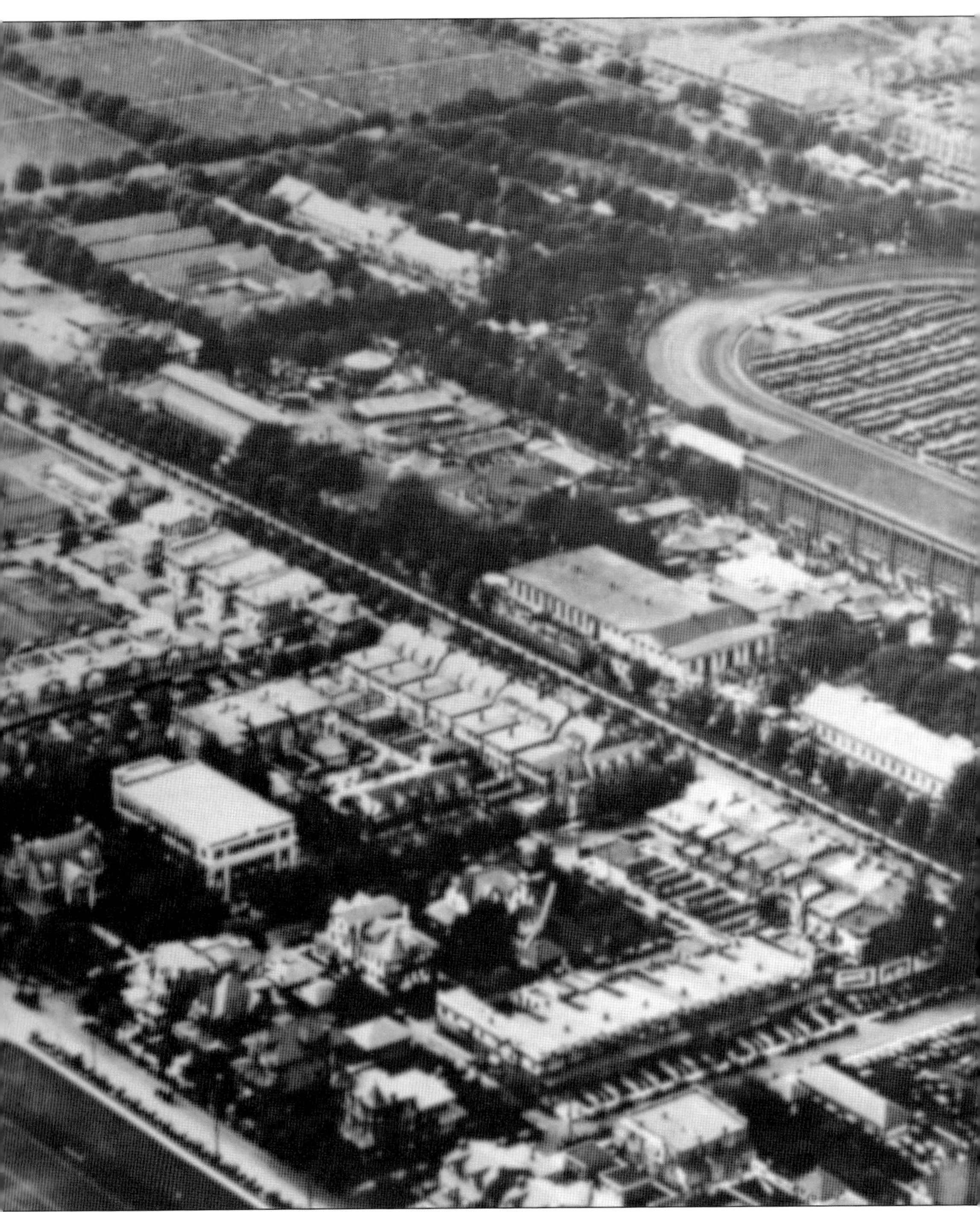

In this 1920s aerial, the original fair buildings can be seen. On the corner of Seventeenth and Chew Streets, toward the bottom of the picture, is the main entrance gate aside of the tree-filled Grove. Following Chew Street to the left of the grounds is the octagonal Floral Hall, then Mechanics Hall, and then the main Exhibition Hall. The domed cross-shaped Horticultural Hall sits aside of that with the poultry barns next. Moving across the grounds toward Liberty Street to

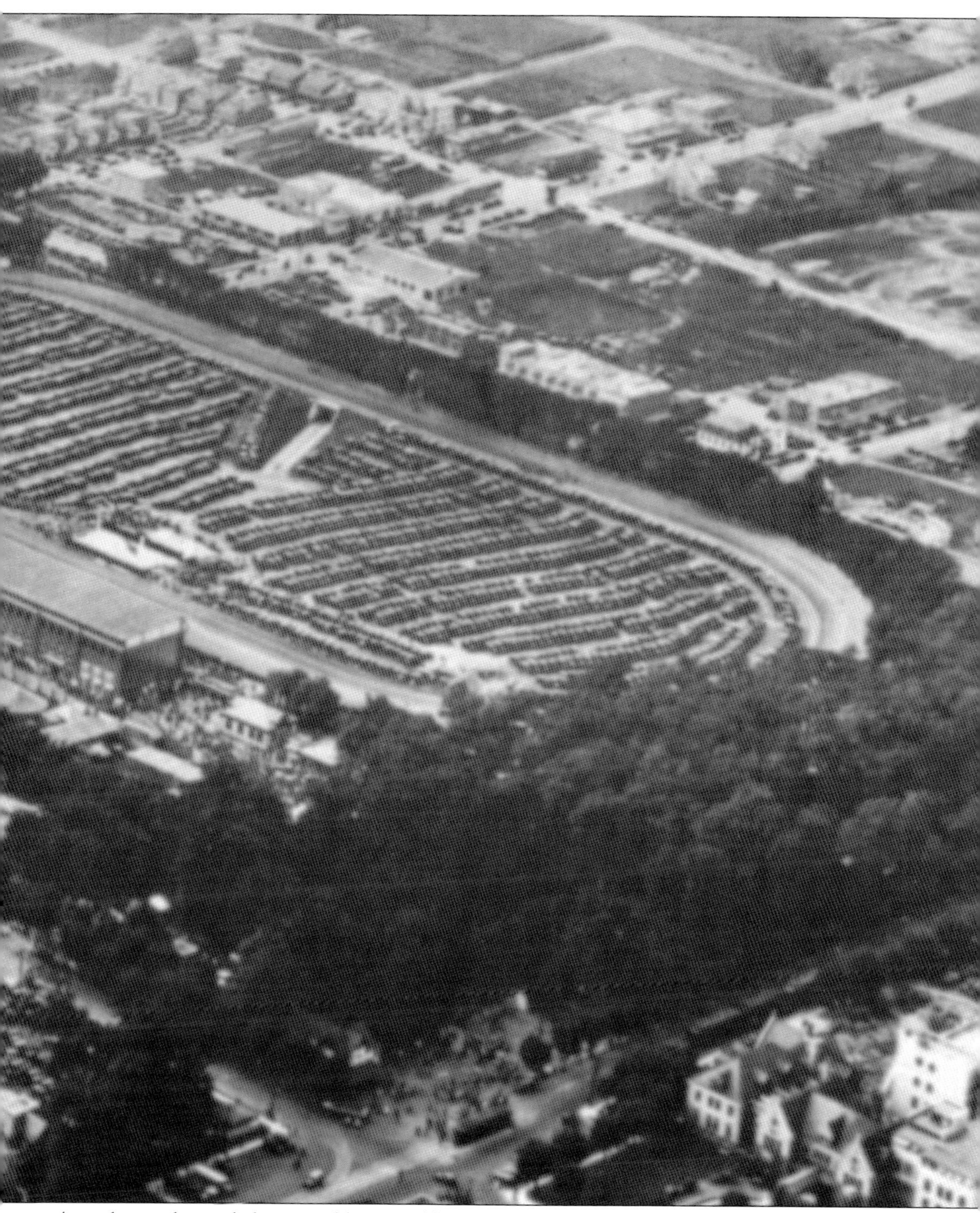

the right are the cattle barns and horse stables. The cattle barns create a square with an open pen in the middle. Peeking above the trees are the turrets of the Horse Exhibition Hall. The infield of the track is filled with cars that gained entrance through the tunnel leading from Liberty Street under the track.

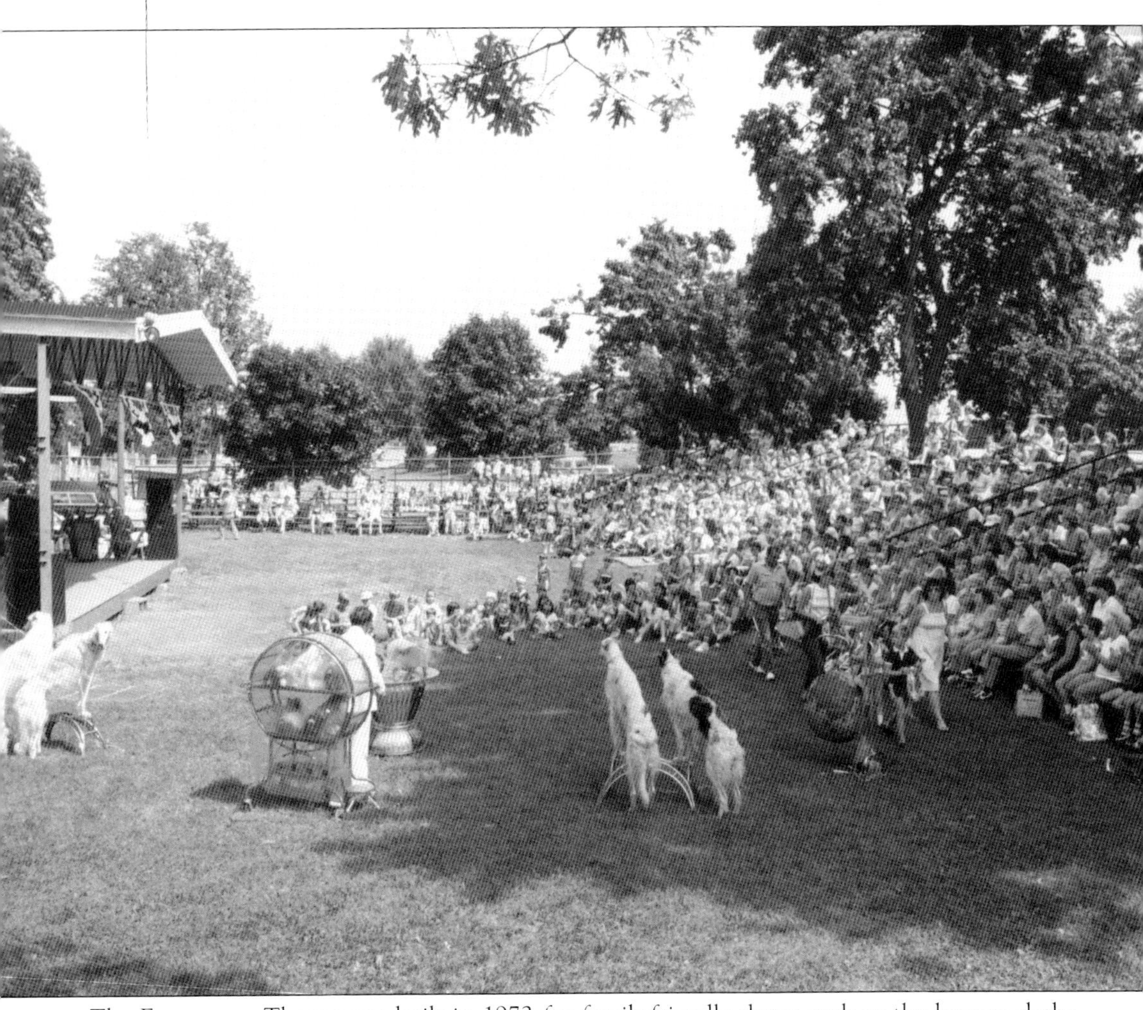

The Farmerama Theater was built in 1972 for family-friendly shows such as the banana derby, where monkeys rode ponies. Other animal acts, like this dog circus routine, filled the bleachers with anxious children. Several of the original performances in 1972 were spoken in Pennsylvania Dutch. Focusing on the Pennsylvania Dutch traditions, other events that week included potato-picking contests, milking contests, and pie-eating contests. There was even a "liar's corner" for the best liars in the county to compete. As the years went by, the Farmerama Theater continued to offer family-friendly entertainment, all free to fair patrons. Talent shows, skill contests, animal performances, and the annual Miss Allentown Fair have filled the Farmerama Theater each year. In 1988, Las Vegas act the Cold Nose Five appeared, showcasing tricks from Clark McDermott's famous performing German shepherds.

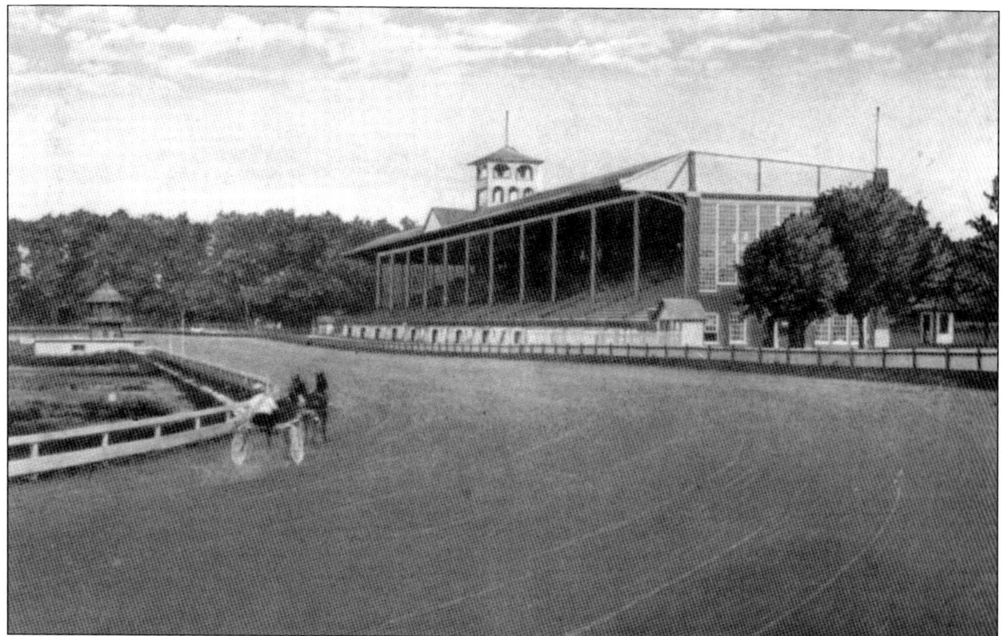

When world-famous Dan Patch came to race at the fair in 1905, his stable was elaborately decorated. His stall was fitted with a double-layer floor to prevent dampness, and an awning was hung over his doorway with lace curtains inside. His racing harness was kept in a white trunk and displayed so visitors could see the gold inscription of his name. (Courtesy of Kelly Ann Butterbaugh.)

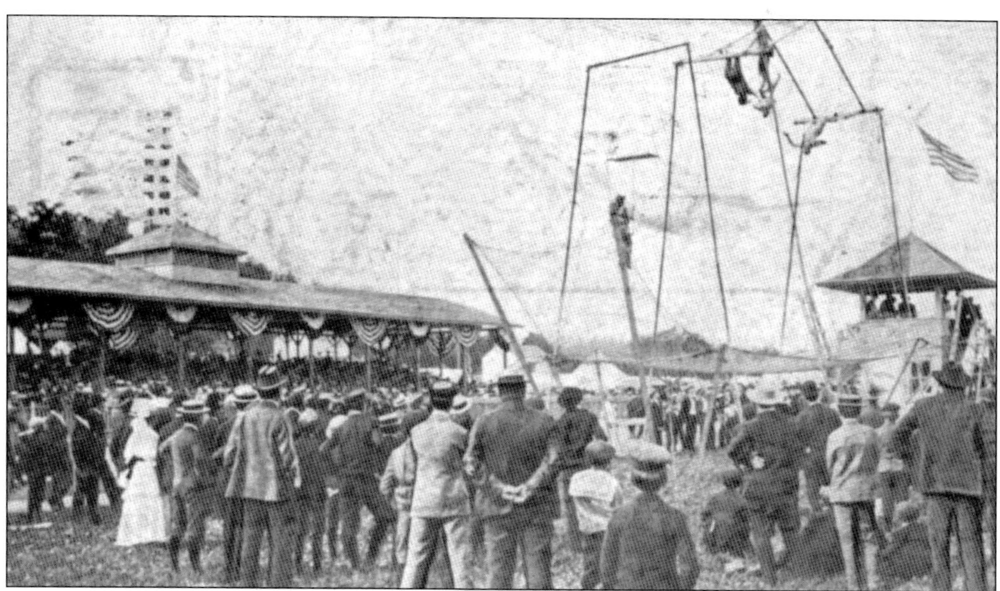

Vaudeville and trapeze acts perform in front of the original grandstand. These acts performed between the harness races. In 1926, the Flying Condonas performed their trapeze act without a net. In 1934, a tightrope walker named Costica Florescu stood on his head on top of a swaying 114-foot pole before swinging from a rope by his teeth. (Courtesy of David Bausch.)

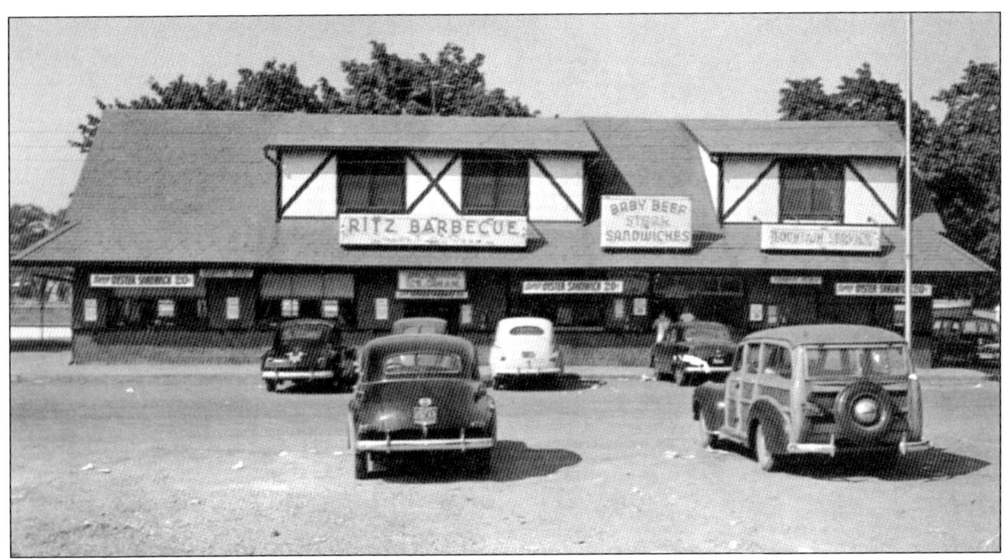

The Ritz restaurant began in August 1927 on the fairgrounds when William Ritz started selling hot dogs, baked beans, barbecue, and ice cream at the fair. He then expanded and opened his barbecue shop in a 30-by-30-foot shed on this site, expanding to the current building in 1937. Very little changed at the Ritz over the years, even when William Ritz sold his locally famous business in July 1956.

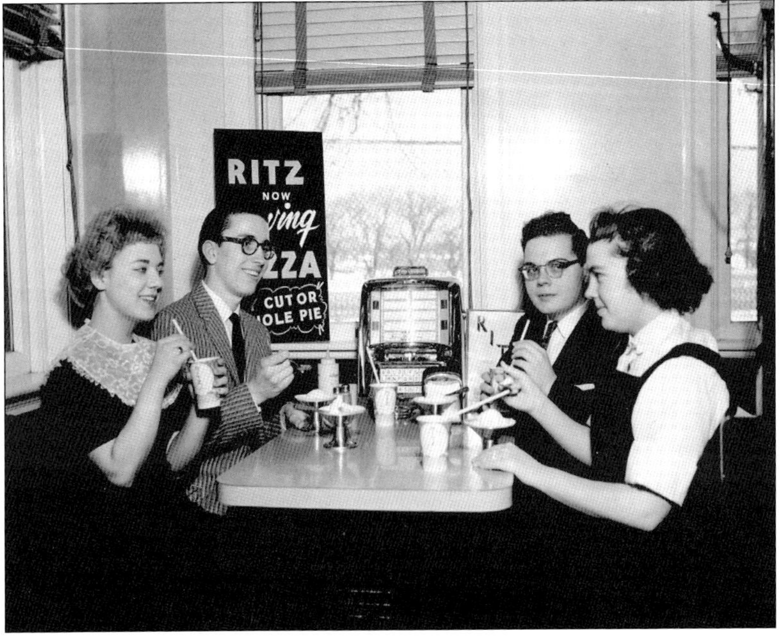

From its opening, the Ritz drew crowds for its food, atmosphere, and ice cream. Billy Ritz was known to hang out the window of the restaurant to look at the line and then turn and tell his workers, "I can't see Chew Street yet." Many teens remember "cruising the circuit" in the 1960s and ending their night at the tables of the Ritz.

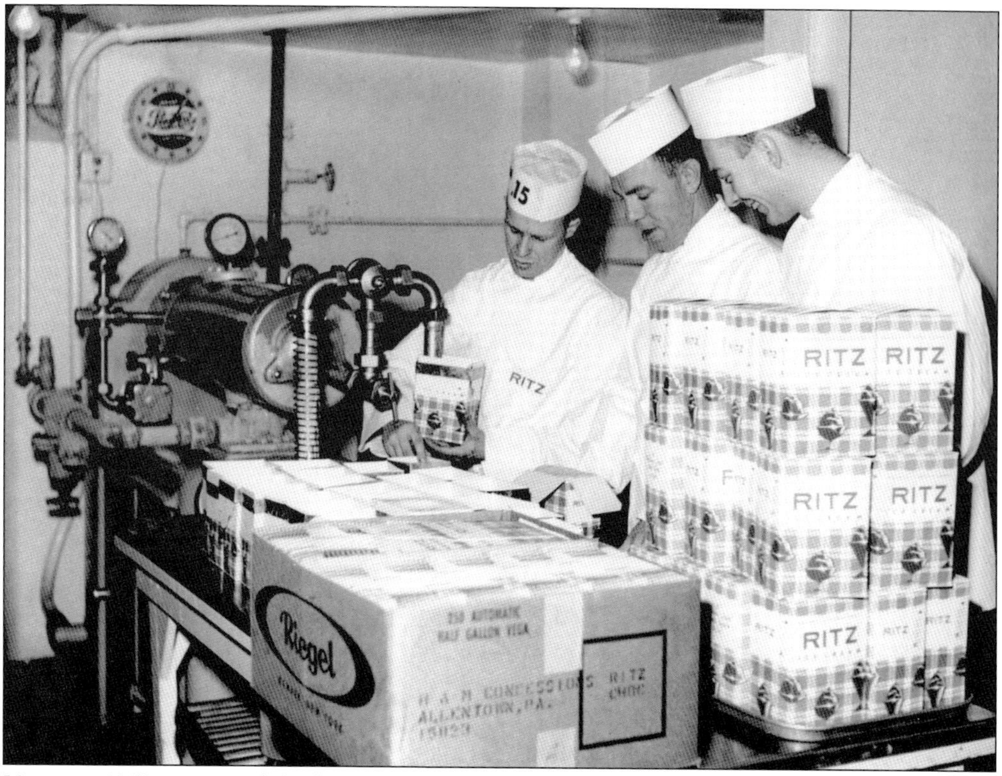

Here, in 1952, Warren "Skip" Schmidt (left) and his coworkers use the 1951 Cherry Burrell machine to make the ice cream that draws crowds to the Ritz every week. The machine is capable of producing 160 gallons of ice cream in an hour, useful for the 800–1,000 gallons the restaurant needs each week. The machine survived the fire on June 14, 1998, that destroyed most of the building. Among those who extinguished the flames that night also stood fans of the restaurant watching with tears. With hard work, the restaurant was open in time for the fair that same year, serving its first meal to the firefighters who had worked on the blaze a few months before.

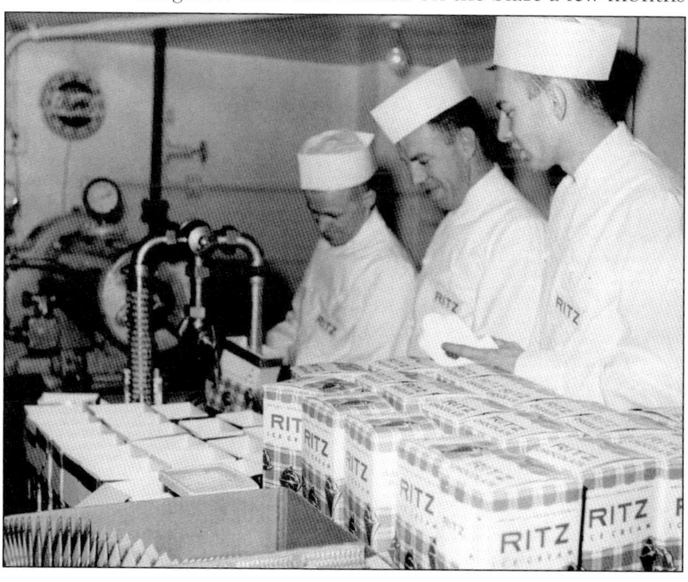

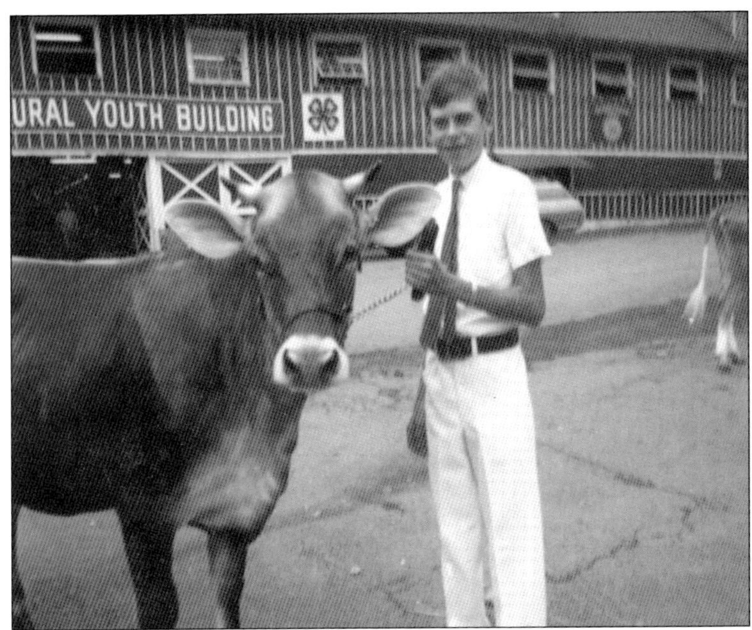

The Rural Youth Building was constructed as an L-shaped barn in 1901 at the southwest corner of the track. In 1964, it was converted into an exhibition building for the 4-H and Future Farmers of America clubs, which held meetings upstairs and kept stables below. Daryl Urmy, a member of the 4-H, stands in front of the building with his Brown Swiss dairy cow. (Courtesy of the Urmy family.)

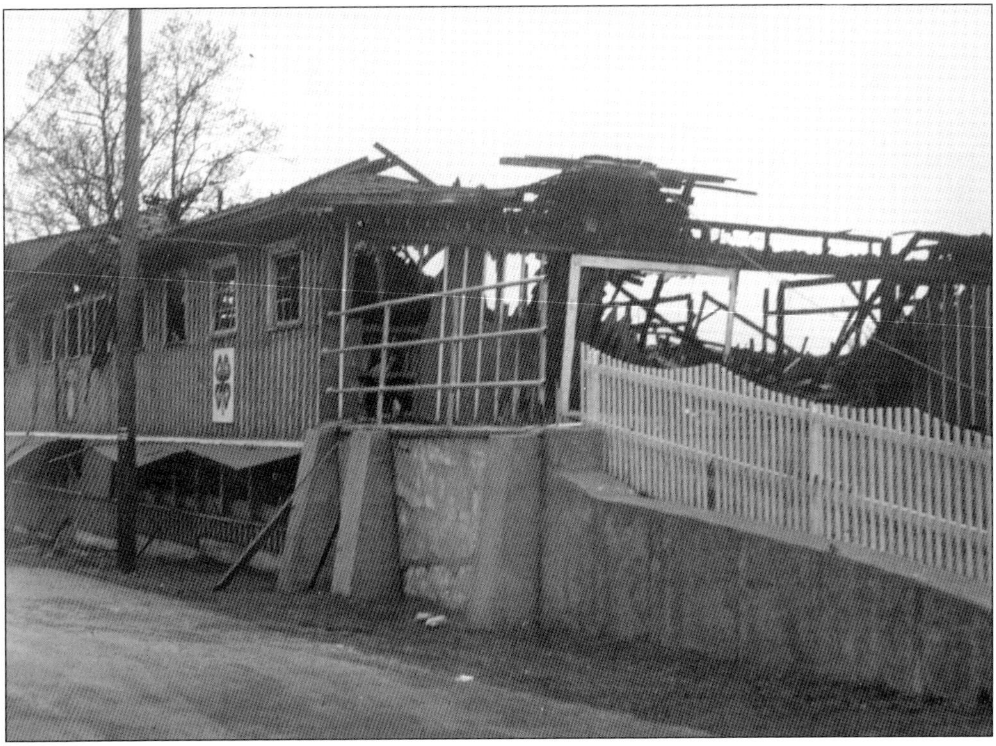

Late at night on May 5, 1974, a three-alarm fire sparked in the fair's Rural Youth Building. All 10 sheep and the two racing horses that were kept inside were saved. An antique racing sulky as well as harnesses and equipment were lost to the flames, as was a large collection of fair memorabilia and records. The 200-foot-tall flames destroyed the wooden building within an hour.

Two

The Fair's Early Years

The Allentown Fair had humble beginnings as discussions about forming an agricultural society and hosting a fair began as early as 1850. Then, on January 24, 1852, a group of citizens gathered in a meetinghouse in Egypt to discuss and organize the fair for that year. The Lehigh County Agricultural Society was founded on February 3, 1852, and the fair was planned for October 6–8, 1852. Admission would be 25¢. The rented lot was surrounded by a seven-foot-tall muslin screen so only paying customers could see the exhibits. This drew great curiosity from those outside. Inside, Stephen Lentz paraded his Flying Coach, a horse-drawn wagon with a quasi-orchestra in the back. This first fair was a great success, and a second fair was held September 28–30 the following year. Harness racing was central to the early fairs, while entertainment acts were booked to perform between each race. In 1888, the races drew enough spectators that 59 special trains were designated to bring visitors from out of town to the fair that week. It was clear that the fair had outgrown its location.

In 1889, the Lehigh County Agricultural Society moved to the present location. The first fair at the new fairgrounds was held during a rainy week in 1889. Though the rain cancelled the horse races on the new track, the fair was still a great success and continued to be successful as the new century arrived. Entertainment such as vaudeville acts, trapeze artists, and sideshows drew people to the new promenade known as the midway. Exhibition buildings overflowed with entries of livestock and domestic goods. Thousands of dollars in premiums were awarded, and the Allentown Fair continued to grow in popularity. The Allentown Fair commenced its 50th anniversary celebration in 1901 and continued through 1902, a great milestone celebration that spanned two years. To add to the festivity, the fair borrowed exhibits that year from the Pan-American Exhibition, the New York World's Fair. The Great Allentown Fair has continued almost without disruption to the present day.

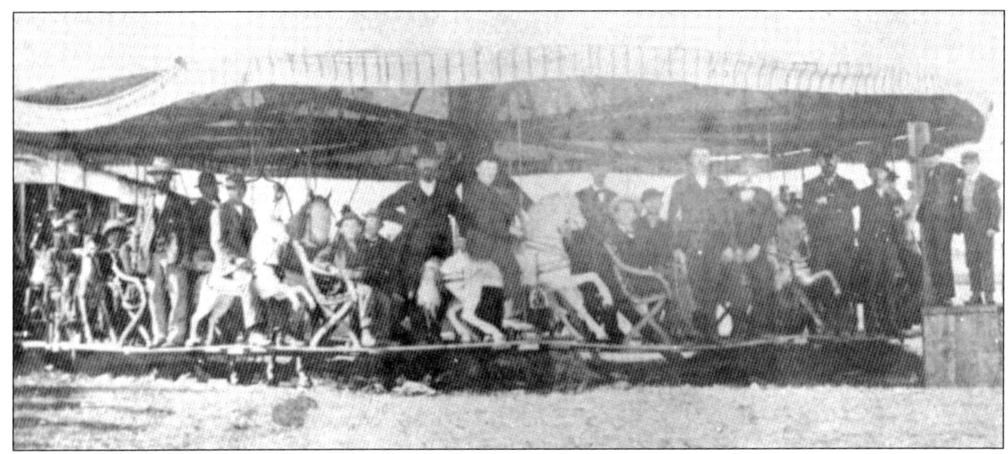

The second Allentown Fair ran from September 28 to September 30 in 1853 at the "old fairgrounds." A popular attraction was the Lentz Flying Coach. This early merry-go-round was powered by one horse in the center that walked in a circle and moved the platform that held the stationary horses and benches. A local minstrel provided music for the riders. The ride was constructed and designed by local Allentown resident Lewis Lentz.

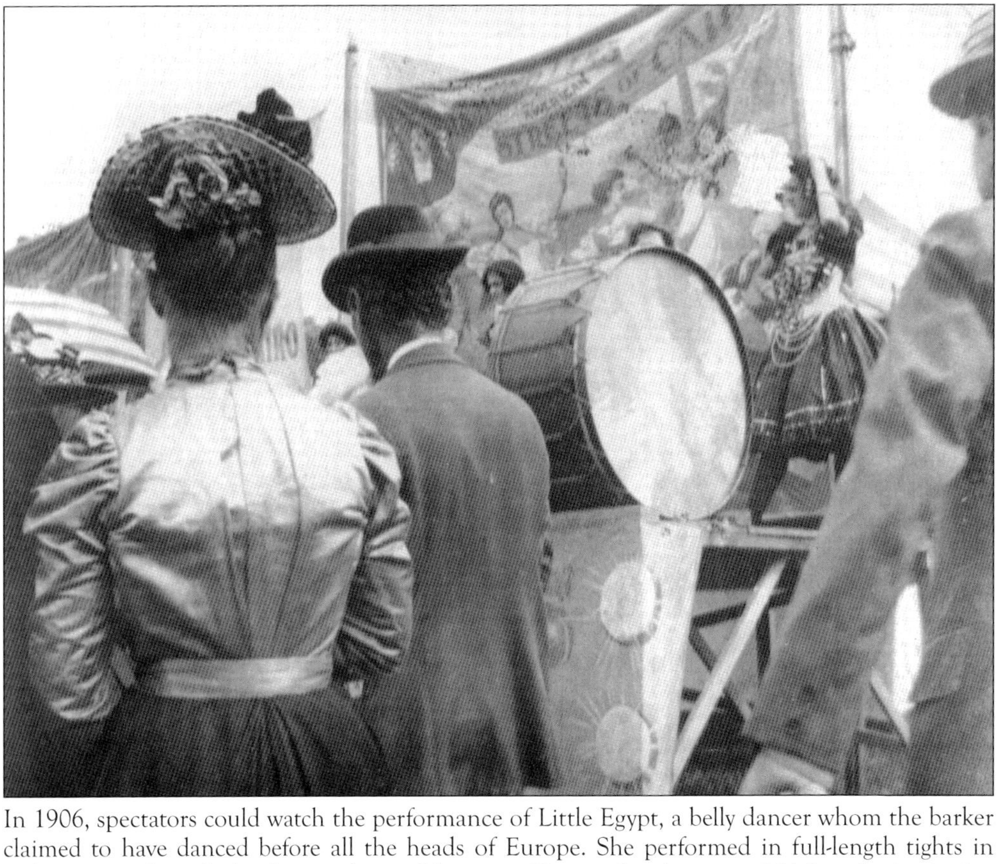

In 1906, spectators could watch the performance of Little Egypt, a belly dancer whom the barker claimed to have danced before all the heads of Europe. She performed in full-length tights in order to comply with the decency laws of the time. Her regular show cost 10¢, but the intriguing "after-hours show" cost 25¢. Spectators were disappointed to learn afterward that both shows were exactly the same.

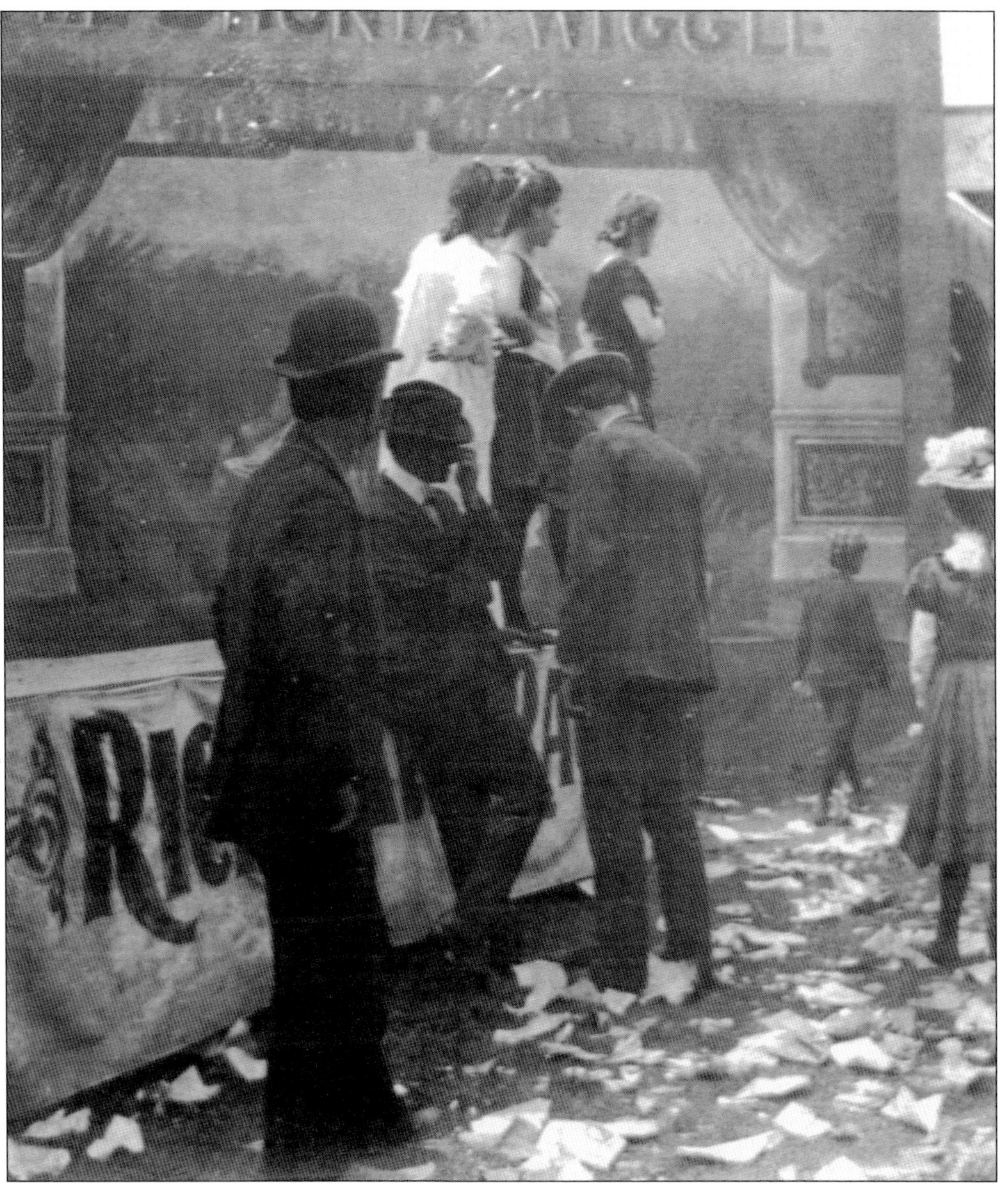

This 1904 photograph captures the interest in the midway dancing shows that were often subject to scrutiny. Known locally as the "hootchy-kootchy dances," the scantily clad girls performed routines that boasted of exotic attire and dancing, often claiming to be from the streets of Egypt. Their dances were called muscle or wiggle dances, but today they would be called belly dances. One show tempted customers to pay for a show to see Lady Hamilton in her "bear skin," but most customers did not notice the play on words and were disappointed to see her emerge wrapped in the fur of a bruin. Every year, one of the shows was closed by town officials midway through the week after it was declared improper or the crowds got too rowdy. In an effort to have the "cleanest" fair in its history, the dancing girls were banned in 1905. Not to worry, the midway saw its shows and antics return in 1906.

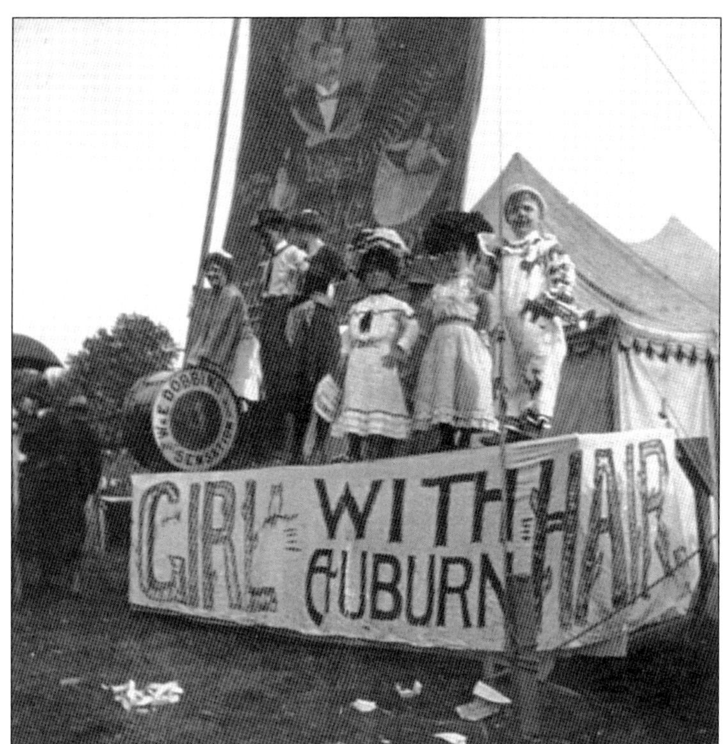

W.E. Dobbins Sensation was one of the midway attractions early in the 20th century. Fairgoers' curiosity was piqued by displays of physical rarities such as five-legged cows, hairless draft horses, notably overweight men, and people short in stature. Illusionists, boxing kangaroos, jugglers, and dancers were other attractions in the tents along the midway. Sometimes, wordplay trickery was employed to tempt visitors to pay for entrance to the shows.

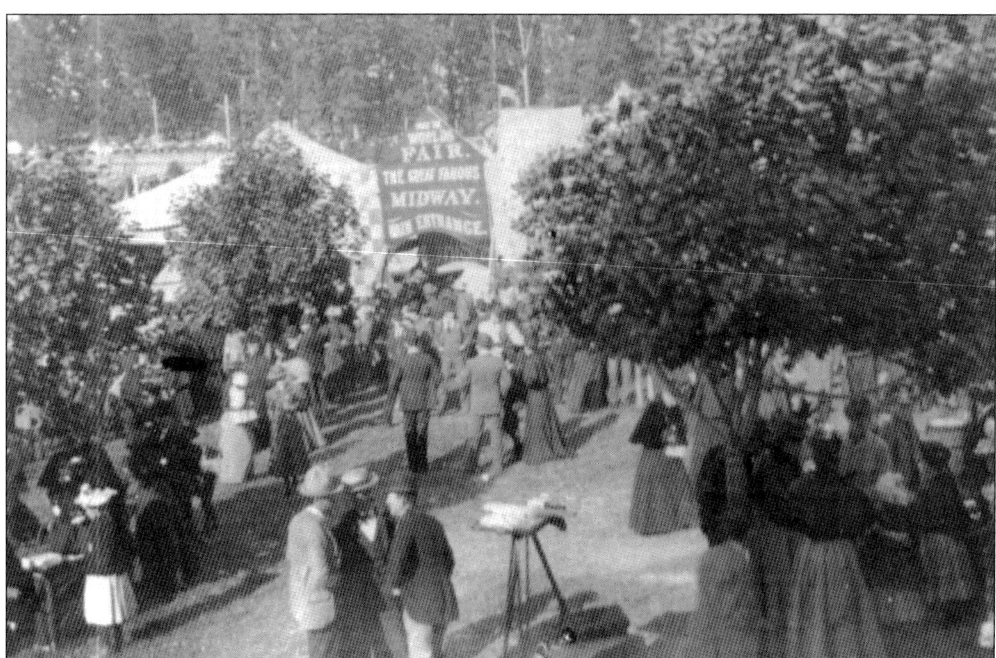

Once larger fairs closed, promoters like George Hamid recruited their performers and exhibitions for local fairs as part of nationwide tours. In 1934, acts from the recently closed Century of Progress International Exposition, the Chicago World's Fair, traveled to the Allentown Fair. Performers from the New York World's Fair came to Allentown in 1939. Over time, the eager crowds turned the grassy midway to dirt before paving began.

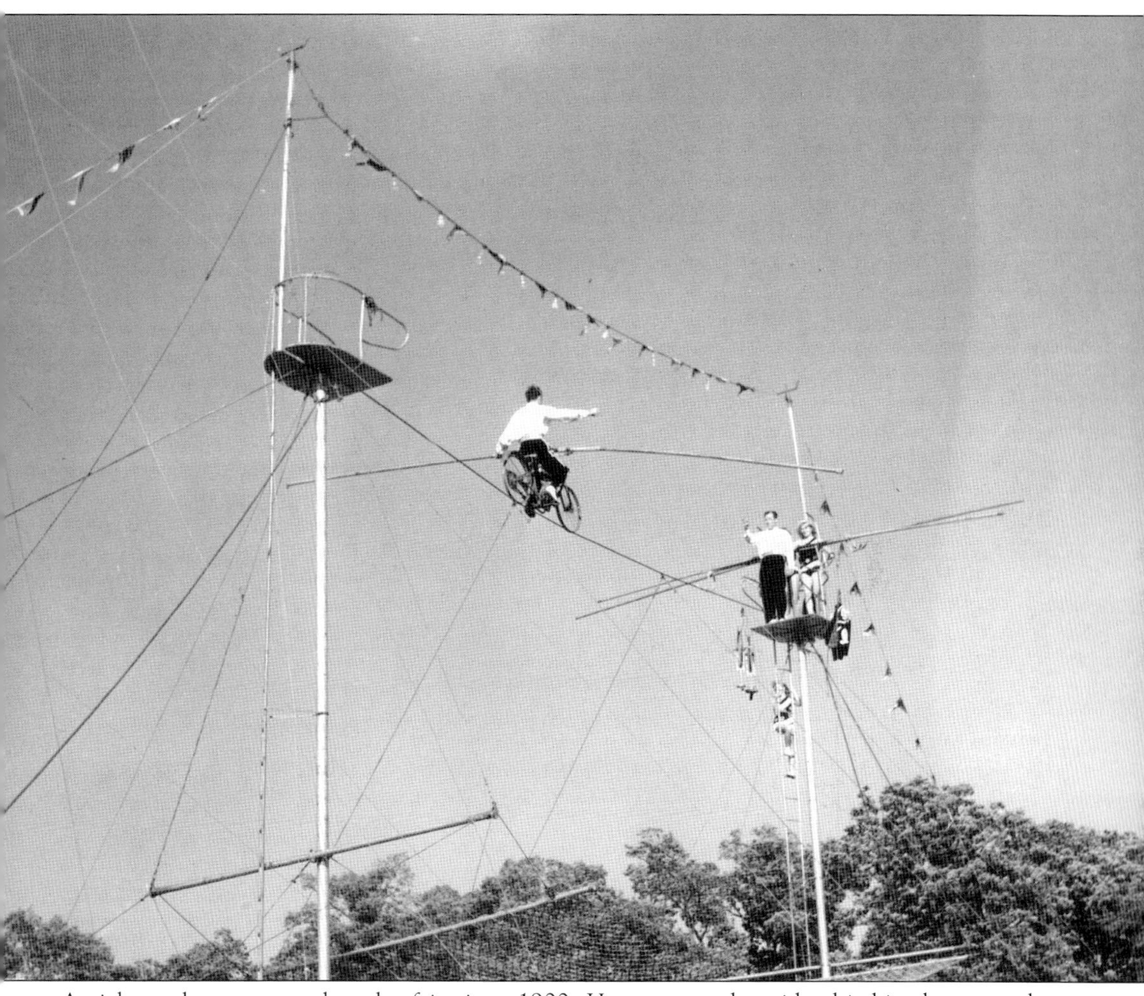

Aerial acts have appeared at the fair since 1900. Here, an acrobat rides his bicycle across the tightrope. This routine was originally performed in 1900 by the Martel family and repeated again in 1916 by another tightrope cycling act. Other acrobatic routines that have towered above the audience include the dancing couple Benny and Betty Fox jitterbugging on a pole with a two-foot-wide platform.

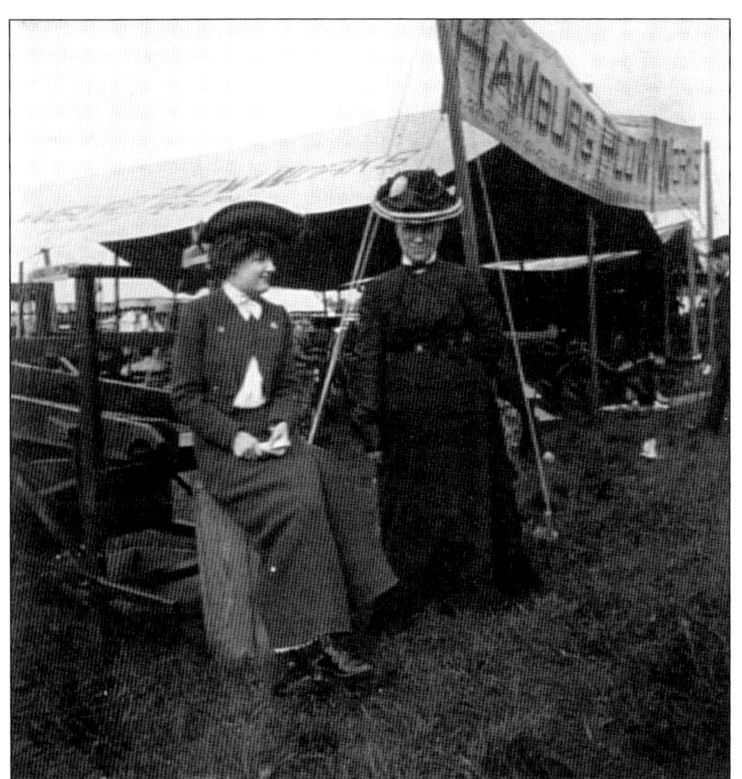

These ladies take a break outside the farm equipment displays at an early-1900s fair. The exhibits in the northwestern section of the fair included gasoline engines, corn huskers, and milk separators. Just behind the ladies is the Hamburg Plow Works display. The company is known today as Hamburg Manufacturing Inc., but when it was founded in 1882, it primarily produced plow equipment and some other farming needs, like troughs.

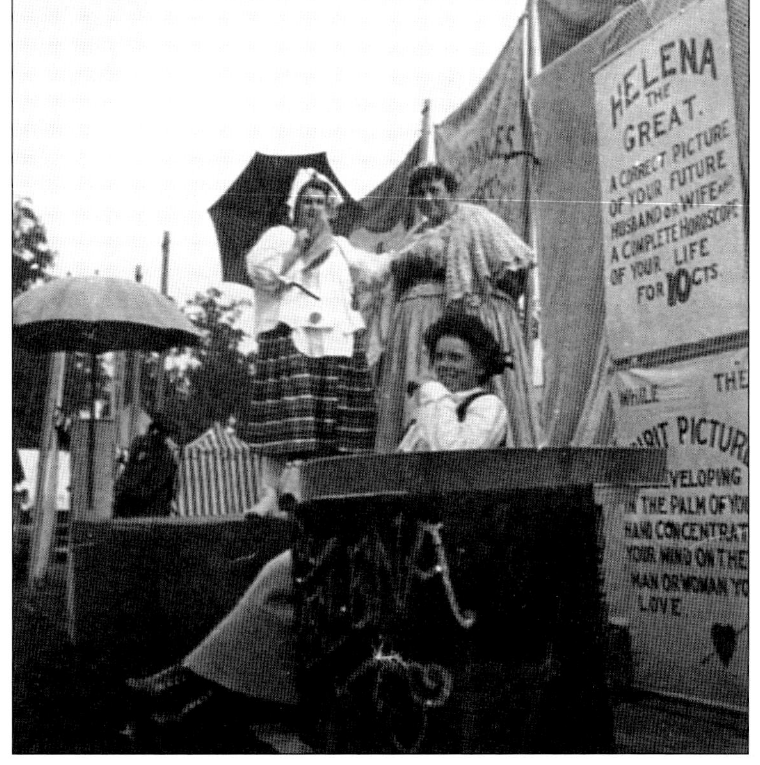

Shows on the midway drew people to see a woman with three hands, a family that was half-bear and half-human, and people performing unheard-of feats. Between those shows, fairgoers could visit the stands of mystics like the fortune-telling Helena the Great, seen here, ready to read the palm of anyone who paid 10¢ to know of his/her future spouse.

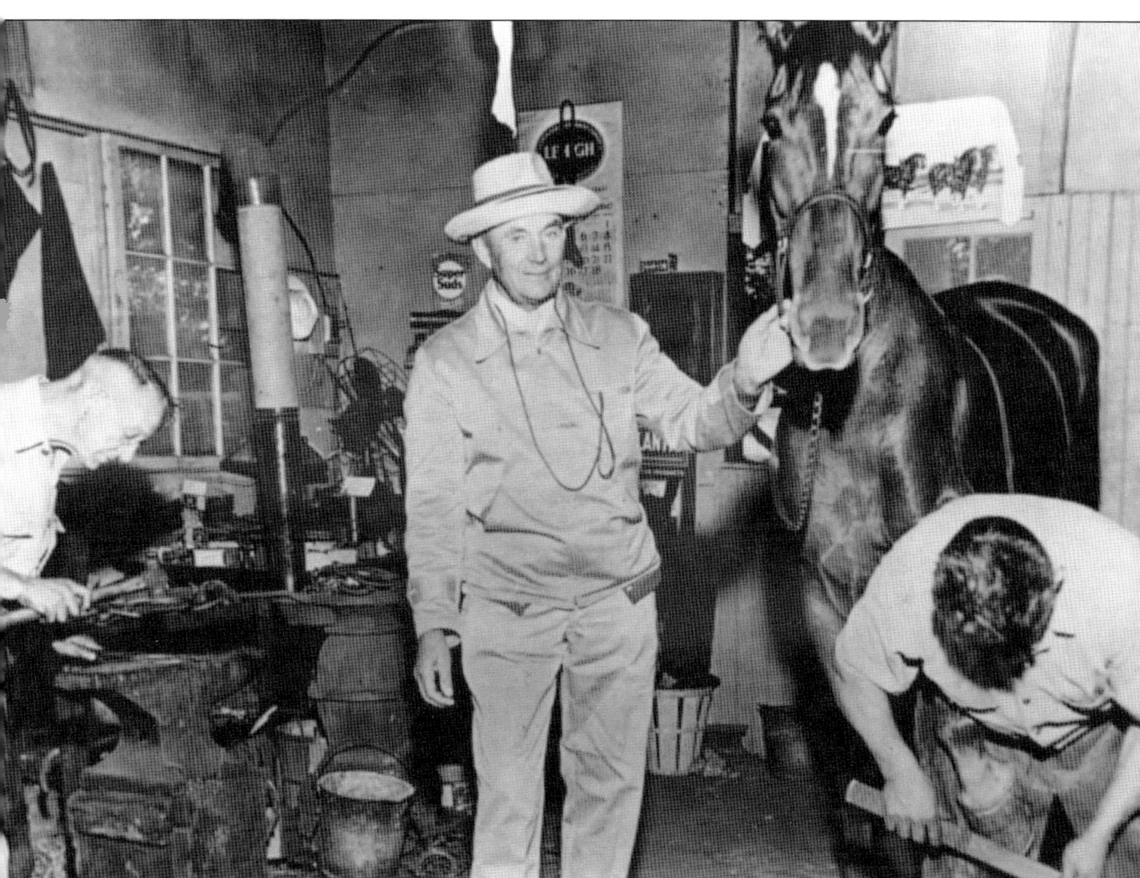

With the number of horses on the fairgrounds each year, it made sense to have a farrier on-site. Situated near the stables, the farrier on duty replaced shoes on the racing horses throughout fair week. For the best racing results, horses were shod within a week of racing, keeping the track farrier busy. Here, William E. Miller holds the mare Pearl Gantle as she receives a new set of shoes in 1951. Miller owned and raced the pedigreed standardbred who won on tracks along the East Coast. Harness racing continued to grow from its start at the fair, increasing to its highest numbers in the early 1900s. In 1914, there were 200 race horses stabled at the fair. This increased to 324 horses at the 1915 fair, the biggest year for harness racing. (Courtesy of Clarence Jones and LCAS.)

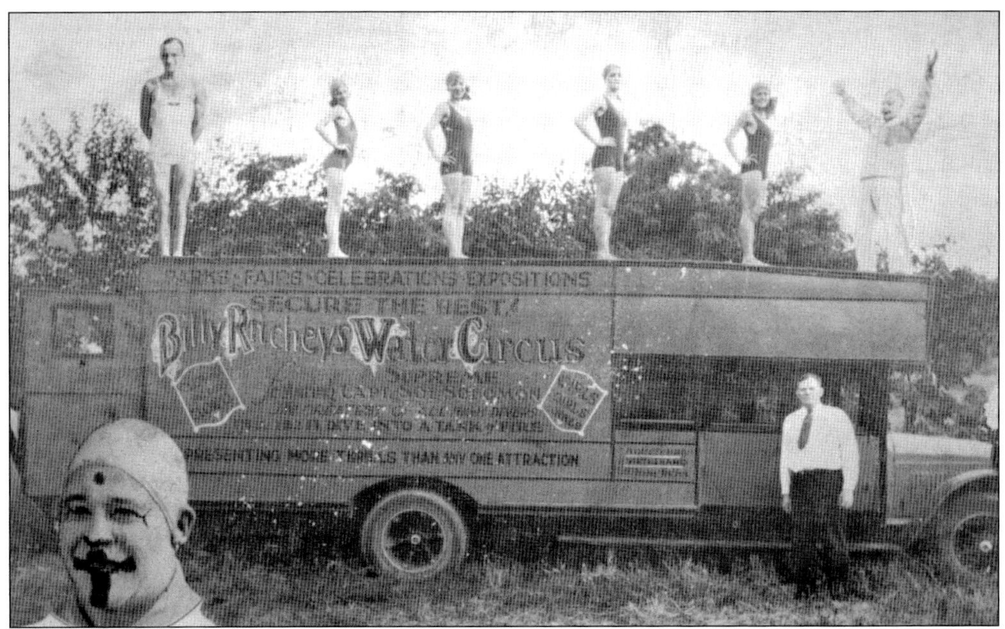

Billy Ritchey was a well-known diving performer across the state throughout the 1930s. His shows featured high dives not only into water but flames as well. Like many acts, Ritchey was promoted by George Hamid, who was always on the lookout for new performers. Hamid supported the 1936 World High Diving Championship in Palisades Amusement Park, New Jersey, and guaranteed the winner a minimum six-week booking.

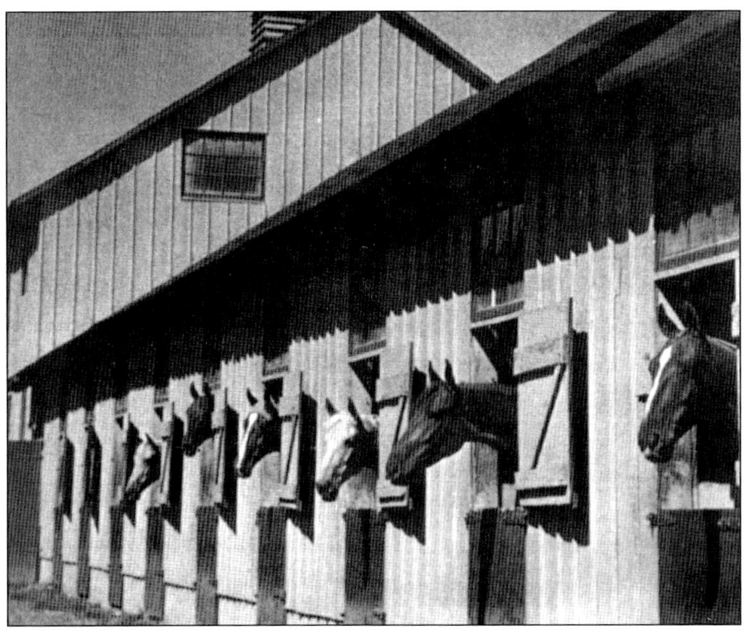

The horse sheds from the original fairgrounds were moved to the new fairgrounds, but more were needed. These new box stalls, 50 total, were built for the racing horses in 1910. In addition, there was a large exhibition building for individual horses and teams, and racing stalls lined Liberty Street for the harness racers. In the 1950s, a two-story stable was proposed for the race horses but never completed.

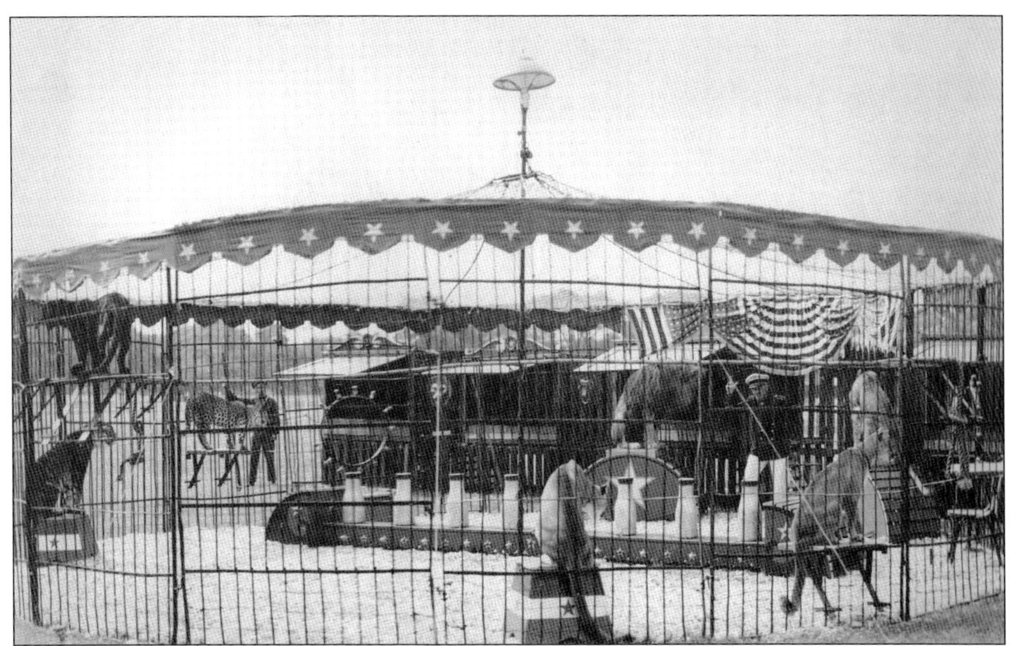

Exotic animals have been a constant exhibit at the fair. In 1954, a circus featuring a giraffe, camels, rhinoceros, and primates joined the midway. In 1959, the Strates Circus and Wild Animal Acts joined the fair, and the Hanneford Circus came from 1970 to 1972. While these were smaller circuses that came during fair week, the Ringling Brothers and Barnum & Bailey Circus came to the fair as one of the year-round fairgrounds grandstand shows. They filled the grandstand seats on June 7, 1950, and again on June 11, 1953. In 1953, a black mare named Starless Night with her rider, Capt. William Heyer, visited the fair after performing for years with Barnum & Bailey. The dancing mare had been purchased by Barnum & Bailey at the 1941 Allentown fair from her owner, George Person.

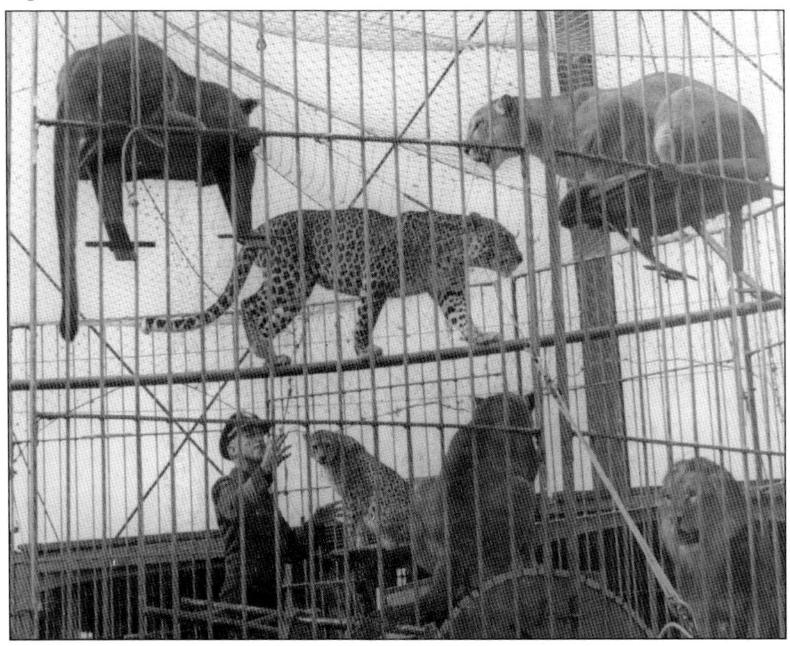

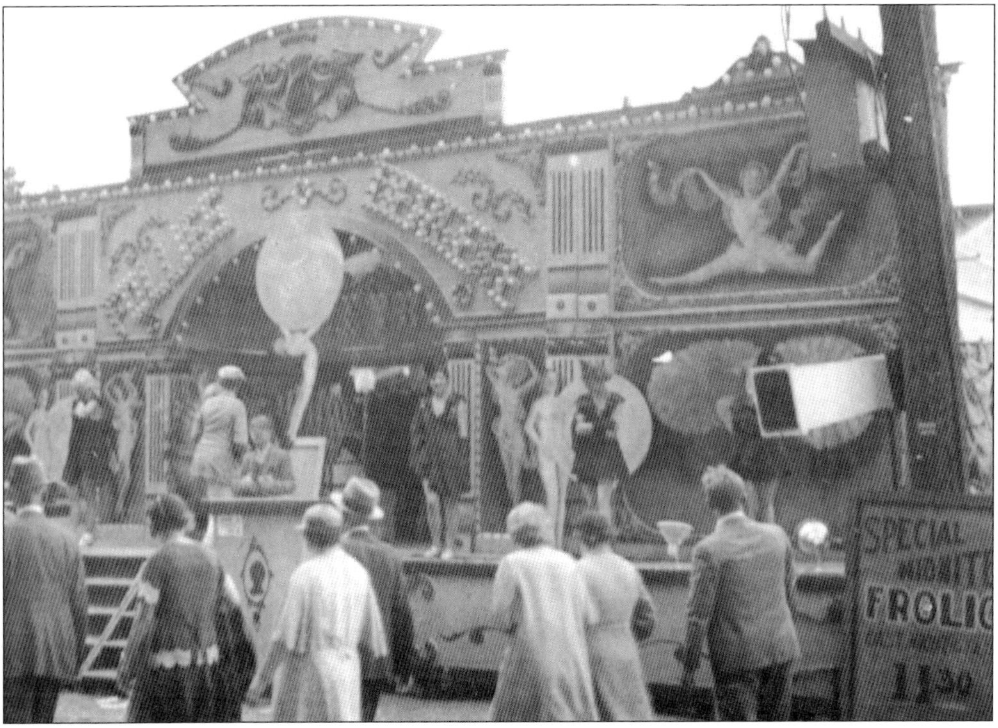

This midway attraction mimicked the Folies Bergère shows in France on the elaborate stage. No doubt, inside it mimicked the Paris attraction with its risqué costumes and provocative cabaret show. The dancing shows at the fair were well-known and, while often criticized, were very popular attractions. In 1916, one of the "whirlie-girlie" shows called "Paris by Night" featured girls dressed in feathered outfits.

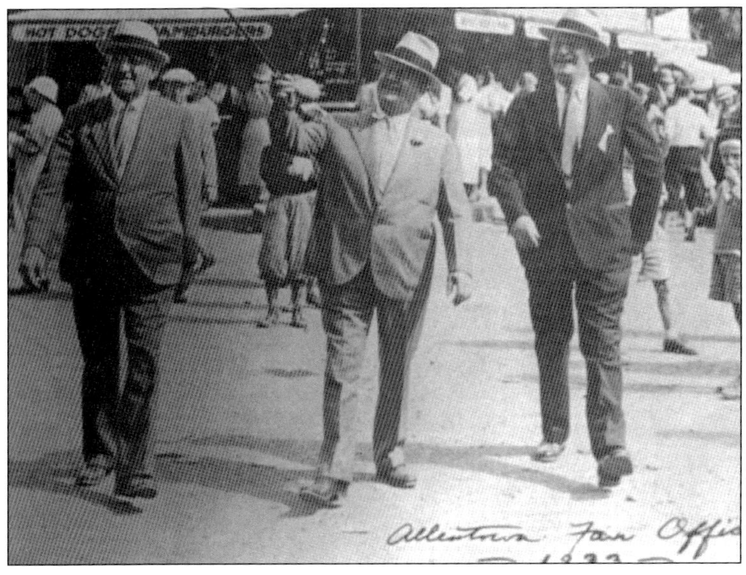

Fair directors tour the midway at the 1933 fair with much delight. This was the first year that the Royal Bengal Tigers, who were featured in front of the grandstand, appeared at any fair in the nation. Special fair days that year were dedicated to children and farmers, and every evening featured Hamid's "Winter Garden Revue" on the grandstand stage.

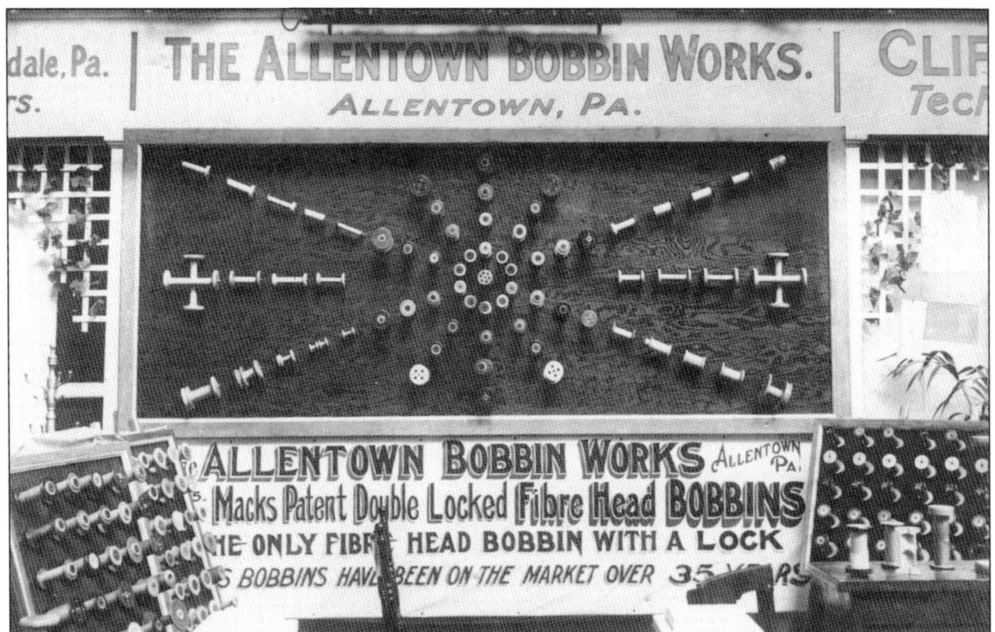

The Allentown Bobbin Works showcases its products in a business display at the fair. When the Lehigh Valley was filled with humming silk mills, the Allentown Bobbin Works was established in 1904 to manufacture the wooden bobbins needed to hold the silk threads on the mills' machines. Today, the Bobbin Works factory on Fourteenth Street in Allentown still stands. (Courtesy of David Bausch.)

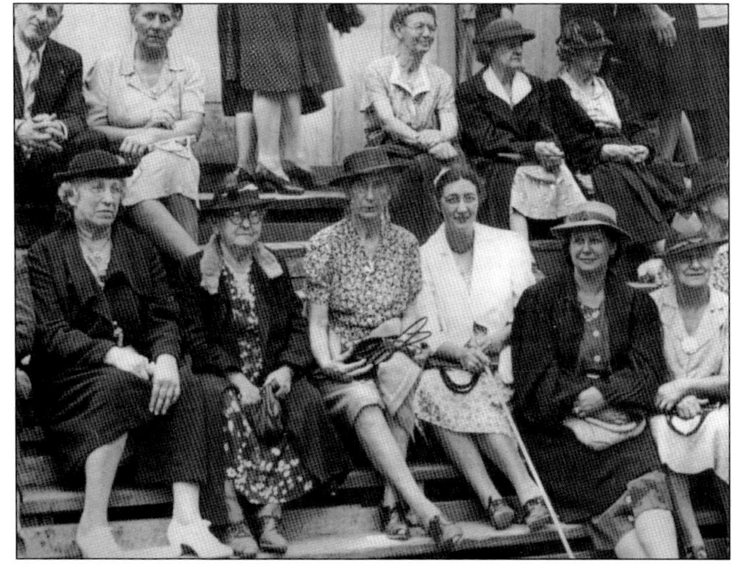

Fairgoers gather to take a break on the steps outside of one of the exhibit halls during Big Thursday at the fair in the late 1930s. Perhaps they await the cavalcade, a traditional daily parade of the best exhibitions of horses and cattle that had always been held at 10:00 a.m. on the track. However, in 1929, the cavalcade moved to 4:00 p.m. to accommodate the larger afternoon crowds.

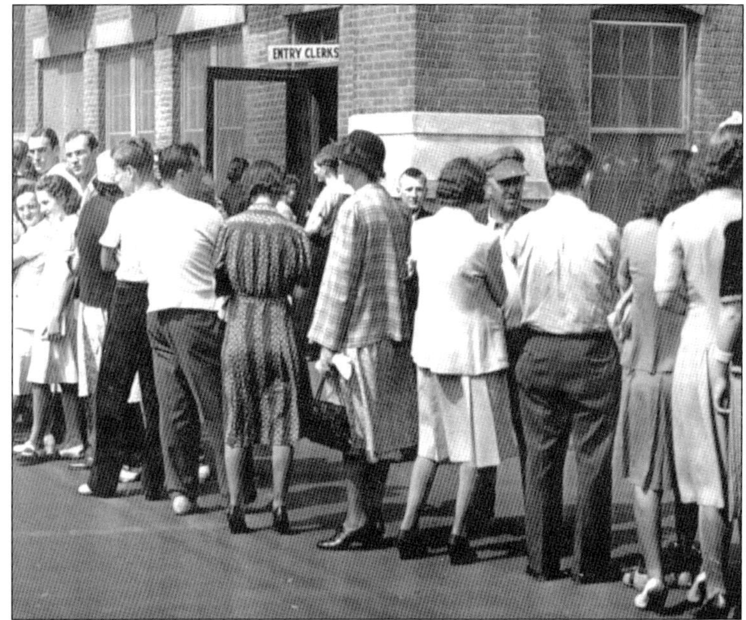

The home and culinary contests at the fair have always drawn a crowd. Here, a crowd lines up at the entrance under the grandstand to secure their entry tickets. Edward Johnson is the first man in line, waiting with his mother to enter baked goods. Thousands of entries filled the exhibition halls every year, and every winner's name was published in the local newspaper after the fair week.

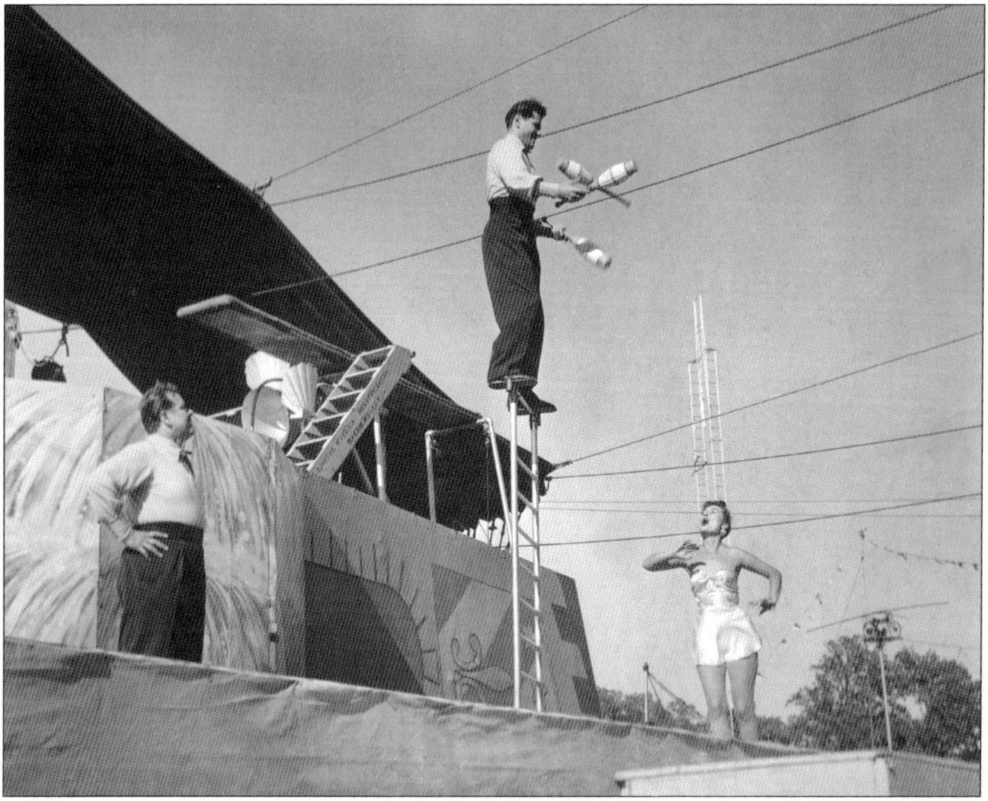

Jugglers perform as part of the Lottie Mayer Disappearing Water Act. Lottie Mayer Warfield began her vaudeville career in 1907 after earning merits as a long-distance swimmer and high diver. She toured nearly every major fair and theater in the country during her 50 years of performing trick dives into a small tub of water.

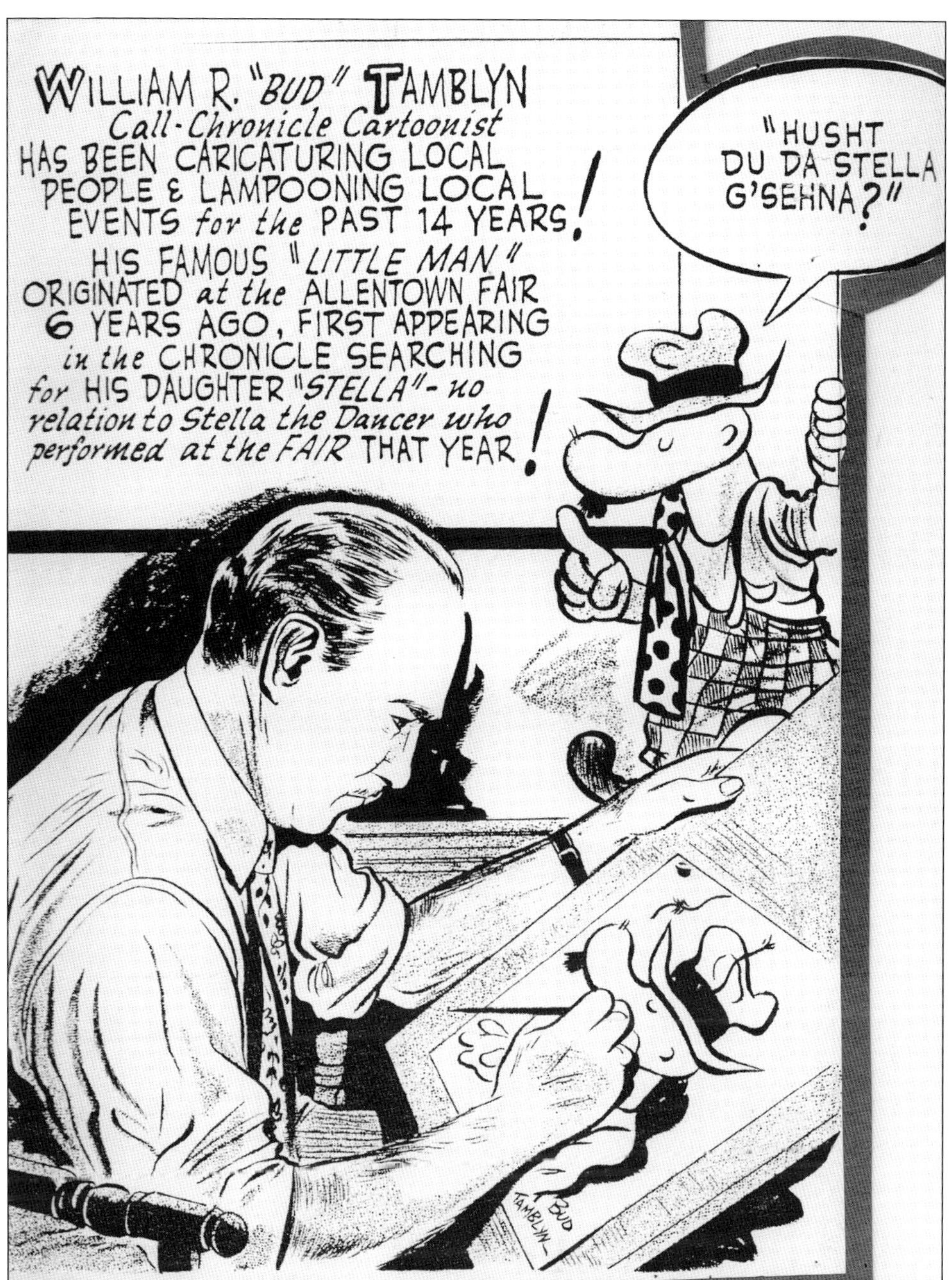

Artist Bud Tamblyn featured the Allentown Fair in his *Morning Call* caricatures from 1937 to 1985 before retiring. Each fair week, Tamblyn would draw a daily cartoon collage about the events at the fair. Known to everyone who read his cartoons was Drew P. Turtlederfer, his character known as Little Man. Little Man first appeared in 1945 when he began looking for his daughter Stella at the fair. Every day, Little Man asked in Pennsylvania Dutch, "*Husht du da* Stella *g'sehna?*" ("Have you seen Stella?") The fictitious Stella was a joking reference to a midway dancing girl with the same name. Whether there really was a dancing girl from Emmaus named Stella in 1945 is a mystery, but Little Man's famous question became a well-known quip at the fair. Little Man had adventures beyond the fair, as he was a bit of an alter ego for Tamblyn and his trademark character.

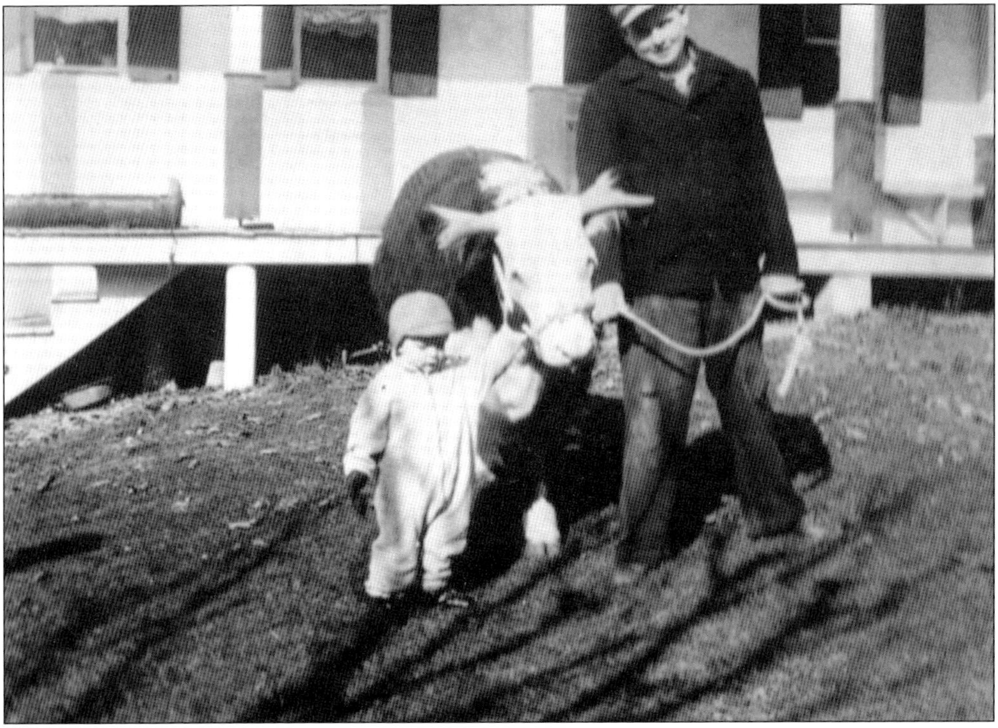

Fourteen-year-old Henry Gruber (right) poses with his younger brother Harry (left) and his Herford steer, Tony, at their home in New Tripoli. The steer was entered in the 1947 Allentown Fair 4-H competition, winning ninth place. Henry Gruber went on to receive 4-H awards at the county, state, and national levels and served as a 4-H beef club leader and 4-H livestock judge. (Courtesy of Beverly Gruber.)

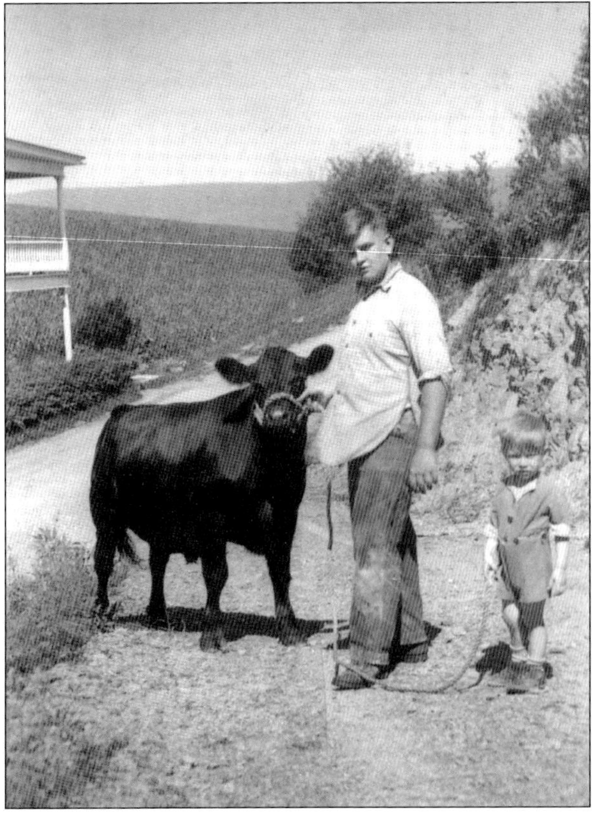

Henry Gruber (left) prepares his Black Angus steer for the 1949 4-H competition. His brother Harry Gruber holds the lead. In later years, Henry Gruber helped to organize and to judge the livestock entries at the fair and served on the fair's executive committee. He was also a former president of the Lehigh County Agriculture Extension Board. (Courtesy of Beverly Gruber.)

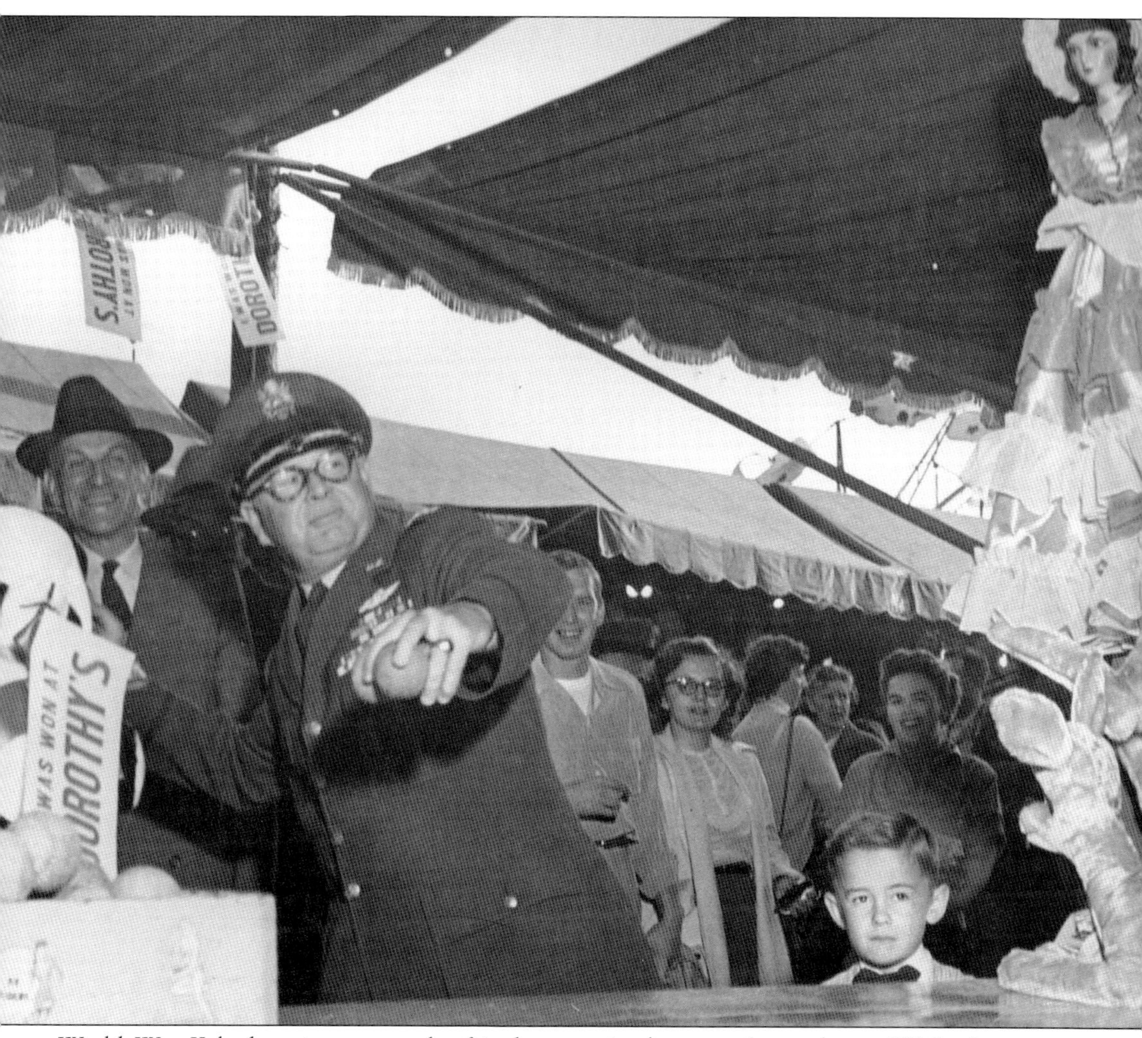

World War II had an impact on the fair, but not in the way of attendance. While those in Washington, DC, advised that the public avoid events like fairs, people like this soldier playing a game on the midway flocked to the 1942 Great Allentown Fair. The thought in Washington was to save tires and, therefore, save rubber by curtailing travel. However, the thought of those at the fair was to use the fair to help the war effort. Not to contradict the government request, fairgoers were encouraged to use the trolley cars to get to the fair. Once there, a war stamp and bond drive was organized by the fair officials and radio station WSAN. It was all hands on deck as the dancers from George Hamid's stage production stepped up to help with the campaign. On Big Thursday, traditionally the day of the fair with the largest attendance, 122 men marched into the grandstand after being newly sworn in to the Navy.

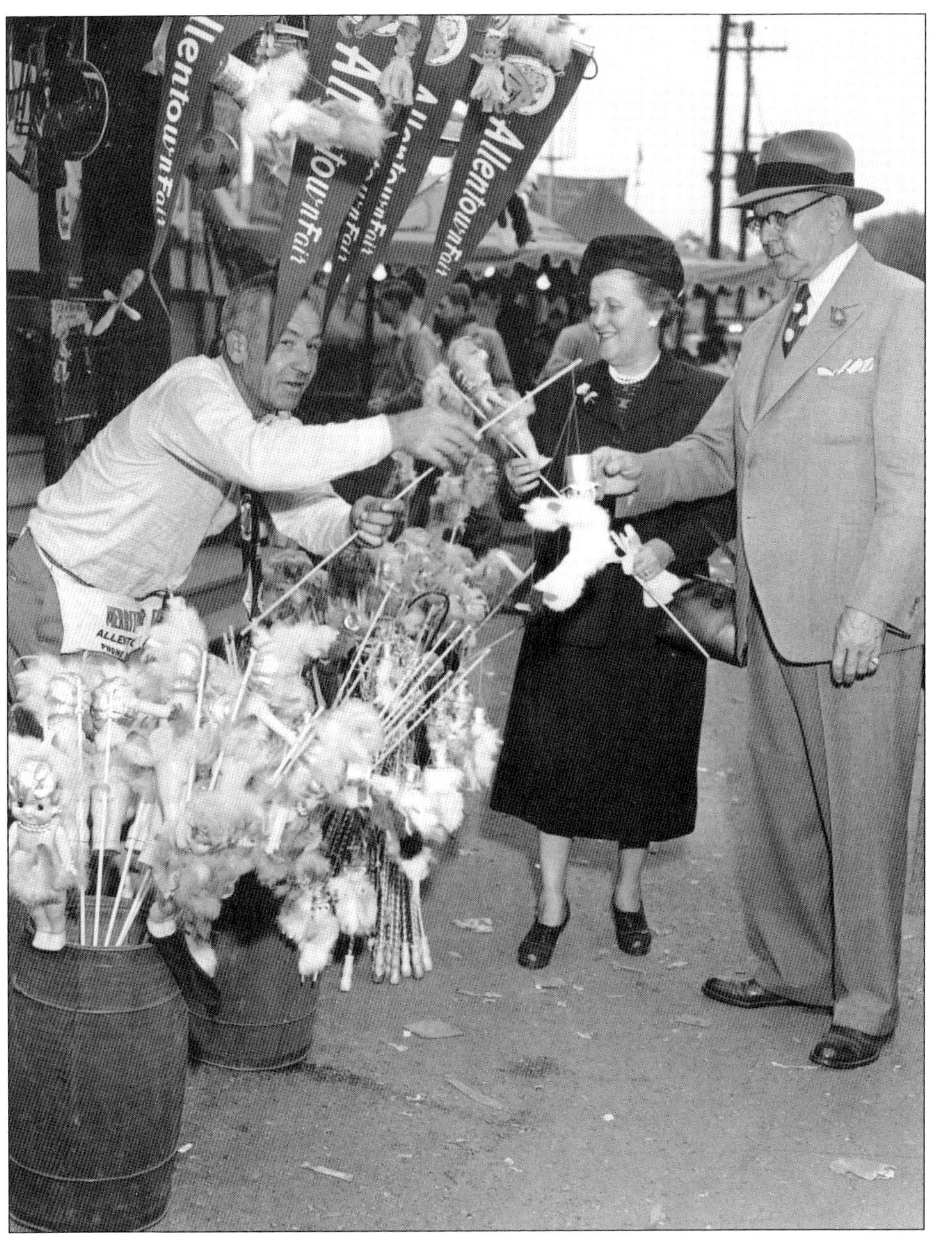

Howard Singmaster and his wife enjoy a trip down the midway. Singmaster served as LCAS president from 1949 to 1956. During his time as president, Singmaster sought to improve the Allentown Fairgrounds. He proposed to move the fair out of the city to allow for more expansion as needed, and as a result, the LCAS purchased a tract of land off today's Emmaus Avenue. This tract was never used for the fairgrounds, and it was later sold. Singmaster also proposed the building of a multipurpose arena that could house all of the fair's activities. This structure that was never meant to be would have been called the Coliseum. Singmaster did get to see the fairgrounds enter into the phase of renovation that began in 1956. This renovation saw most of the original buildings razed in order to provide more exhibition space, more concessions space, and better pathways through the fair. The original plan proposed in 1956 was to take place over several phases for the next 25 years and involved the construction of several new exhibition halls.

Three

The Great Allentown Fair

While the Allentown Fair is known for its traditions that remain from its early days, the 1950s saw great change for the fair. Not only did the fairgrounds itself go through extensive renovations and modernization, but the overall look of the fair itself began to shift. New thrill rides started to fill the midway, and business displays in the exhibition halls showcased more modern, state-of-the-art products. Fair executives felt that crowds had grown tired of George Hamid's vaudeville-like shows and transitioned into more nationally recognized performers. This earned the grandstand the new name "Home of the Stars." Changes occurred in the grounds as well. During the late 1950s, most of the original Victorian-style buildings were razed and replaced with more modern facilities that provided better viewing and more comfort for the animals. The large agricultural complex present today replaced the specialized exhibition buildings, allowing for year-round use of the complex for other functions such as trade expos and community events.

The central heart of any fair is the midway, and when looking back at the history of the Allentown Fair, the midway reflects the changes to the fair in general. At its earliest, the midway was known as "the pike" and filled with independently run shows. By the 1930s, the entire midway was run by one company, the World of Mirth carnival company, which continued to run it for two decades. The shows were a collection of exotic performers that brought the far corners of the world to the small town of Allentown. In 1959, the midway was taken over by a new company that traveled by rail and was owned by James Strates. This was a more modern midway that transitioned to Gooding's Million Dollar Midway in 1964. That year, it featured a double Ferris wheel and bigger thrill rides like the Himalaya, which debuted in 1968. By 1984, S&S Amusements took over the midway. The focus on thrill rides shifted away, knowing that it could not compete with nearby Dorney Park, and instead focused on games of chance and other amusements.

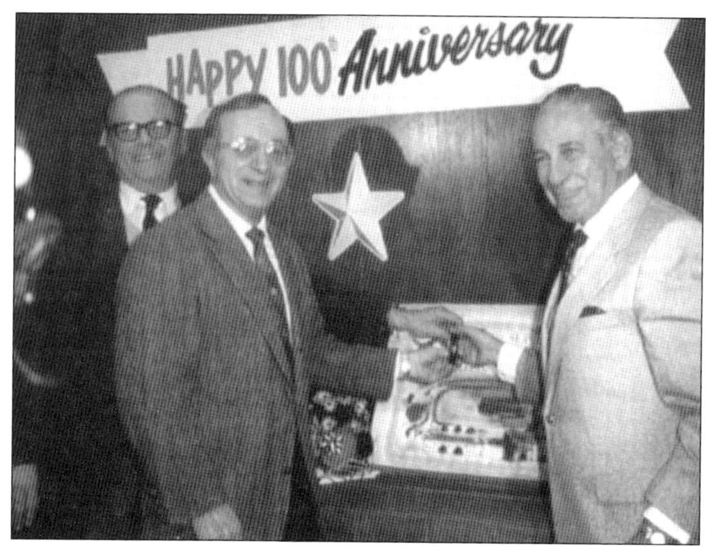

From left to right, fair directors David K. Bausch, Joe Daddona, and Ed Charles celebrate the 100th anniversary of the current fairgrounds. The fair moved to its current location between Seventeenth, Chew, and Liberty Streets in 1889. Unfortunately, the first fair at the new location was rained out, and the sulky races were cancelled that year. In 1989, the weather for the centennial celebration of the grounds was more cooperative.

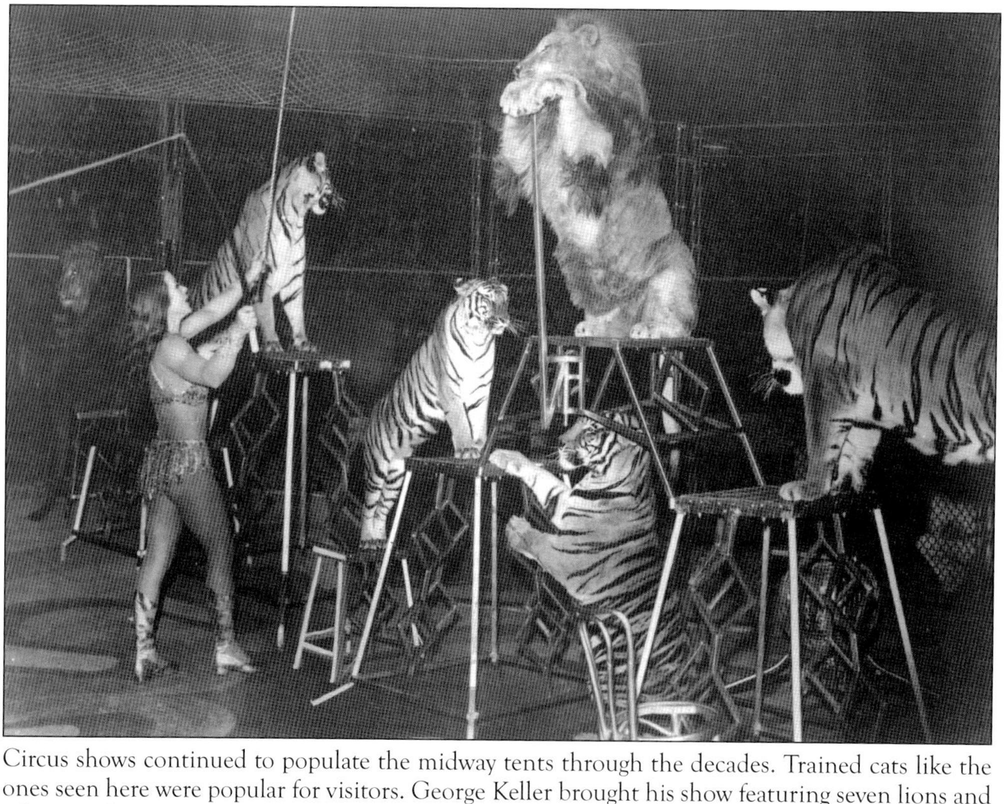

Circus shows continued to populate the midway tents through the decades. Trained cats like the ones seen here were popular for visitors. George Keller brought his show featuring seven lions and other jungle cats to the 1952 fair, where he ended the show by putting his head in the mouth of a lion. Here, a female trainer poses her big cats for the audience.

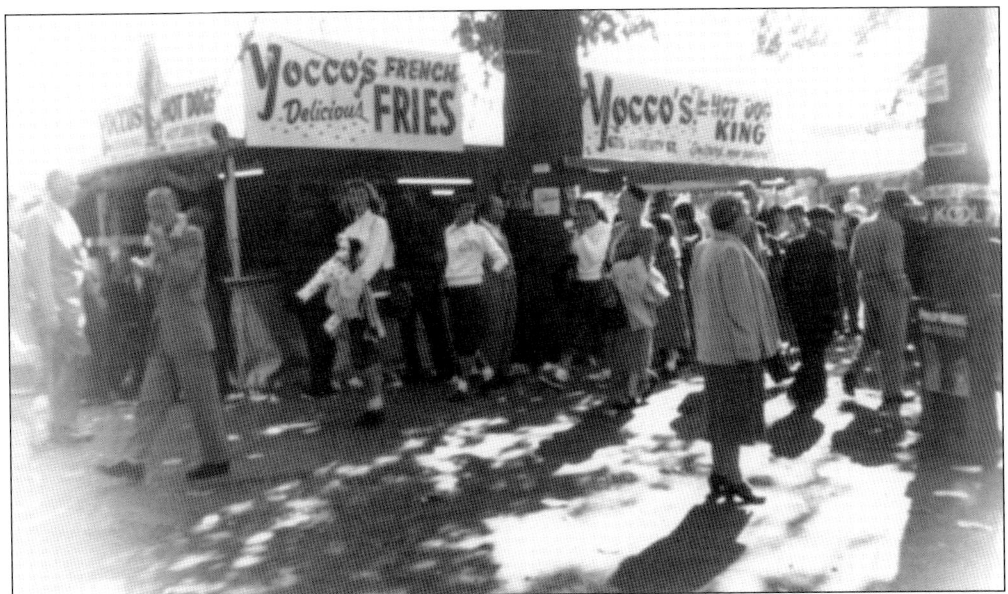

Patrons in the 1940s enjoy a stop for Yocco's hot dogs and its famous secret sauce. Owned by the Iacocca family, Yocco's hot dogs first appeared at the Allentown fair in the 1930s. A decade later, 12-year-old Joseph Daddona worked at Yocco's during fair week. When Daddona served as the mayor of Allentown, he declared June 2, 1987, "Yocco Hot Dog Day in Allentown." (Courtesy of Gary Iacocca.)

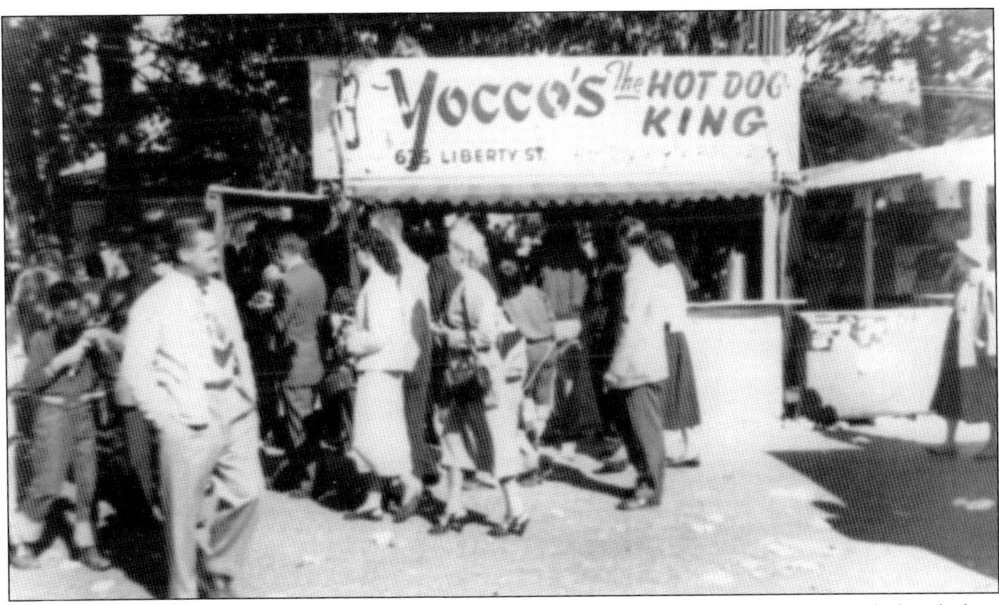

In 1922, Theodore Iacocca ran a convenience store named the Liberty Grille and decided to add hot dogs to its menu. From that day forward, Iacocca's store was known for its hot dogs. As popularity rose, the Doggie Pac, a complete at-home kit for 12 hot dogs, was created. The Doggie Pac has been shipped around the world to those who miss the local legend. (Courtesy of Gary Iacocca.)

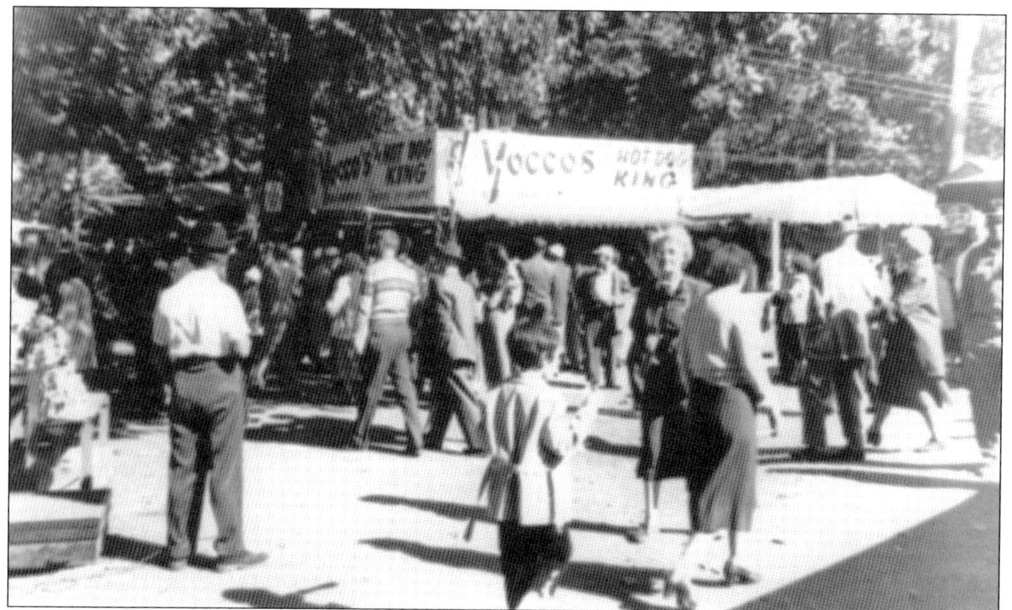

While the business was originally named for its location on Liberty Street, German locals had trouble pronouncing "Iacocca" and referred to it as "Mr. Yocco's Place." This nickname reflected the way they pronounced the Italian last name, sounding like "Yacoca." One day, the family painted the name "Yocco's" on the store window, and the name stuck. The Iacocca family continues to operate the franchise today. (Courtesy of Gary Iacocca.)

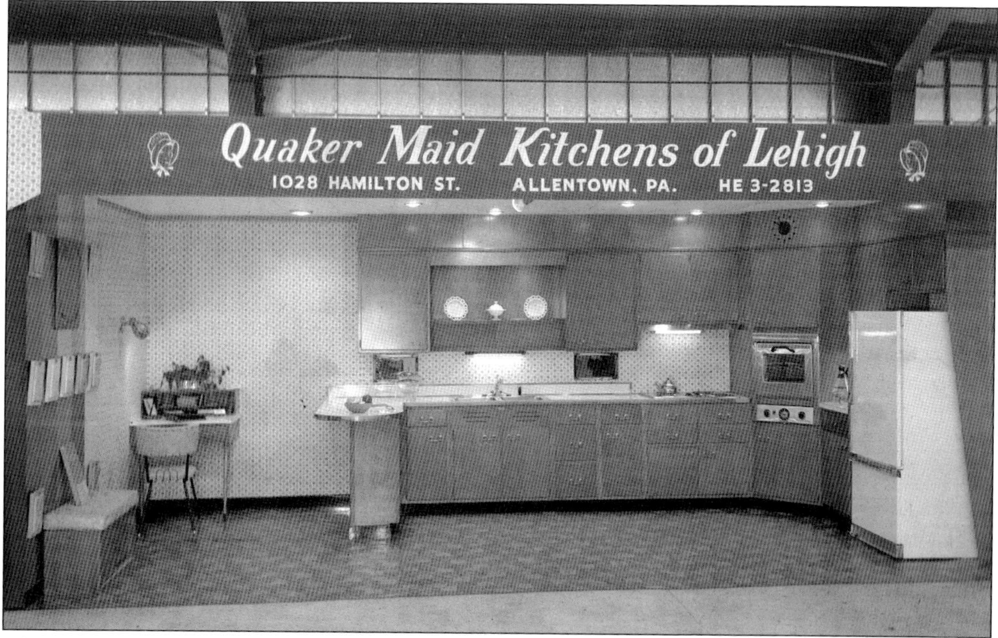

Thanks to the new Agricultural Hall, business displays flourished, and the QuakerMaid Kitchen Company built an entire kitchen with modern appliances for its 1950s fair display. The company was known for designing complete custom kitchens, and many visitors to the fair no doubt left desiring a custom kitchen of their own. The company, once on Hamilton Street in Allentown, has since closed. (Courtesy of Kelly Ann Butterbaugh.)

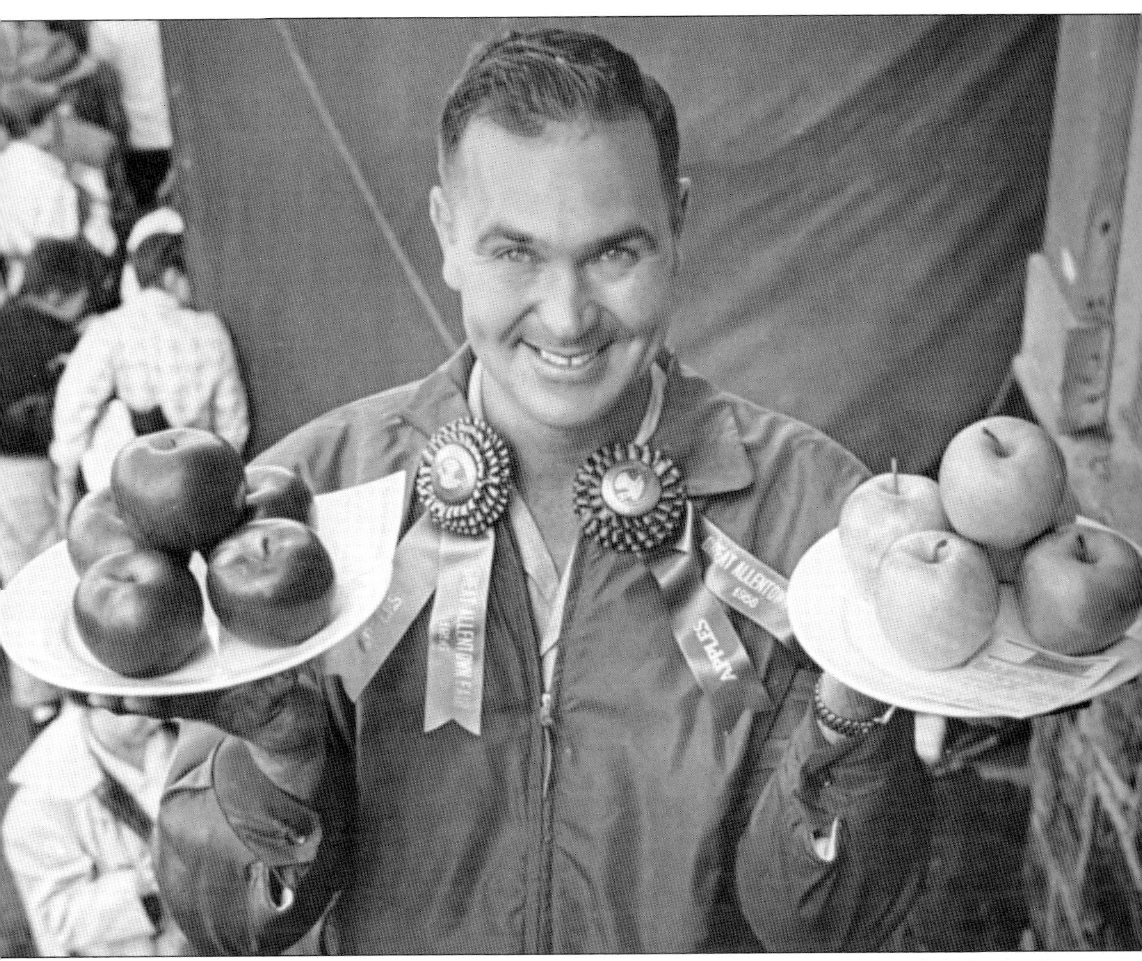

Rewellien "Rudy" Mohr proudly shows his prizewinning apples in the 1956 fair. Mohr's Orchards spanned 500 acres in Fogelsville and gained attention with its slogan "Eat Mohr Fruit." Mohr served as a director for the fair, organizing the pie-eating contest at the Farmerama Theater. Both his father, James Mohr, and his son, Karl Mohr, served on the executive committee for the fair as well. (Courtesy of Karl Mohr.)

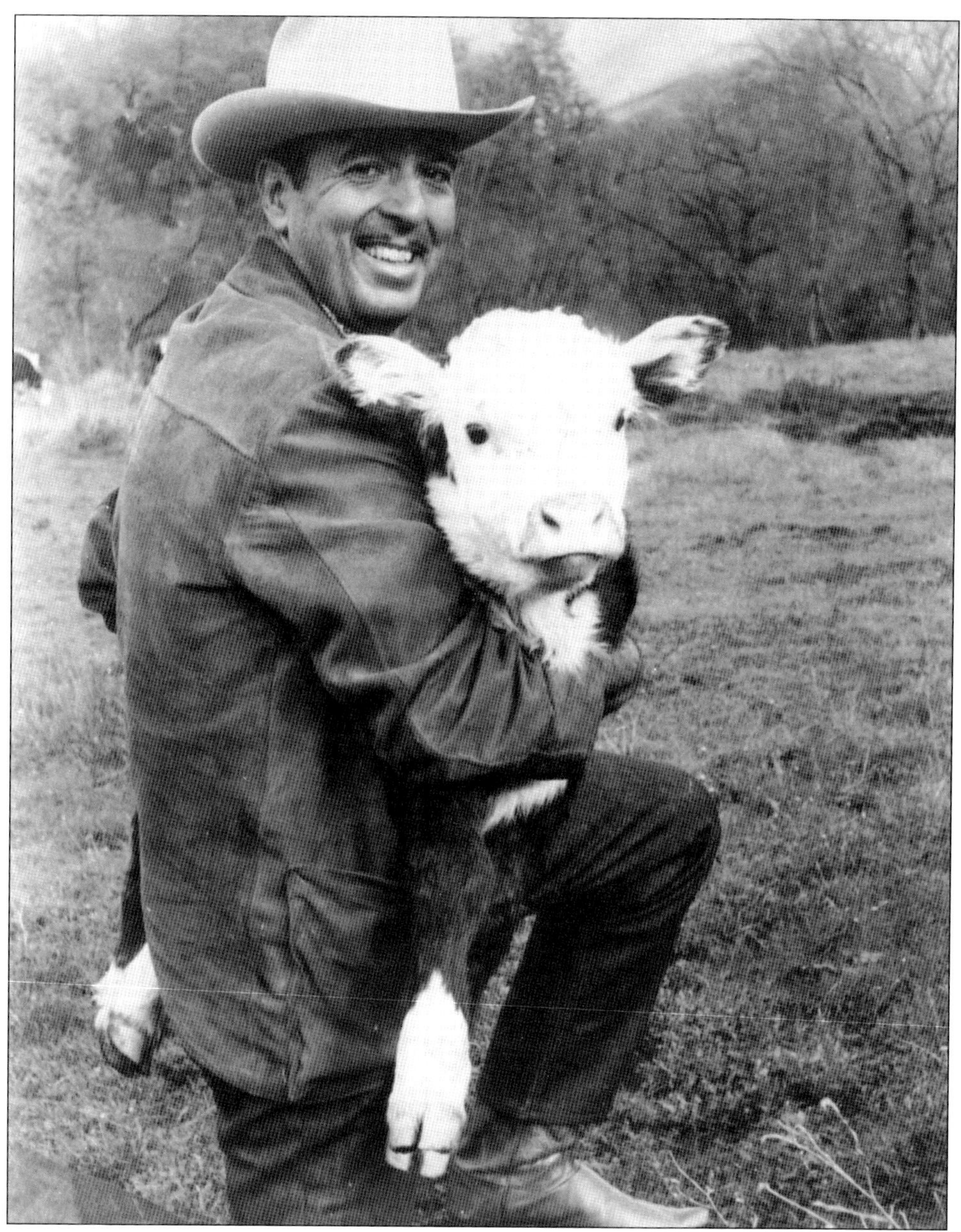

Martin Ritter officially became involved with the Great Allentown Fair in the 1950s, but his family holds ties back to his great-grandfather, who served as the first fair president in 1854. During his time working with the LCAS, Ritter served as a member, a board member, vice president, chairman of the executive committee, general manager, president from 1980 to 2004, and president emeritus. However, what he is most known for is his ability to book stars for the stage that were difficult to negotiate. His favorite booking was Olivia Newton-John in 1974; he booked her before her first hit song and negotiated a superstar for a rising star price. Ritter also became friends with Roy Rogers and Dale Evans when they visited the fair. Because of his contribution to the talent that performed on the grandstand stage, on July 29, 2004, the grandstand at the fairgrounds was rededicated as the Martin H. Ritter Grandstand, "Home of the Stars." At that event, Ritter joked that he had been at the fairgrounds the day the grandstand was built in 1911.

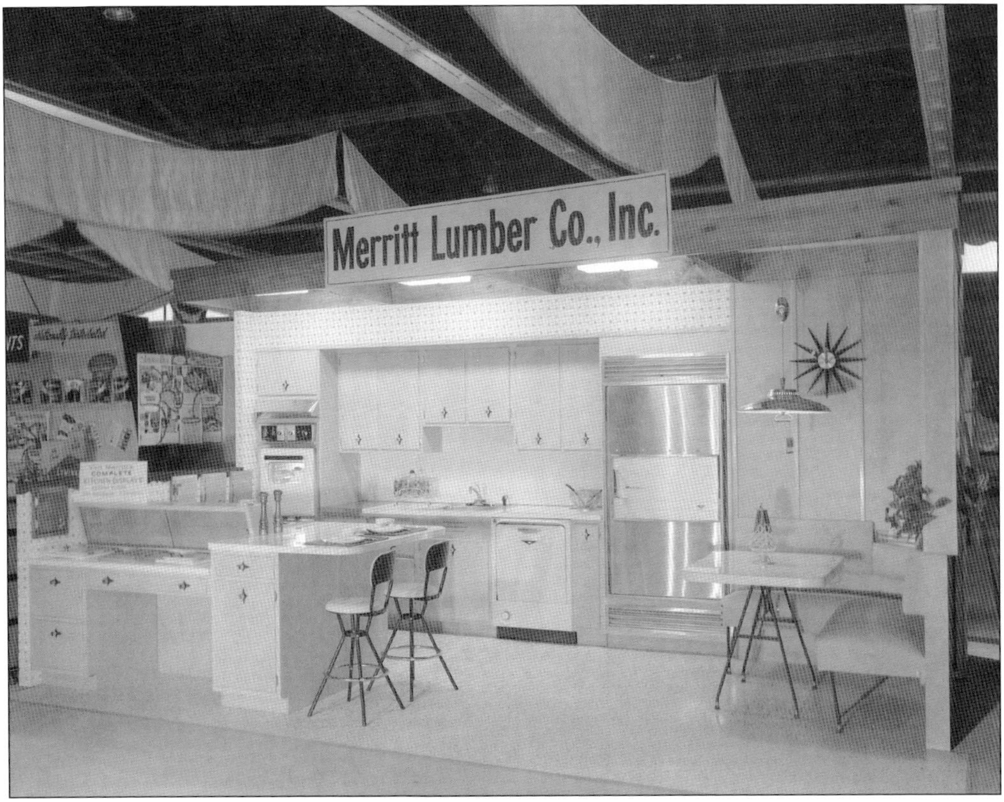

During fair week, the inside of the Agri-plex is transformed into displays from local companies. This 1948 display is from Merritt Lumber, a company that originated in 1880 by Thomas and Howard Merritt and in 1944 opened a branch on Hamilton Street in Allentown. Yet even this new exhibition hall grew crowded, and additions were made over the years. (Courtesy of Kelly Ann Butterbaugh.)

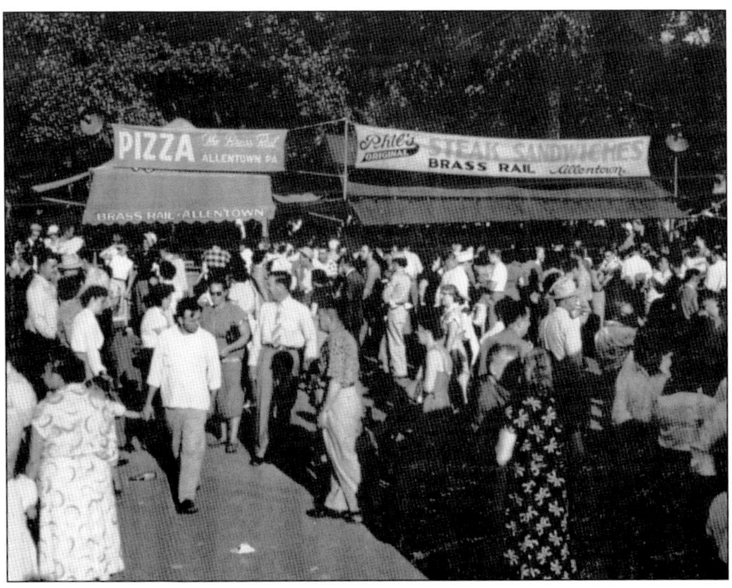

The Brass Rail has been a staple at the fair for decades. It began in 1931 as a hamburger and hot-dog stand owned by Philip Sorrentino. Two years later, he opened a restaurant on Hamilton Street. In 1937, he added steak sandwiches to the menu for 15¢ each. Utilizing a local bakery for its rolls and adding the signature sauce, it became a town favorite. (Courtesy of Mark Sorrentino.)

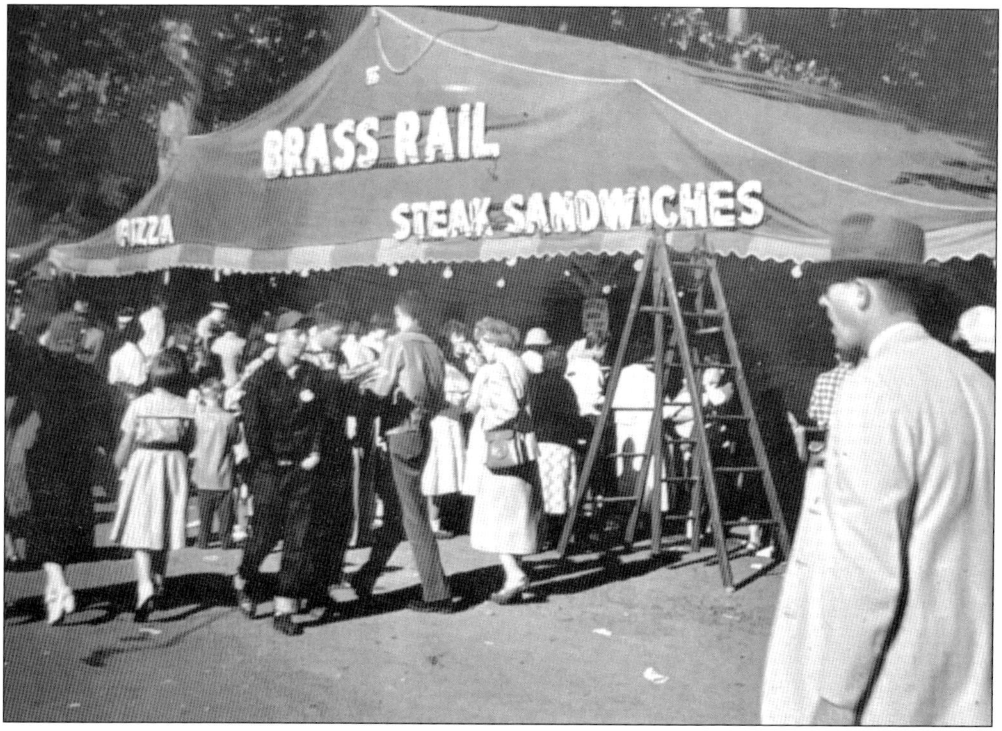

Known for its cheesesteaks and pizza, those who craved Brass Rail food after the fair could visit the bar and restaurant on Hamilton Street. In 1961, a second location opened on Lehigh Street. The Hamilton Street location closed in 2001, and the Lehigh Street location closed in 2022. However, in 2024, the restaurant reopened in the farmers market under the grandstand at the fairgrounds. (Courtesy of Mark Sorrentino.)

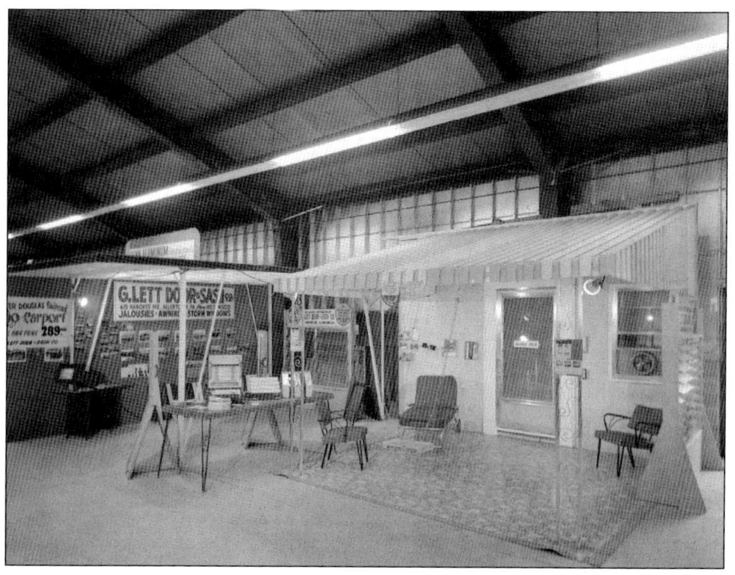

G. Lett Door and Sash Co. constructed an elaborate display for the business showcase at the fair in the 1950s. The popular jalousie windows and doors were all the rage of the company's display, as was the sturdy aluminum patio/carport awning. The display invites visitors to test the strength of the awning by sitting on the swing suspended from the aluminum. (Courtesy of Kelly Ann Butterbaugh.)

The Pennsylvania Farm Bureau (PAFB) set up a tent at the Allentown Fair to promote products that reflected the needs of its members. The pennants in the bureau's stand show products that are endorsed by the PAFB. The display of FADA televisions shows its full endorsement of the company, founded in 1920 by Frank Angelo D'Andrea, who named the company by his initials. (Courtesy of Kelly Ann Butterbaugh.)

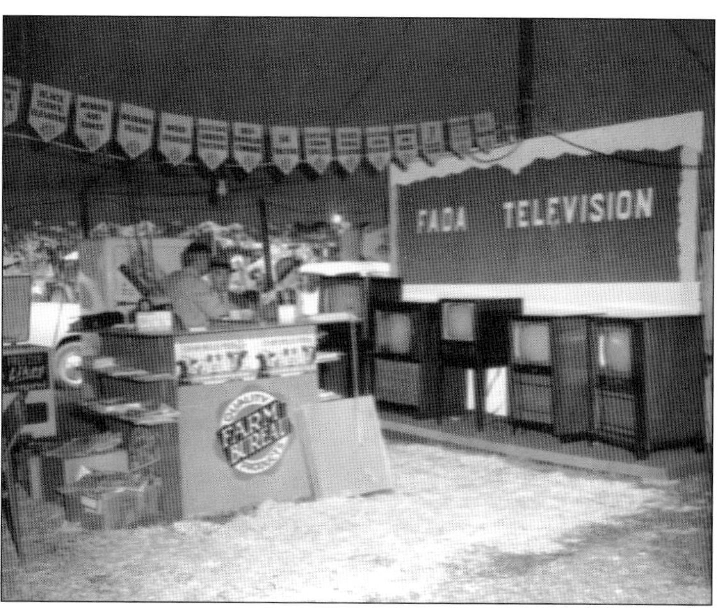

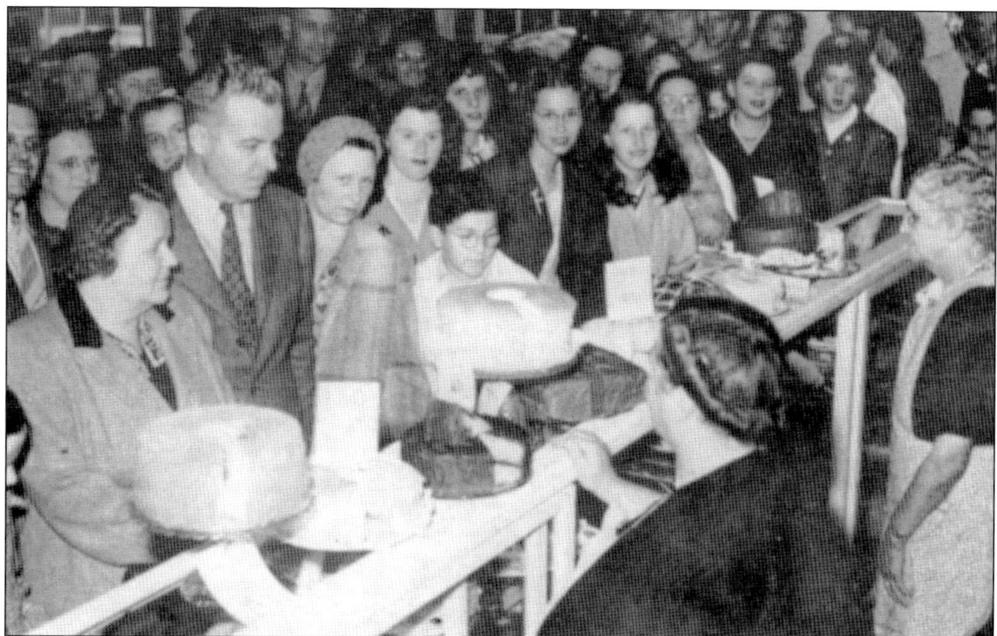

Here, in 1968, onlookers admire the premium winners on display inside of Ag Hall. Entrants have the opportunity to enter needlework, baked goods, and antiques during the fair. Not only are the colorful award ribbons sought after but so are the premiums. In 1963, the award premiums for agricultural, domestic, and fine arts exhibits totaled more than any other fair in the state. (Courtesy of David Bausch.)

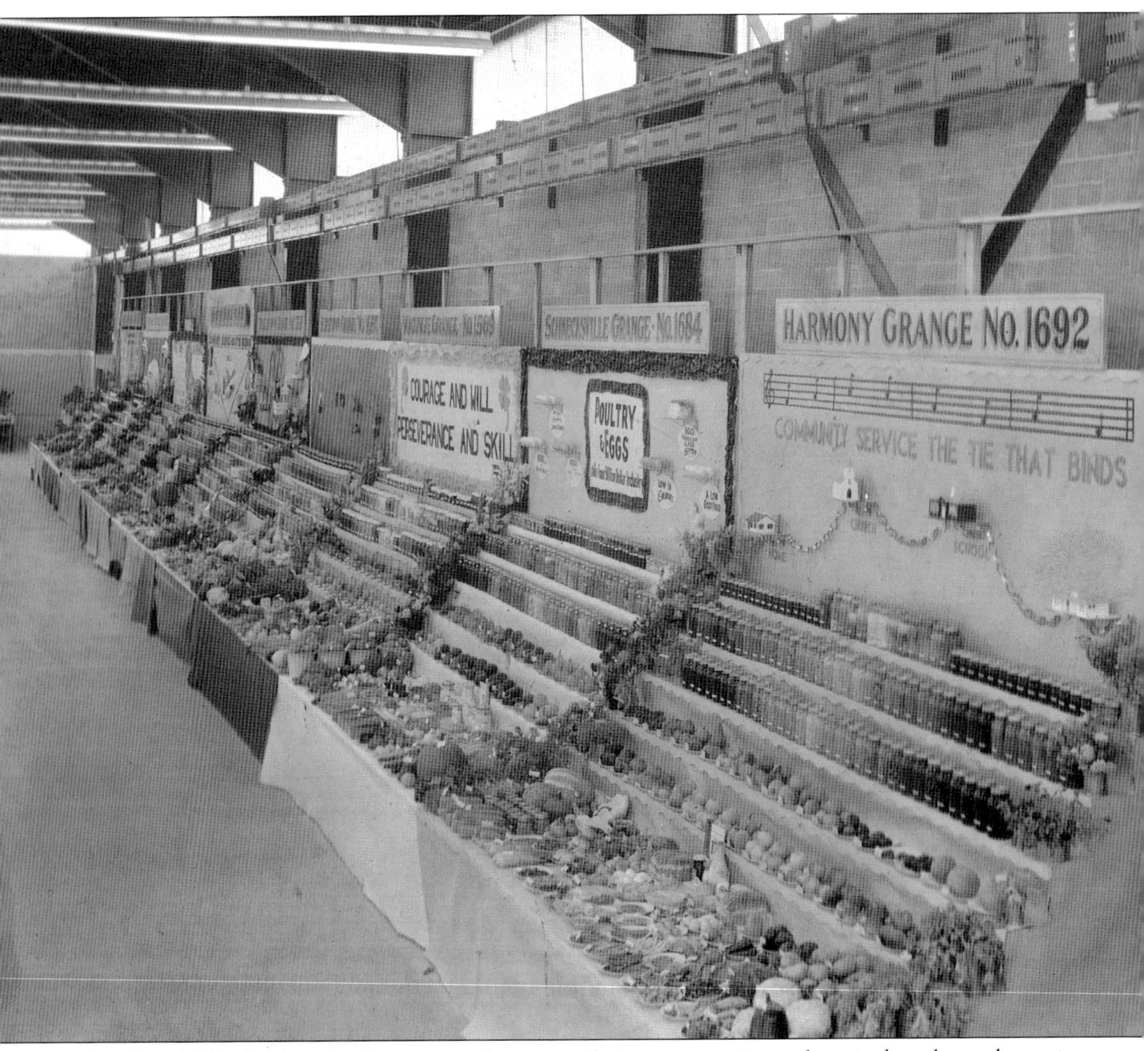

In this 1957 display, local granges showcase their preservation of agricultural products in alignment with a selected theme. The winner at this year's fair was the Harmony Grange No. 1692 of Northampton with its 114 jars of preserves. A close second place this year was the Hanover Grange No. 1698 of Northampton. Harmony Grange saw its largest membership on record in 1957 with 350 members. By 1977, grange memberships in the area were low, and Hanover Grange merged with Harmony Grange. The other granges displayed here are Central Grange No. 1650 of Germansville, Seipstown Grange No. 1657 of Fogelsville, Trexlertown Grange No. 1755 of Wescosville, Macungie Grange No. 1569, and Schnecksville Grange No. 1684. Granges are organizations dedicated to helping rural communities through education, fellowship, and community service. As the population of Lehigh County and its surrounding area moved away from agriculture, the focus of the remaining granges has shifted from agricultural education to community service. (Courtesy of Kelly Ann Butterbaugh.)

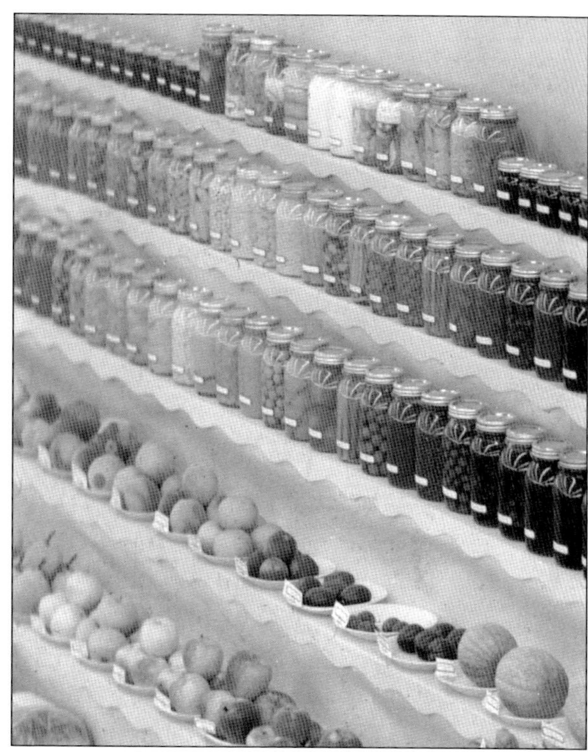

The first year that grange displays were at the fair was 1920. That year, 12 area granges were invited to display orchard, garden, and farm products. At the end of the fair, the products from the grange displays were sold. Prizes ranging from $75 down to $25 for the top three granges went to Upper Saucon, Trexlertown, and Macungie. (Courtesy of Kelly Ann Butterbaugh.)

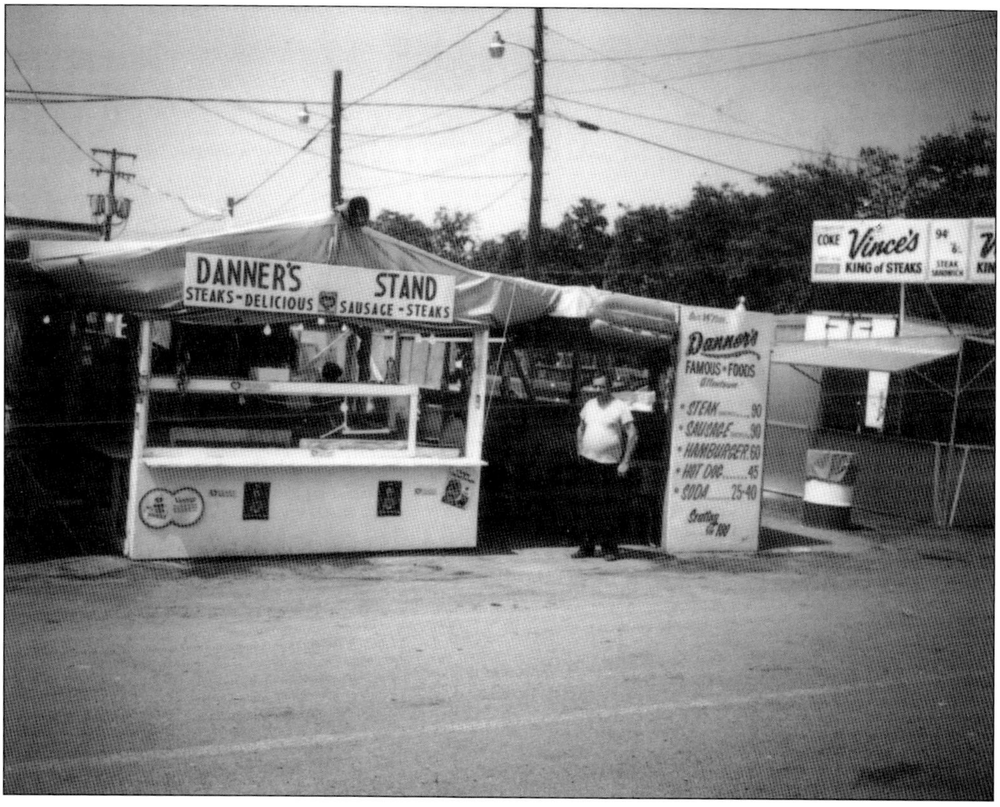

Danner's concession stand and Vince's cheesesteaks are set to open and feed the thousands of visitors at the fair. While Danner's sold a variety of foods, Vince's focused on cheesesteaks and sausage sandwiches. Starting its business in 1957, Vince's prides itself on a "Lehigh Valley cheesesteak," a chipped steak sandwich with sauce, pickles, and hot peppers. Both were family-operated businesses. (Courtesy of the Danner family.)

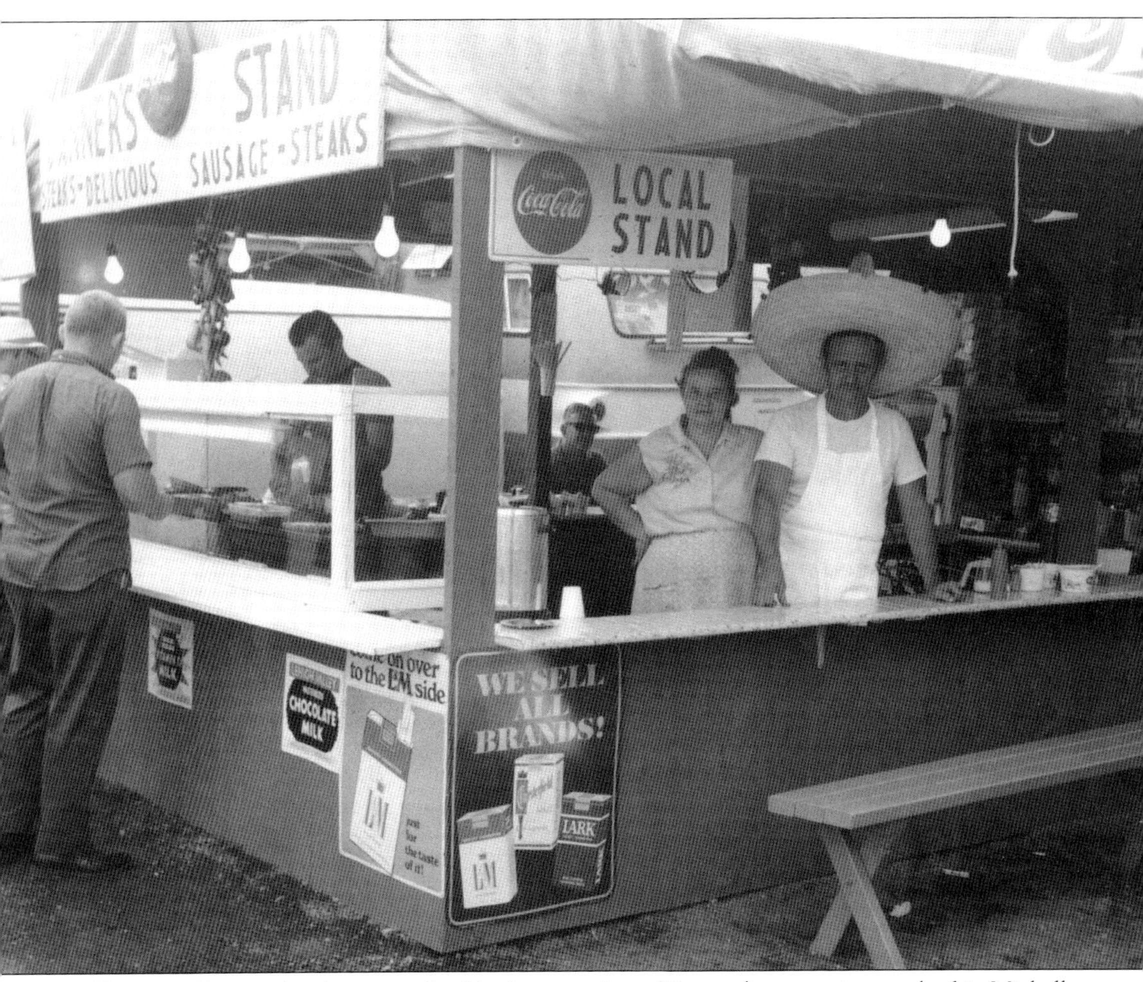

The entire Danner family was involved in the operation of Danner's concessions at the fair. Michelle (Danner) Ritter remembers childhood times spent at the fair with her family's stand. Although the fair closed at night, Danner's concessions remained open to serve those who worked the fair. Michelle Ritter recalls enjoyable evenings playing cards and talking with people who operated other attractions at the fair. Midway performers, other concession owners, and ride operators ate at her parents' stand after hours, enjoying the camaraderie of their fair friends. When the Danner family bought a brick-and-mortar restaurant, they continued to operate their concession stand at the fair, but Danner's concessions transitioned to the Willow Street Pub, taking the name of their restaurant to use for their fair concession stand. The Willow Street Pub served steamed clams and mini lobsters, unique dishes to the fair that drew diners to their stand. (Courtesy of the Danner family.)

The Danner family operated concessions at the fair every year from 1961 to 2021. Roy Danner Sr. takes a minute here for a photograph inside the family stand known as Danner's. Danner's concessions traveled to fairs around the area, employing family members throughout the years. In 2006, the family changed their stand's name to Willow Street Pub to reflect the family's restaurant in Coplay. (Courtesy of the Danner family.)

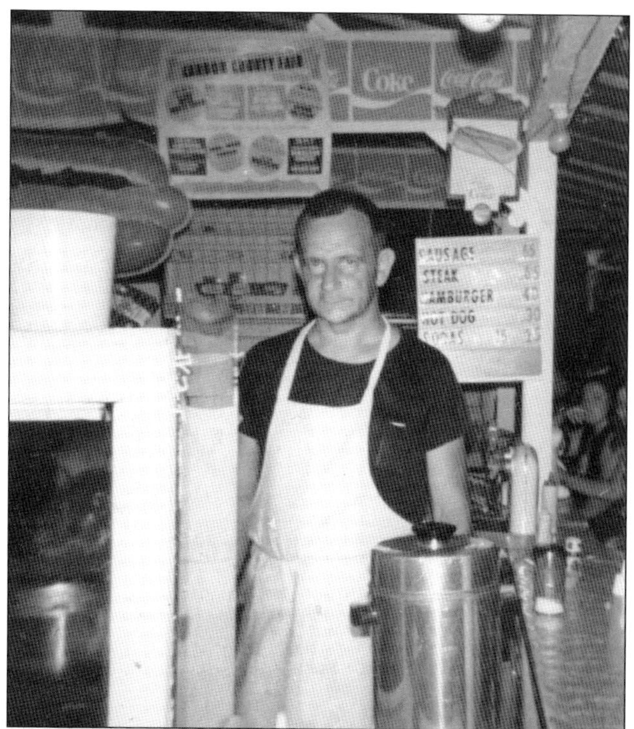

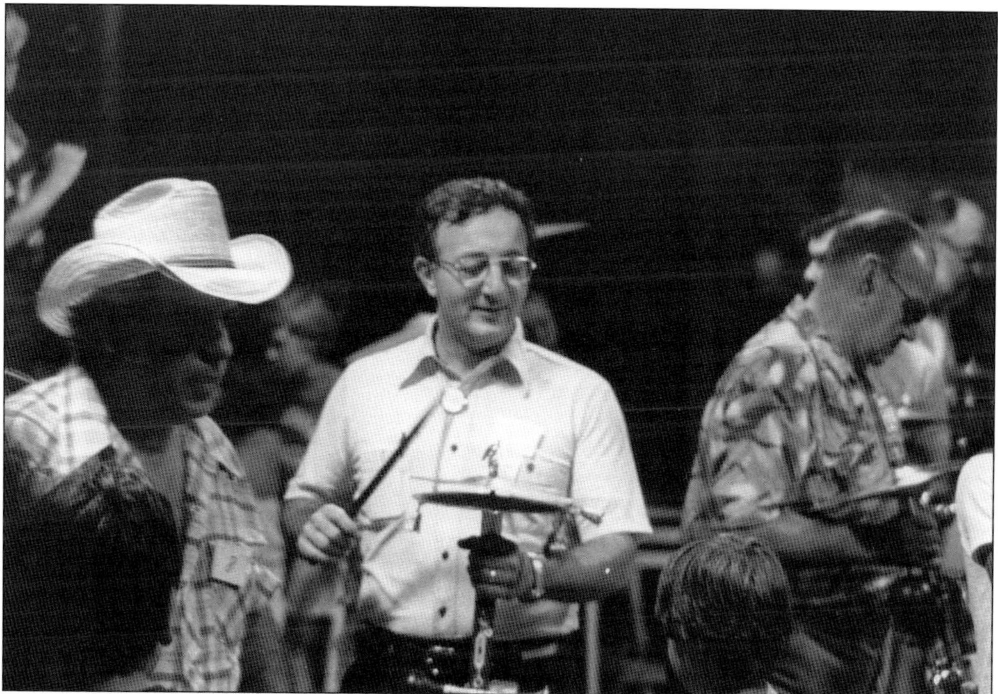

Mayor Joe Daddona plays a "boomba" during one of the contests of the Happy Boombadears at the 1978 fair. A boomba is a one-man band instrument that resembles a pogo stick with sleigh and jingle bells, a tambourine, a cowbell, and a wooden block attached to it. Daddona once quipped about his experience learning to play the boomba, "I lost seven pounds and four neighbors."

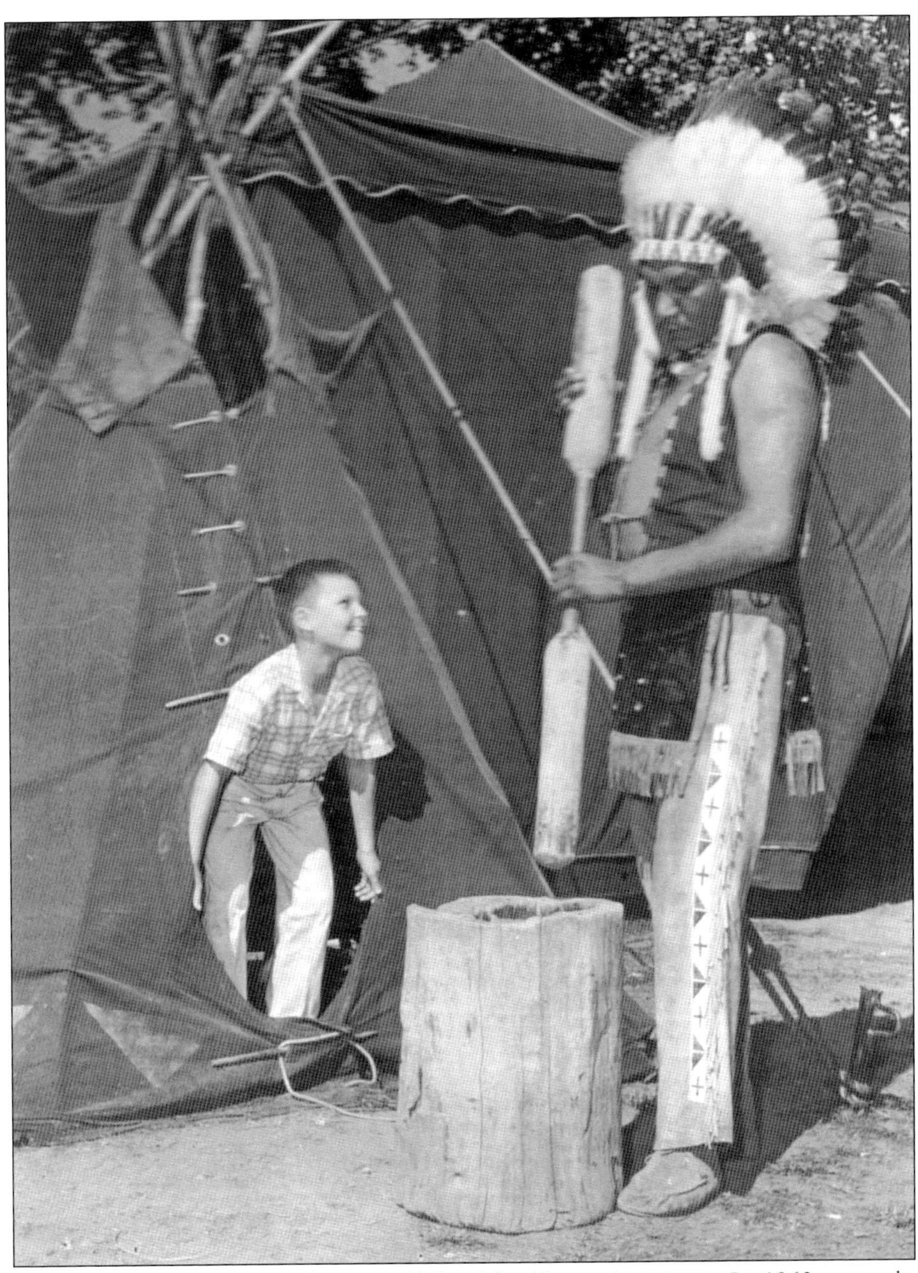

This youngster is excited to see the way of life of the Native Americans. In 1963, an authentic Native American village was constructed with demonstrations like one. Visitors could step into the past as they explored the village and its intricate craftsmanship. Performances featuring Native American dances and music also gathered a crowd. The draw of the American West endured throughout the 1950s and into the 1960s. Dancing shows featured a western theme, and cowboy entertainers performed in front of the grandstand throughout the decade. The largest cowboy draw to the fair was Roy Rogers, but Tex Ritter's singing also built excitement for the fair. Booked by Martin Ritter, the man responsible for many of the "big stars" at the grandstand stage, Tex Ritter found it amusing that they shared the same last name. As a joke, Tex Ritter signed an autograph for Martin Ritter, calling him "cousin."

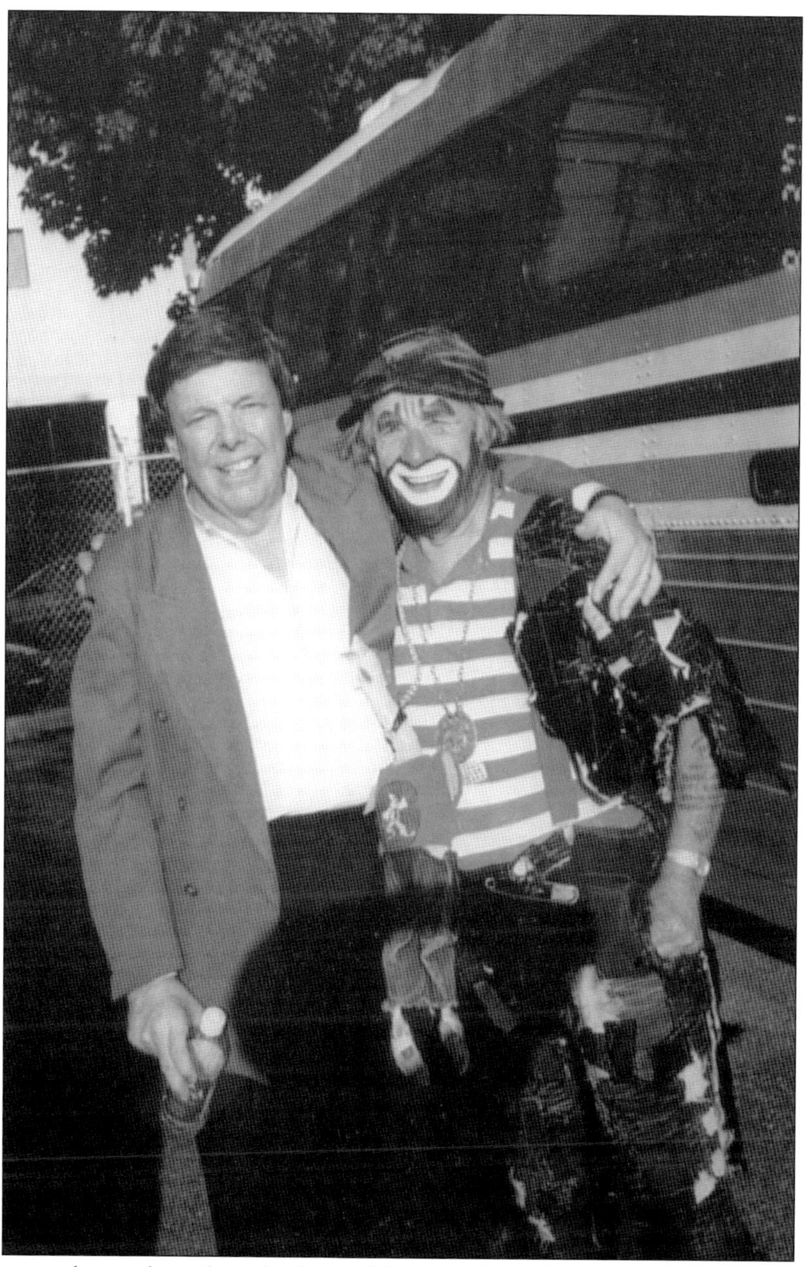

Dapper Dan made people smile at the fair for 37 years. The fair's favorite clown was born in 1966 when Mack Truck electrician Danny Bonner was asked to dress as a clown for a company picnic. He painted his face like Emmett Kelly and dressed like a hobo, falling in love with clowning around almost instantly. Bonner traveled to other fairs in the region and even performed with the Hanneford circus, which also visited the Great Allentown Fair. With a rubber chicken named Cosmos, a pet pig on wheels named Porkchop, and a stuffed skunk that "sprayed" unsuspecting audience members, Dan wandered the fairgrounds during fair week, delighting children and adults alike. One of his many magic tricks was making an egg appear in his mouth or making a random item disappear. Dan performed tricks and handed out tootsie rolls to children at the fair until 2014, when he was 90 years old. His picture was added to the fair's hall of fame in 2000.

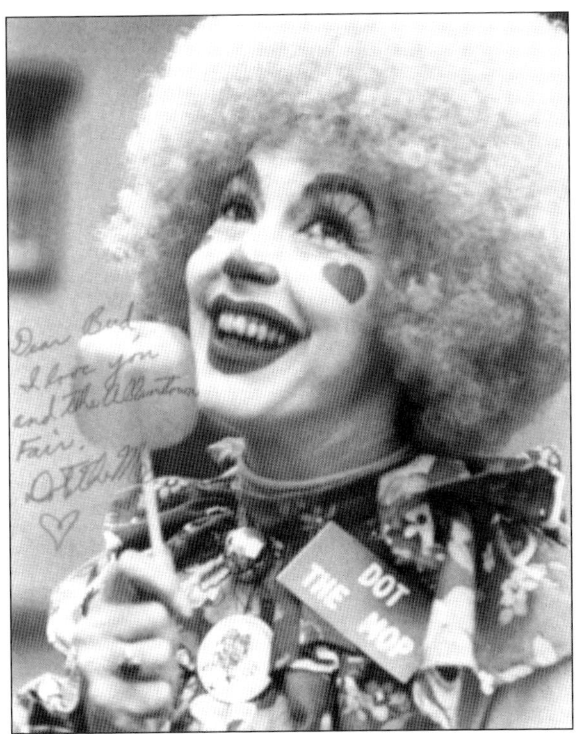

Dot the Mop delighted fairgoers as a walking clown on the midway. In the late 1970s, professional female clowns were rare, and makeup artists only knew how to do male clown makeup. In 1978, Beverly Hoffman did her own makeup and was the only female clown in the country who performed alone as a walking professional clown.

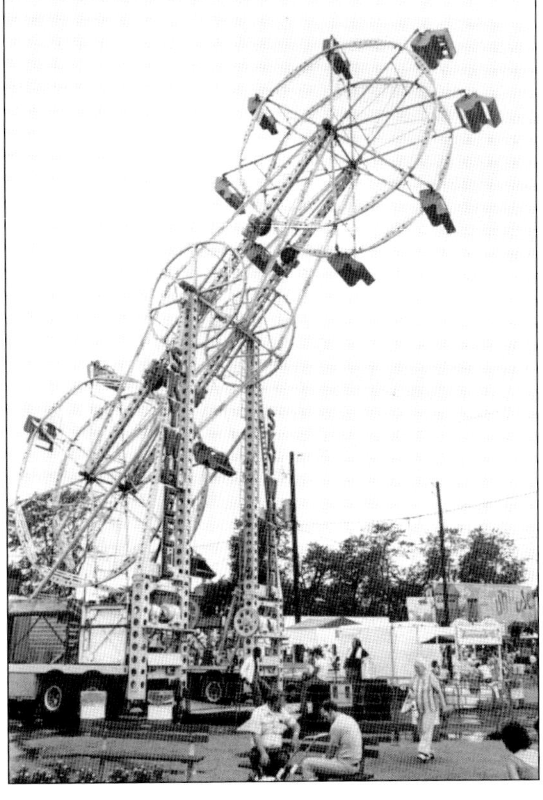

This Skywheel, also known as the double wheel, debuted at the fair in 1964 when Gooding's Million Dollar Midway premiered. Built by the Allan Herschell Company, the wheel towered 140 feet in the air with each wheel spinning in opposite directions. The Skywheel was notoriously difficult to set up, making it a ride that was not seen at every fair.

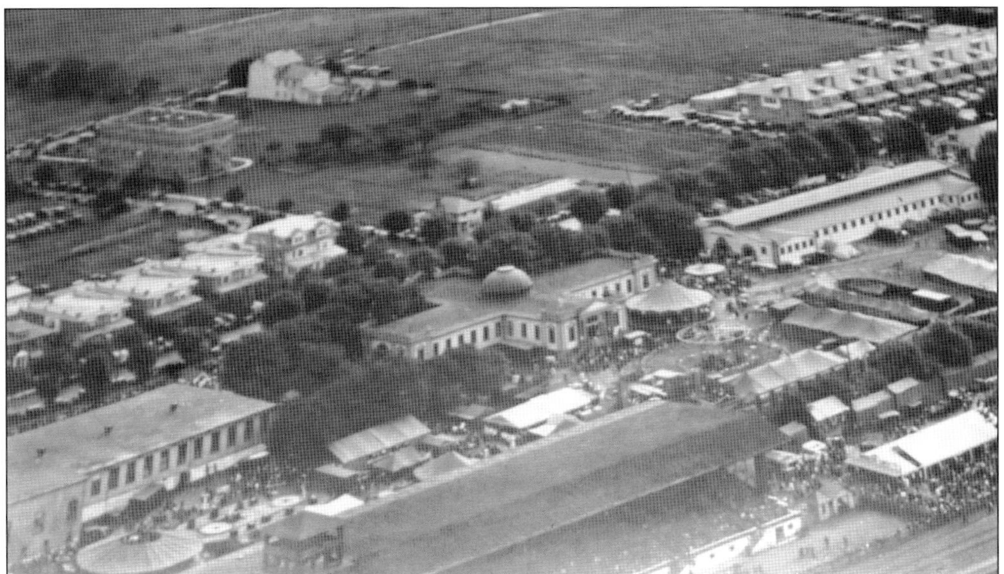

The original exhibition buildings can be seen along the "Great White Way" in 1925. In the center is the cross-shaped Horticultural Hall, to the left is the main exhibition hall, and to the right is one of two poultry barns. A carousel can be seen in front of Horticultural Hall as well as the oblong-shaped Whip ride. A great treat of the fair that year was cotton candy.

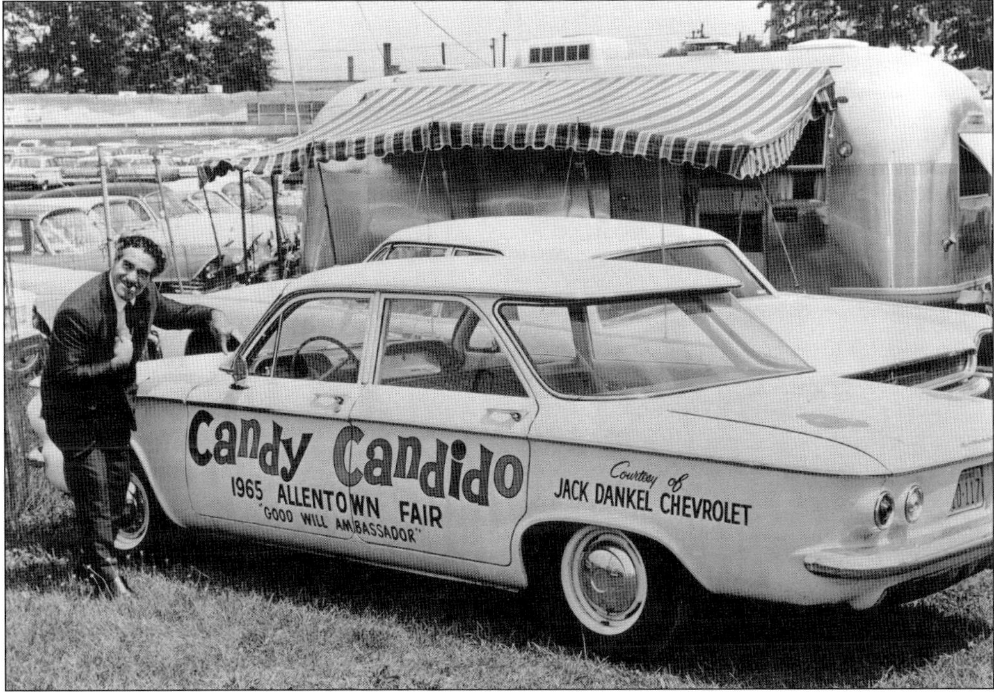

The fair's goodwill ambassador, Johnny "Candy" Candido, stands in front of his Airstream trailer and his touring car. Candido would arrive at the fairgrounds a few weeks before the fair to make appearances that served as advertisements for the fair. Known in Hollywood as "the Man with a Thousand Voices," Candido conducted interviews and escorted celebrities and visitors around the fair.

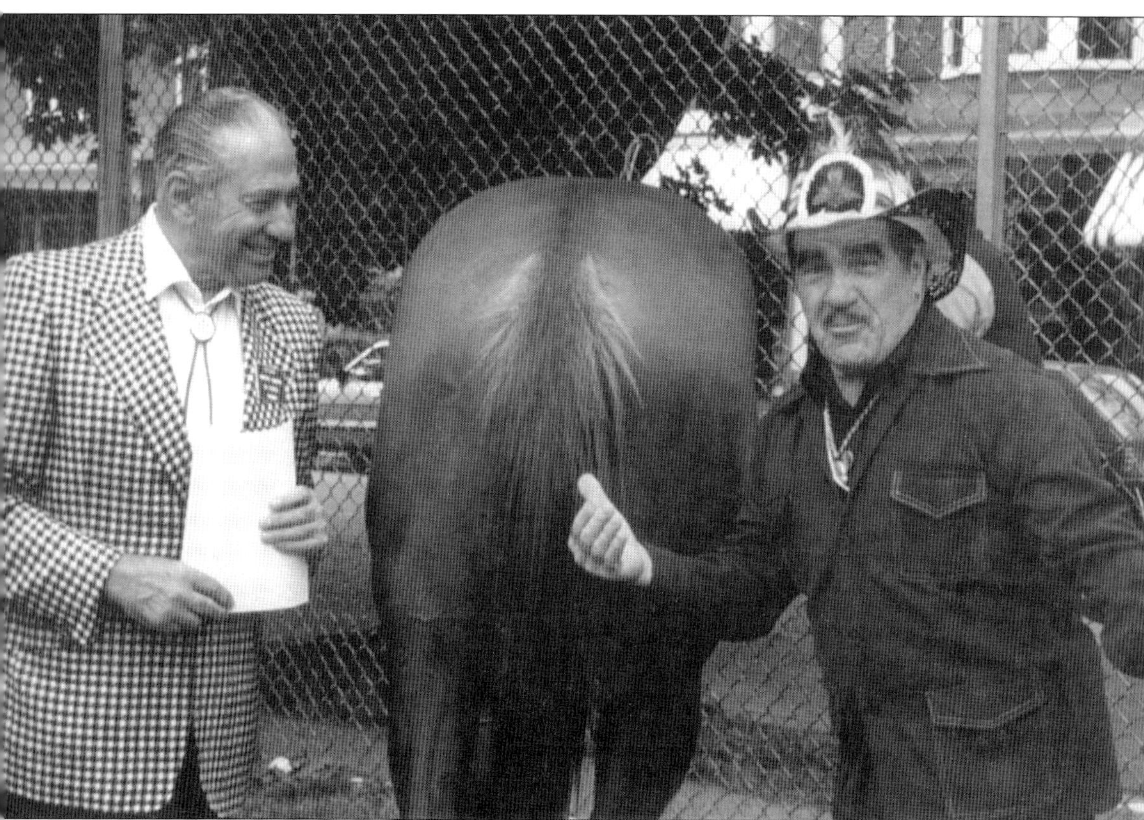

Candy Candido and fair chairman Ed Charles "horse around" at the fair. Candido was a Disney voice actor known for his cartoon voices and his catchphrase, "I'm feeling mighty low." Through connections in the entertainment world, Candido became the fair's goodwill ambassador in 1962 and left Hollywood each year afterward to spend a few weeks in Allentown for fair week. During the fair, he could be found everywhere driving around the grounds in his golf cart and delighting children with his cartoon voices. When Candido could not attend the 1987 fair due to health issues, Allentown mayor Joseph Daddona declared September 1–7, 1987, to be Candy Candido Week. The last year Candido visited the fair was 1993. Candido's photograph hangs next to his friend Dapper Dan the clown in the fair's hall of fame. It was Candido who gave the name Cosmo to the clown's rubber chicken.

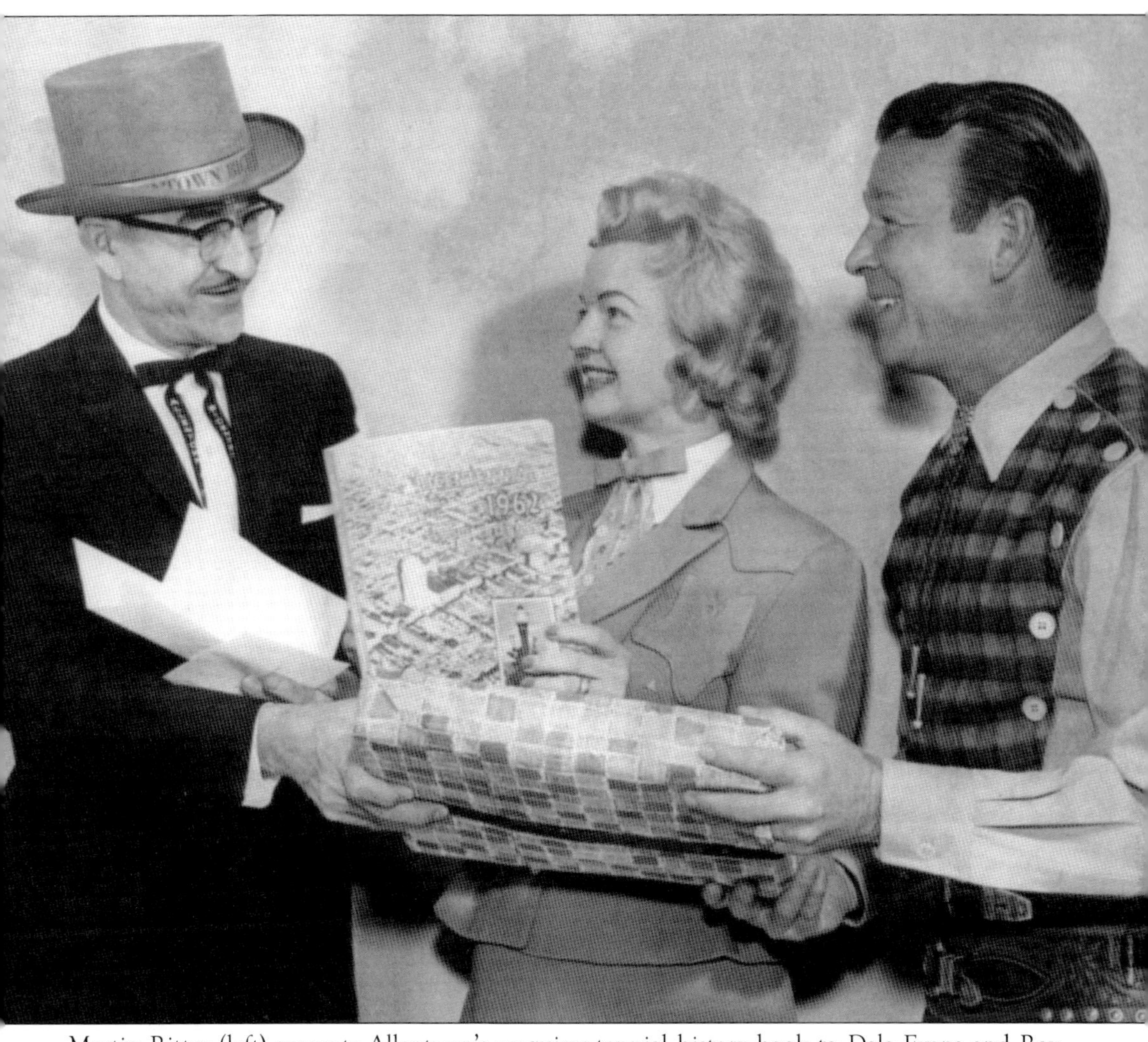

Martin Ritter (left) presents Allentown's sesquicentennial history book to Dale Evans and Roy Rogers in 1962. This was Rogers's and Evans's second time at the fair, and Rogers broke a contract with the New Jersey Fair to instead appear at the Great Allentown Fair this year. Rogers and Evans first appeared at the fair in 1959 with their horses Trigger and Trigger Jr. The singing cowboy couple was the largest draw to the fairgrounds that year. Just before showtime, Trigger became ill, and Emmaus veterinarian Dr. Stewart R. Rockwell tended to the animal, who recovered to the relief of everyone. After the fair closed one evening that week, Ritter took Rogers out to the Livingston Club for a night of bowling. The men returned a little too late for Evans's liking, and she gave Ritter the silent treatment for a few days. All was eventually forgiven when Ritter was later invited to visit the couple at their ranch.

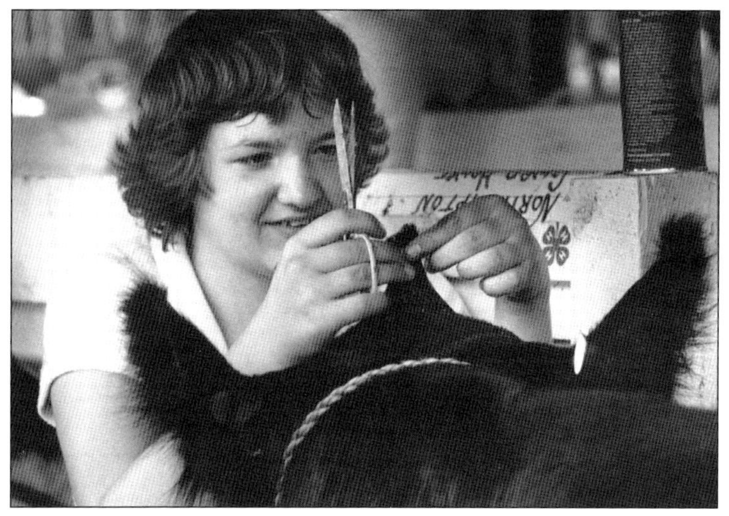

The Hower family began entering Angus steers into the fair competition as early as the 1930s, when Paul Hower used a white halter to show his steer. This halter and the tradition of entering Angus steers in the fair with it continued, and all of Hower's children and some grandchildren were active 4-H members. Here, his daughter Gwen Hower grooms her steer for competition.

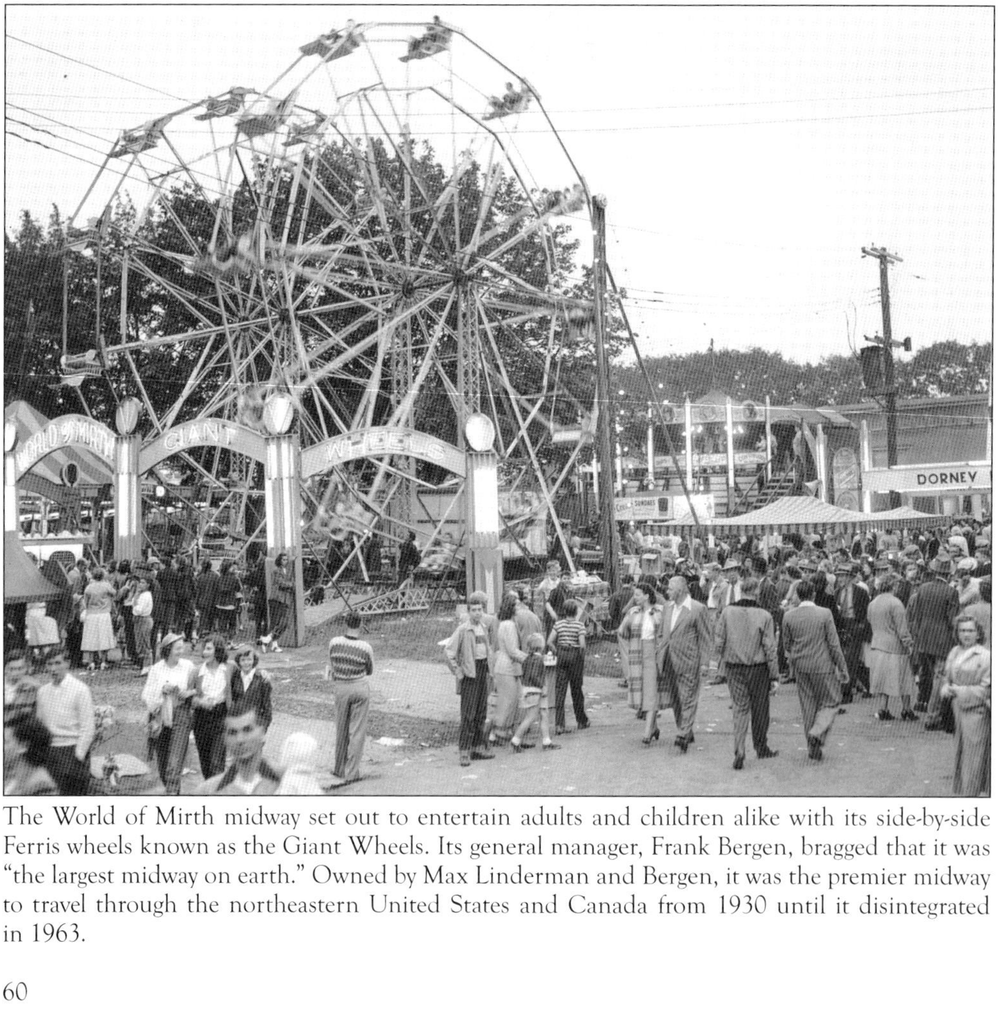

The World of Mirth midway set out to entertain adults and children alike with its side-by-side Ferris wheels known as the Giant Wheels. Its general manager, Frank Bergen, bragged that it was "the largest midway on earth." Owned by Max Linderman and Bergen, it was the premier midway to travel through the northeastern United States and Canada from 1930 until it disintegrated in 1963.

Gooding's Million Dollar Midway picked up in 1964, where the World of Mirth left off, the same time its founder, Floyd Gooding, sold his company to Milt Kaufman. The midway expanded in 1973 to include a children's midway with 35 rides and then hit its largest and grandest size in 1976. In 1979, fair officials parted with Gooding's, knowing that no number of thrill rides could compete with nearby Dorney Park.

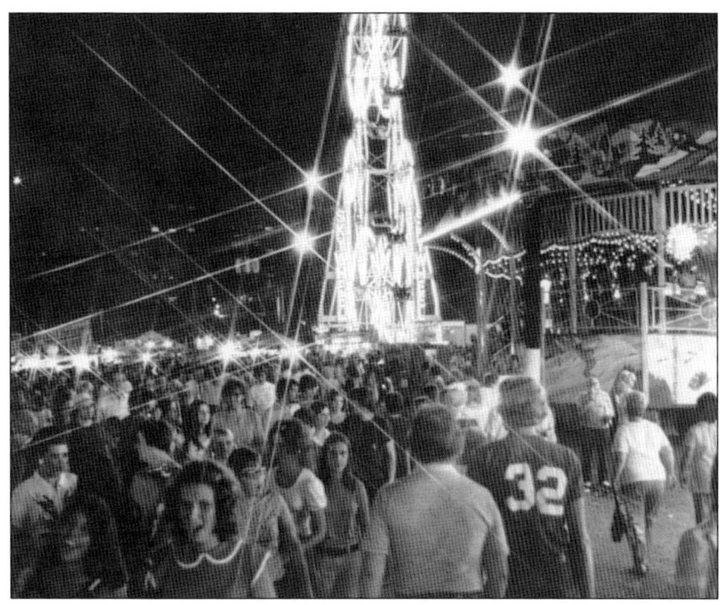

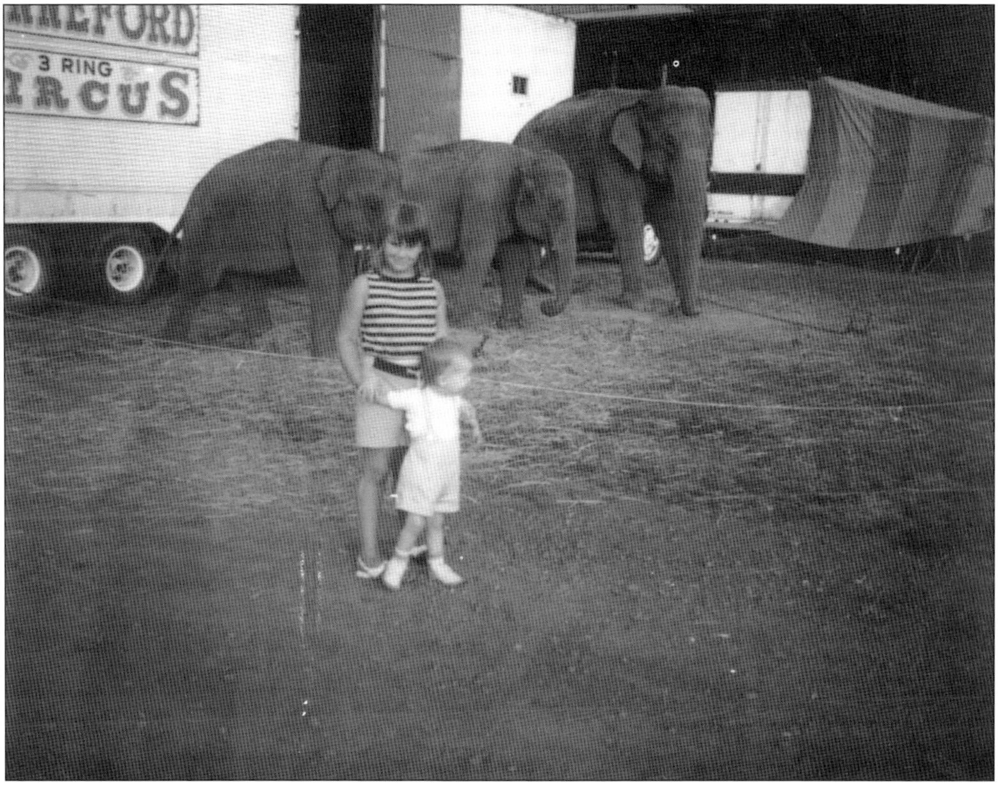

Michelle Danner poses with her little brother Roy in front of the elephants of the Royal Hanneford Circus in 1972. That year, it rained for hours on Romper Day, and the children had to postpone their routines until the last day of the fair. To console the almost 7,000 disappointed children, the circus performed for them in the rain. (Courtesy of the Danner family.)

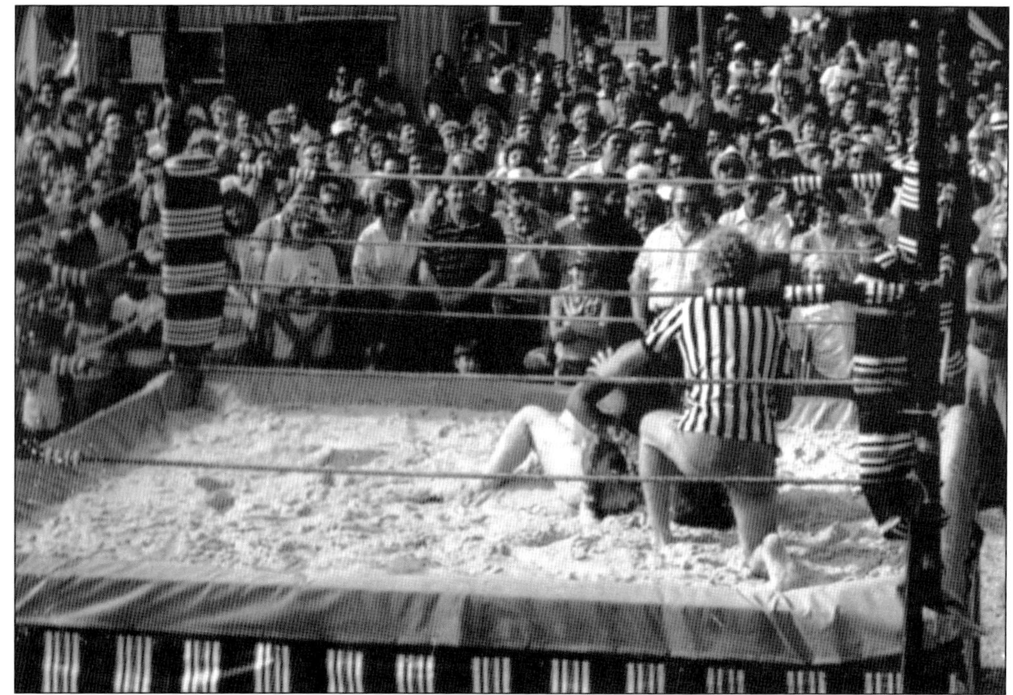

Women's mud wrestling debuted at the fair in 1983. The following year, the four female wrestlers opted to wrestle in chocolate pudding instead of drenched potting soil. The substance changed throughout the years, but the international women's wrestling show continued to put on free performances for the spectators. Sweet potatoes, pumpkin pulp, Jell-O, and oatmeal all filled the ring at times.

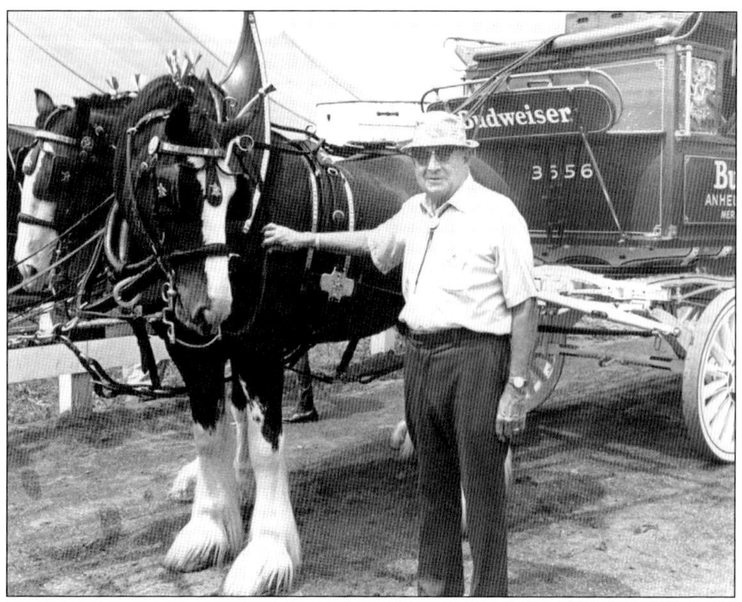

The Budweiser Clydesdales made their third appearance at the fairgrounds from August 4 to 15 in 1971. Each of the eight horses weighed 2,000 pounds and pulled a three-and-a-half-ton wagon as they performed sophisticated drills for the audiences during their daily shows. Special stables were set up for them near the Farmerama Theater. (Photograph by Richard F. Gaal; courtesy of LCAS.)

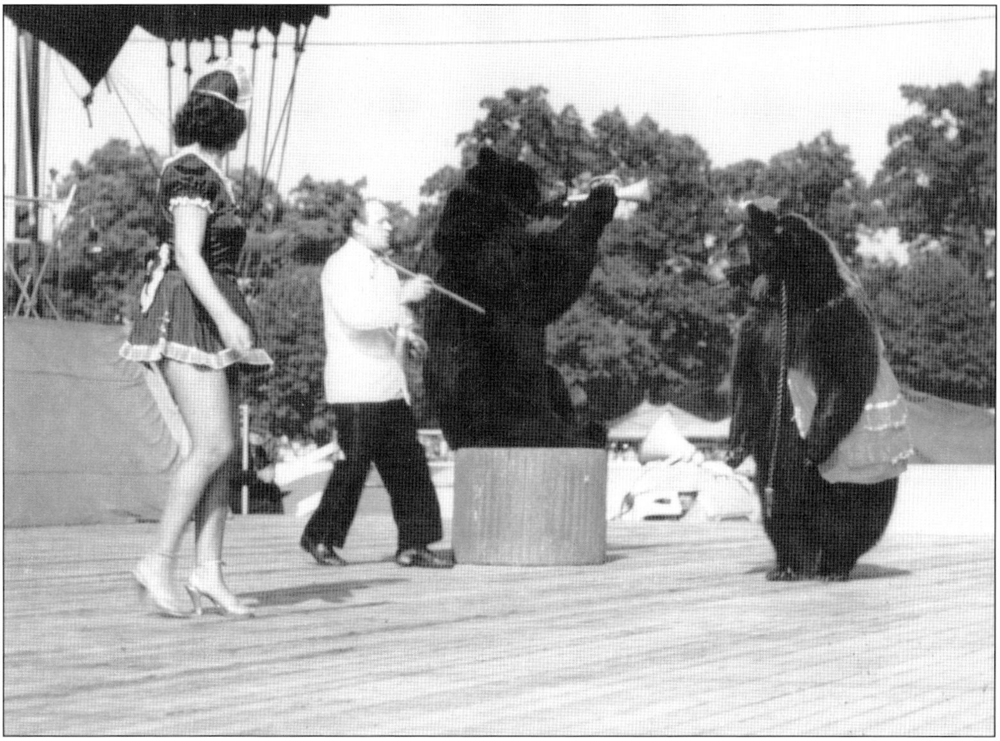

Johnny Welde's famous bears performed on the grandstand stage in 1953. The three brown bears rode tandem bicycles, drove a kiddie car, drank milk from a bottle, and played the trumpet. The louder the audience applauded, the more the gentle bears played, to the point where they were reluctant to leave the stage. (Courtesy of the Danner family.)

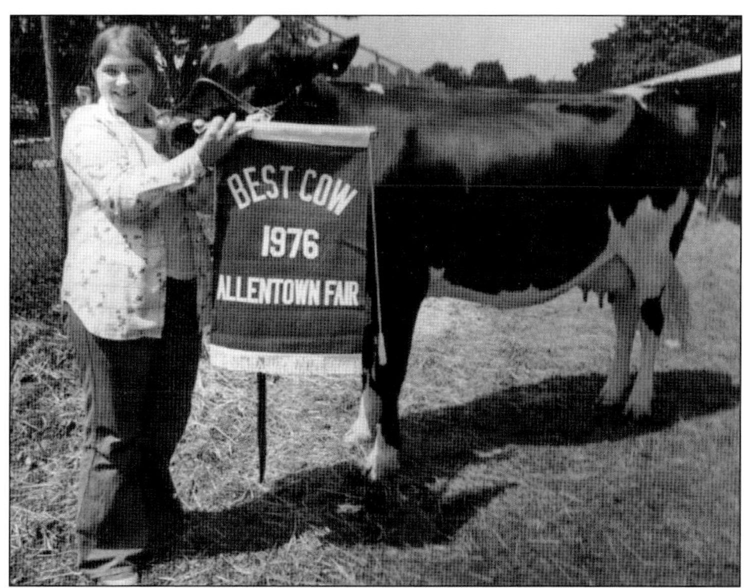

Here, a 4-H member showcases her prizewinning cow in 1976. The first youth fair entries were in 1909, when boys were sent corn seeds to grow and enter into the fair. With prizes ranging from $1 to $10, the contest drew 188 boys. The 4-H was not invited to compete at the fair until 1919, but heavy rain canceled the judging that year, and the first competition was a sow judging in 1920.

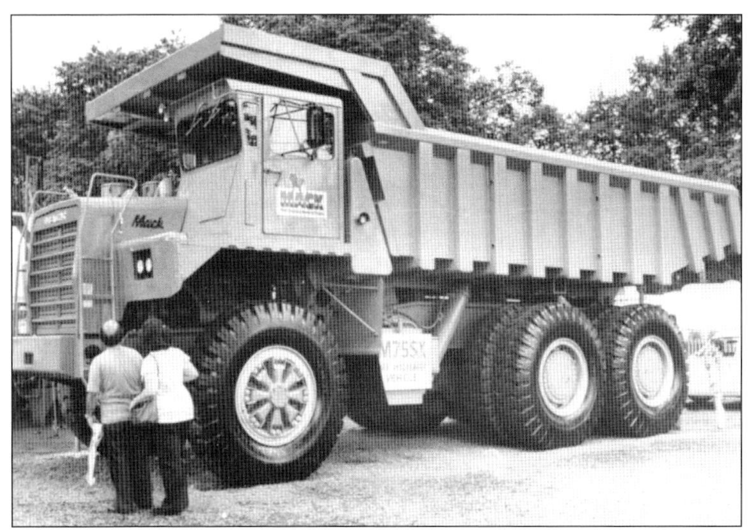

Mack trucks have been drawing a crowd at the fair since 1911. Each year, the local Allentown plant brought trucks to display at the fair. Here, a 1977 MS75SX off-road dump truck is displayed. The model is known as Mack's largest off-road vehicle. The trucks came with 700-horsepower engines and a 75-ton load capacity.

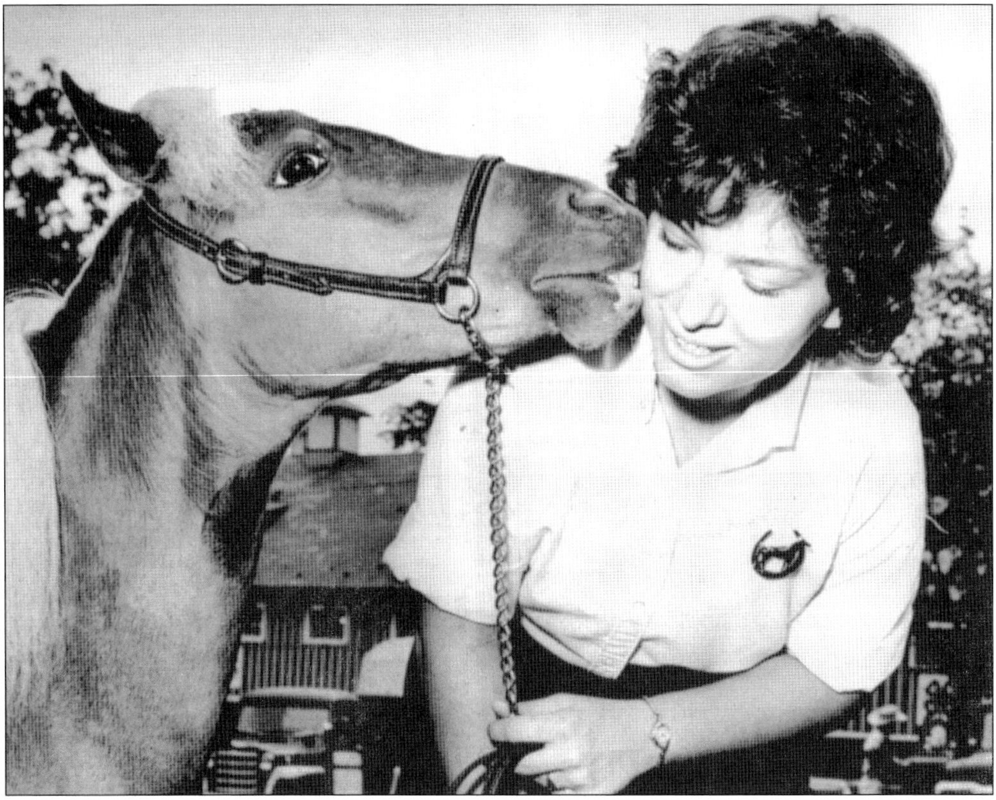

Ruth Rothenberger entered her yearling Shetland pony in the 4-H club district competition held at the fairgrounds in 1963. This photograph was taken just before the competition began in front of the Rural Youth Building. The building was renovated in 1961 to allow for the 4-H Round Up competition to align with the Allentown Fair. The Horse and Pony Club had 75–80 members that year. (Courtesy of Lehigh County 4-H.)

The iconic Ferris wheel joined the Allentown Fair in 1903, and in 1943, three of the largest Ferris wheels were set up side by side on the grounds. As the midway shifted to thrill rides, variations of the wheel (right and left) were more daring. The super loops ride (center), a 55-foot circular coaster, pushes riders forward and backward while inverting them through the loop.

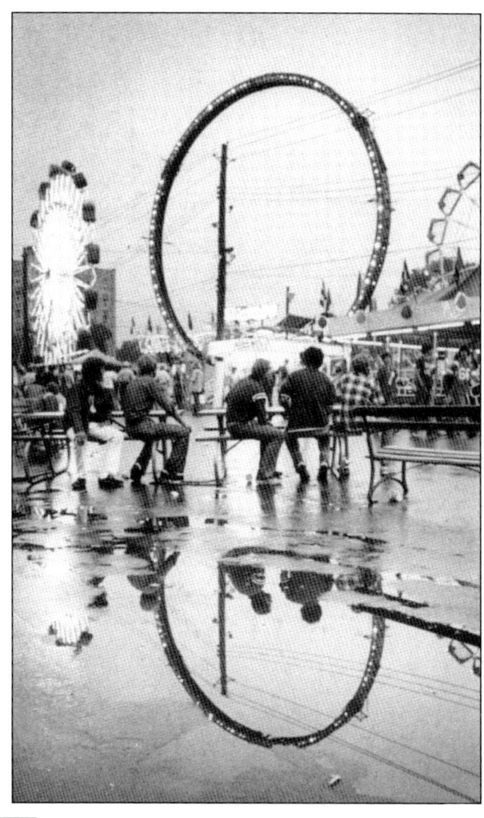

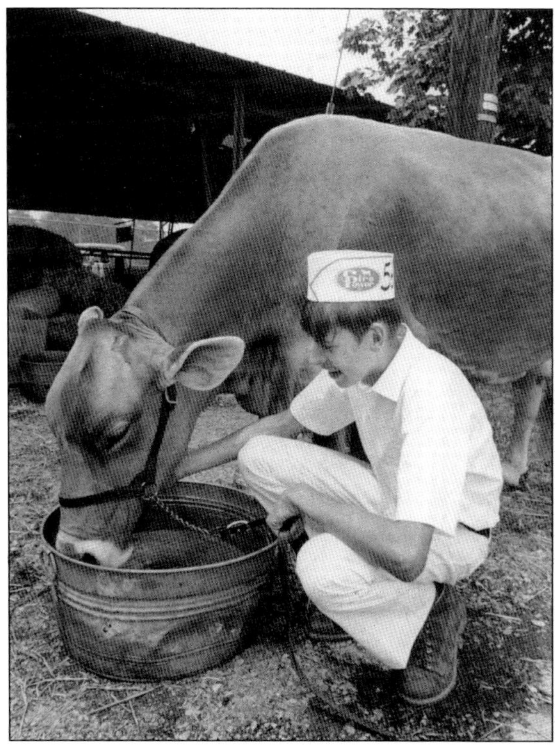

Here, Daryl Urmy, the current LCAS president, is seen with his Brown Swiss cow, Bridget, ready for the 1974 southeast district 4-H competition. Urmy began competing with 4-H in 1966. During his second year of competition, he was the only 4-H entrant to enter two cows, Eloise and Ellie. Both animals won first place in the 1967 competition. (Courtesy of the Urmy family.)

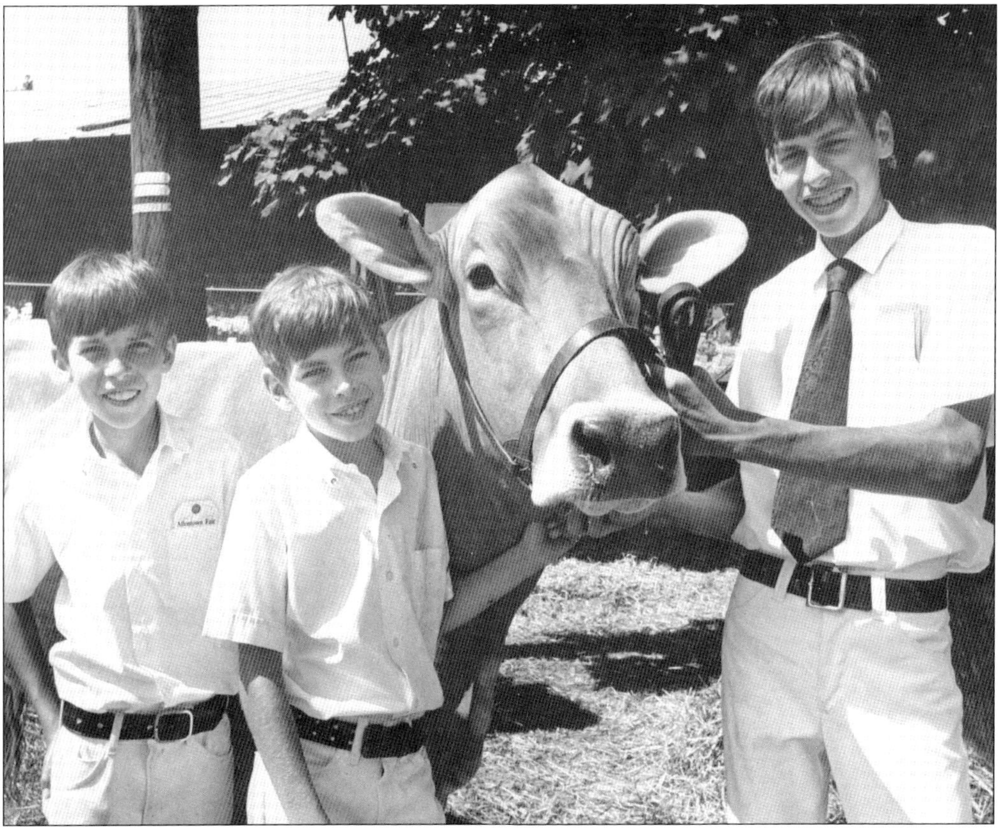

From left to right, brothers Gary, Bryan, and Daryl Urmy prepare Daryl's Brown Swiss cow, Bridget, for the 1975 4-H Round Up at the fairgrounds. The roundup competition winners moved on to the district and then to the state competitions. Each of the three Urmy brothers earned more than one first-place finish during their time competing in the 4-H cattle competitions at the fair. (Courtesy of the Urmy family.)

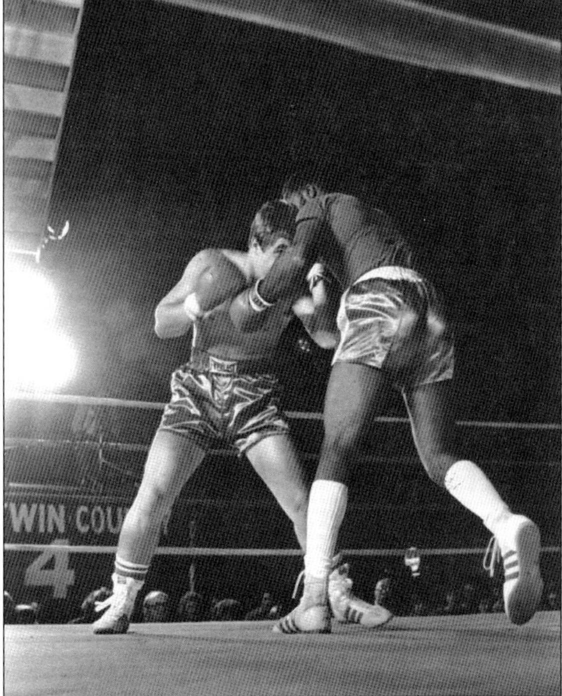

The local Ring 23 amateur boxing circuit held an eight-match event on September 1, 1979. The boxers competed at the Farmerama Theater. Several split decisions and a technical knockout decided the winners that night. All Farmerama events have always been free to fair patrons. That night, roughly 1,000 visitors stopped by the theater for the fights.

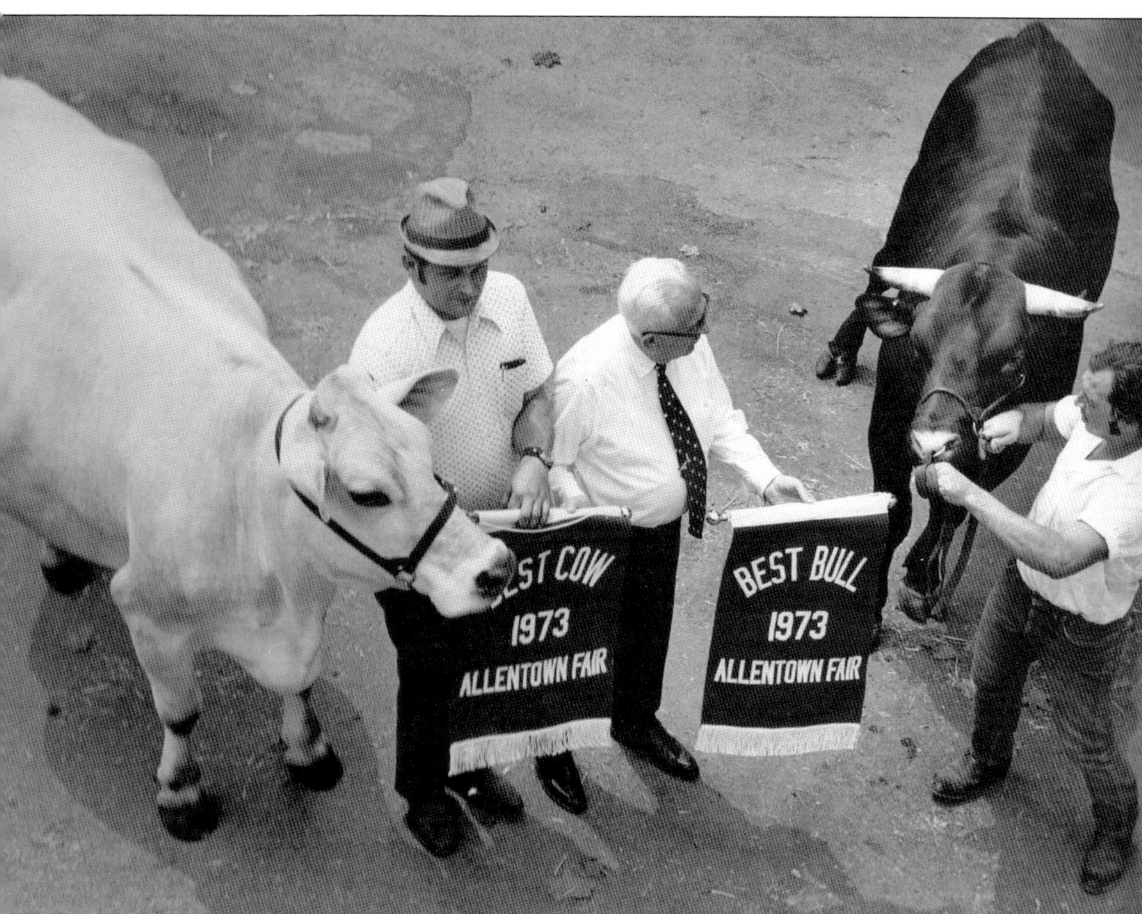

Myron Ritter (center), supervisor of livestock, announces the "Best Of" winners for the 1973 fair. The Best Bull winner was a Milking Shorthorn from Three Springs Farm. He stands with his owner, James T. Young (right). The Best Cow winner was a Brown Swiss named Miss Blue, standing with her owner Wayne E. Sliker (left). Two years earlier at the 1971 Great Allentown Fair, Sliker won 12 blue ribbons and both Senior and Senior Grand Champion Cow titles. Sliker continued his career breeding and showing Brown Swiss cows at his farm in Ohio named Top Acres. He won the 1998 Distinguished Dairy Cattle Breeder from the National Dairy Shrine for his work with Brown Swiss cows. A record was broken when he earned his 117th All-American win, and another was broken when he exceeded 100 Reserve All-American titles. In 2017, he won Grand Champion Brown Swiss at the World Dairy Exposition with his cow, Wizard.

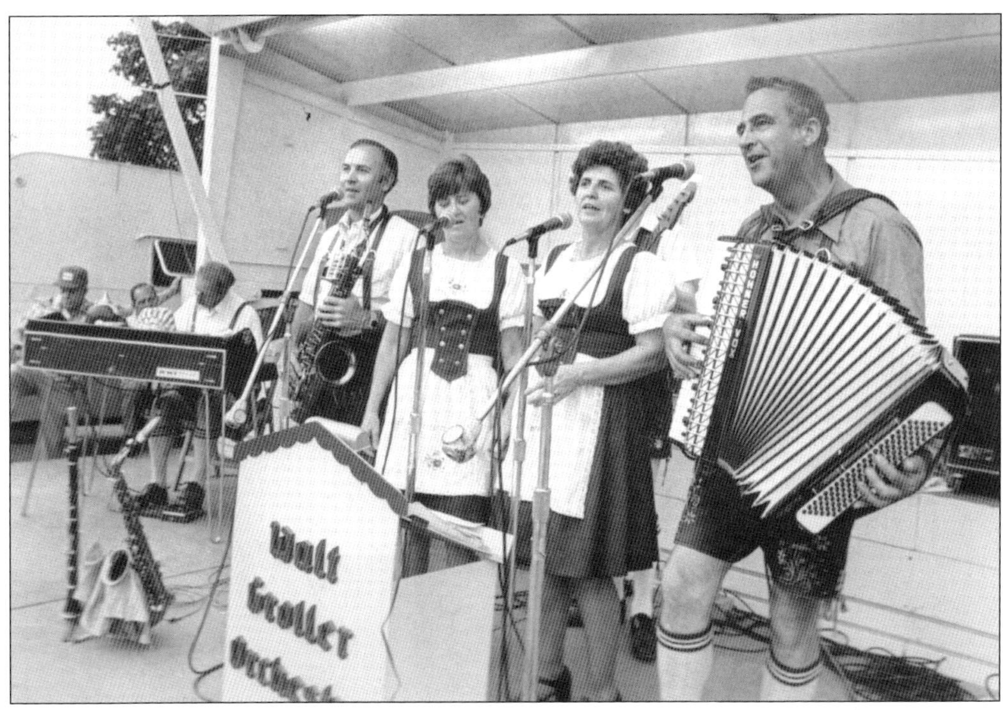

Allentown native Walt Groller was inducted into the International Polka Association's Hall of Fame in 1986 and received commendations from the Austrian government as well as several American presidents. His albums were produced first by Stella Records and then by his own production company in Whitehall, Chalet Records. Groller and his orchestra visited the fair several times, playing here in 1978 at the Farmerama Theater.

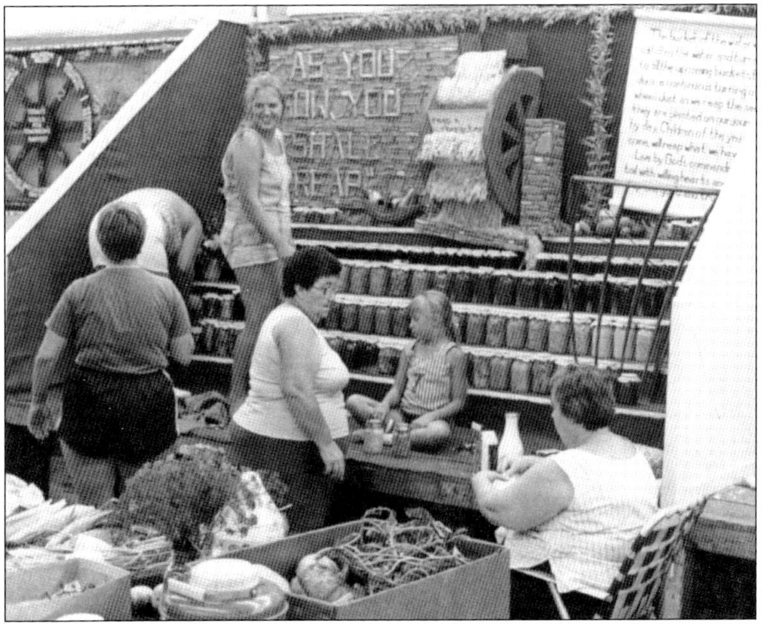

Members of the Harmony Grange are setting up before the 1980 fair begins. The granges put countless hours into their displays, in the past staying throughout the night to finish setting up before opening day. The group displays must align with a self-chosen theme to create unity. Over the years, the number of active granges in the county has decreased.

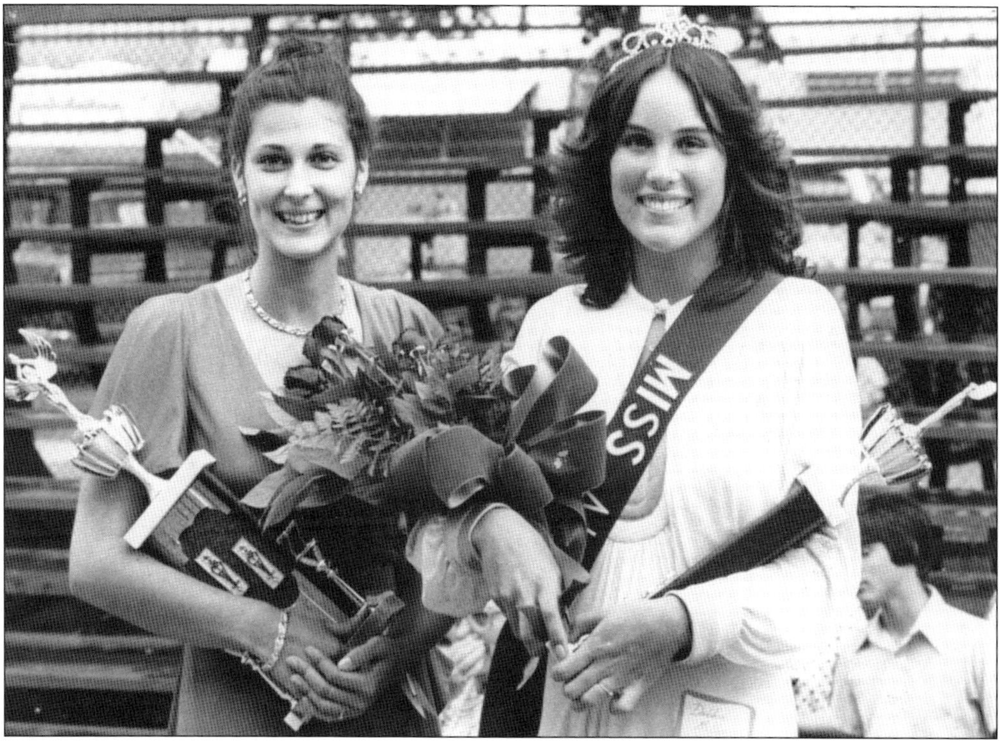

In 1965, the Farmerama Theater held its first scholarship contest, crowning the winner as the Farmerama Queen. The queen reigned for the entirety of fair week and received a scholarship. In 1969, the winner of the contest was renamed Miss Allentown Fair. Here, Debbie Miller (right) is crowned the 1977 Miss Allentown Fair, and Shelia Mack (left) was awarded first runner-up.

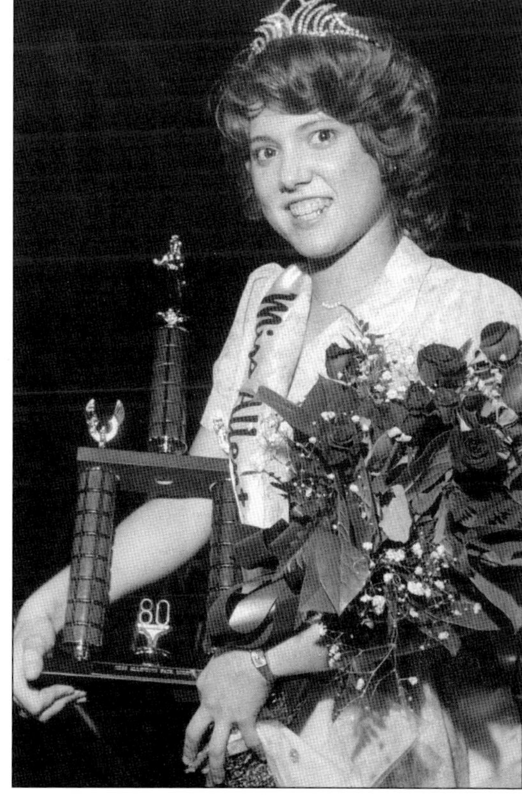

Susan Price was crowned Miss Allentown Fair in 1980. The annual competition took a hiatus from 1991 through 2008 but continues as a scholarship program today. Winners serve as spokespersons for the fair for the year, and the competition includes a presentation outlining why one should attend the Allentown Fair. Contestants also participate in a group community service project before the competition.

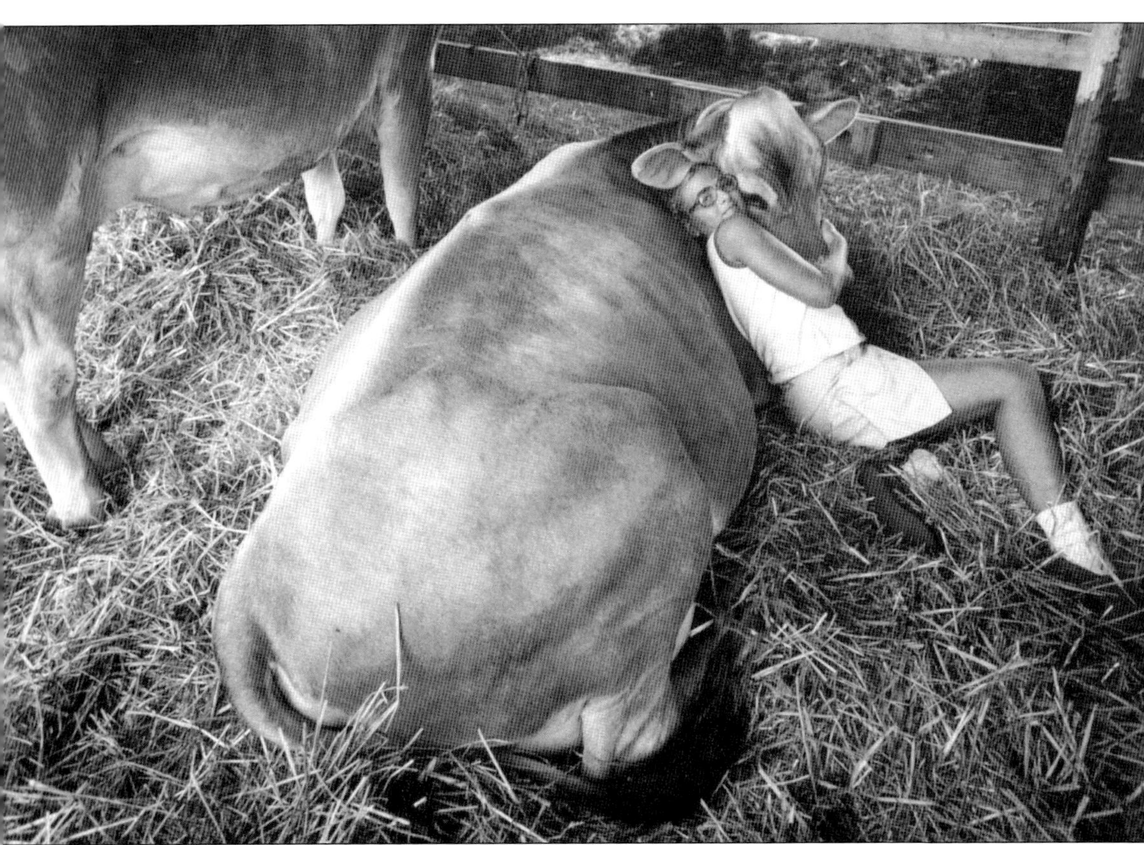

Gayle Urmy takes a break to cuddle her cows during the fair. Like her brothers who competed before her, Gayle consistently earned top-place finishes for her Brown Swiss cows in the 4-H fair competitions. At the 1986 fair, she placed first in several categories of Brown Swiss judging: Junior Heifer Calf, Junior Champion, Two Year Old Cow, Three Year Old Cow, Senior Champion, Reserve Senior Champion, Grand Champion, and Reserve Grand Champion. The Urmy family farm on the border of Upper Saucon and Coopersburg is still operating today. According to former livestock superintendent Sterling Ritter, the Allentown Fair is one of the few fairs that can claim to have hosted all six breeds of dairy cows at the same time: Ayrshire, Guernsey, Jersey, Holstein, Brown Swiss, and Milking Shorthorn. (Courtesy of the Urmy family.)

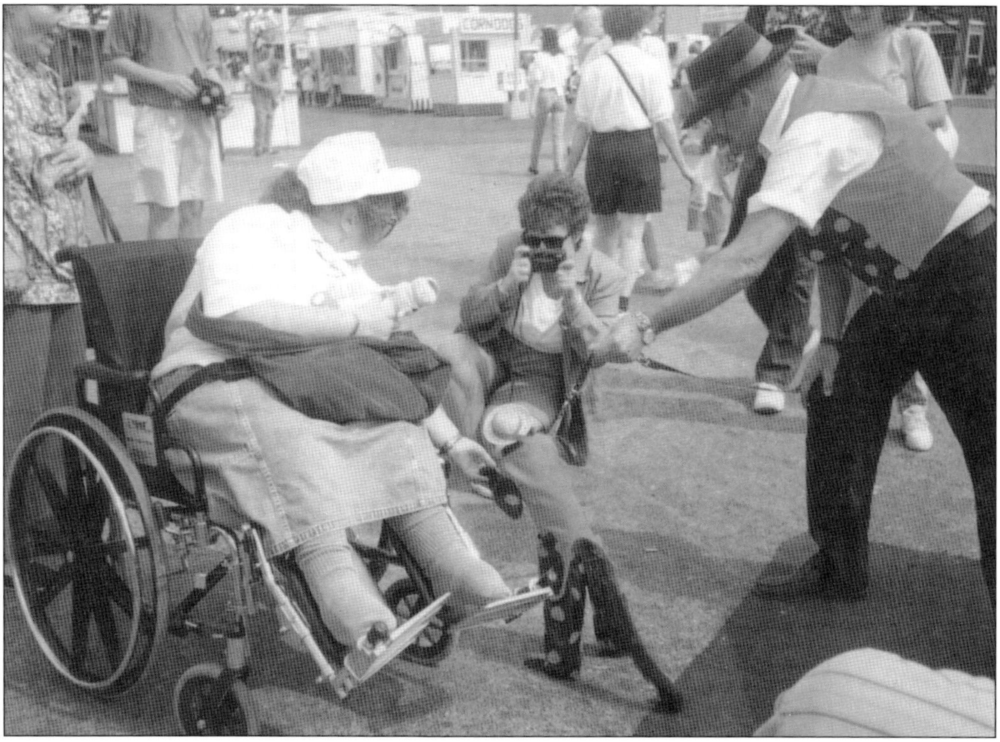

A childhood memory to many is the organ grinder and his monkey. Dressed in a tuxedo, the man played music while the children gave the monkey coins. In 1982, a law banned wildlife from public areas, keeping the monkey and his musical friend out of the fair. The following year, an exemption was granted, and the monkey was allowed to return. (Courtesy of the Danner family.)

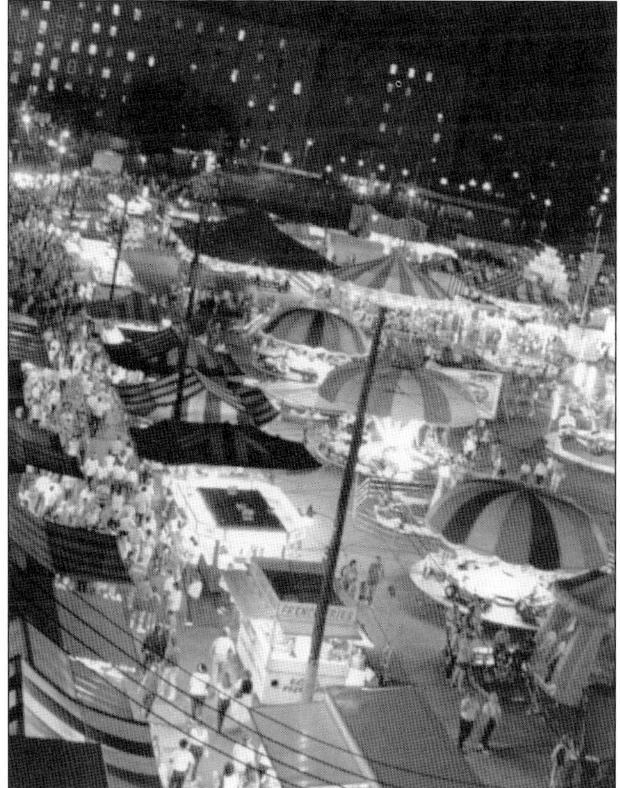

Gooding's Million Dollar Midway sought to entertain the children of the fair and added the familiar parachute-covered cars and planes seen here. The name "Million Dollar Midway" belonged only to the Allentown Fair, as the claim was that it was "a million dollar experience." Unlike the World of Mirth, when these rides, games, and acts traveled outside of Allentown, they were known only as the Gooding Amusement Company.

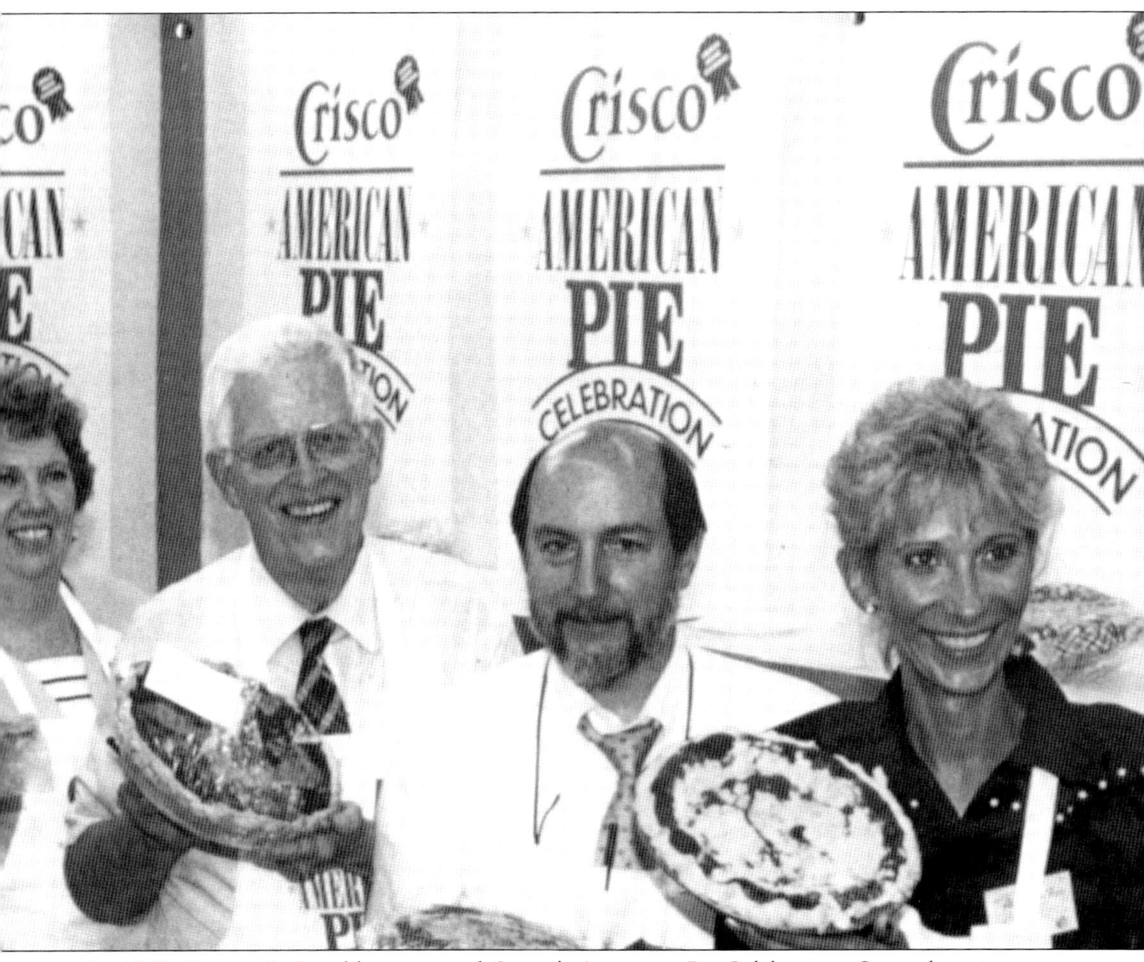

In 1988, Procter & Gamble sponsored Crisco's American Pie Celebration. Since there is no state fair in Pennsylvania, the company chose the Allentown Fair as its state representative for the national competition. The pie of choice was shoofly, and all entries needed to be made using Crisco shortening. This was the first time a culinary competition at the fair was judged in front of a live audience. There were 112 entries, and the winner went on to the national competition. Judges were locally known Bill Albert, Frank Nickischer Sr., Frank Nickischer Jr., Penny Nader (far left), Alan Raber (second from left), Randall Murray (second from right), and Kathy Craine (far right). Each judge had to sample each pie over the course of multiple rounds. The judging lasted from 7:00 p.m. until midnight, and when it ended, judge Kathy Craine could not eat another bite. The next day, during an interview at WFMZ between newscaster Craine, fair marketing director Bonnie Brosious, and fair ambassador Candy Candido, Candido teased Craine by bringing her a shoofly pie.

Four

Camp Crane

The Lehigh County Agricultural Society has donated its land twice for military use during wartime. The first time was in 1862 during the Civil War. Because of the overall devastation brought by the war, the Great Allentown Fair was suspended that year, and seven companies of the 176th Pennsylvania Militia occupied the fairgrounds before being mustered and then departing from the Lehigh Valley train station to active duty. The second time was from May 28, 1917, until April 10, 1919, when the Allentown Fairgrounds was known as Camp Crane.

On May 28, 1917, the US Army Ambulance Corps (USAAC) was given a lease to use the fairgrounds as a training center. The training center was organized by Elbert E. Persons, who received the Army Distinguished Service Medal for his actions. Persons served as the commanding officer of the camp from June 1917 until May 1918, leading many to refer to the base as Camp Persons. The base was officially named Camp Crane in honor of Brig. Gen. Charles H. Crane, Army surgeon general from 1882 to 1883.

Service at Camp Crane fulfilled draft requirements for those who wanted to help with the war efforts but were not interested in direct combat. Those who served in the USAAC provided a great deal of help in France and Italy, and many were awarded with honors when they returned from service. Enlistment in the service also proved risky, as many of the men were sent into dangerous territories to help wounded soldiers and found themselves in danger as well. The men at Camp Crane were known to locals as the USAACs.

During the military occupation of the fairgrounds, improvements to the grounds were made. The Army altered already present structures to fit their needs and added steam heat to the buildings. What remained of the grassy lawns was stomped into dirt, and a few new buildings were added. When the camp disbanded in 1919, the agricultural society set to work to prepare their property for the fair a few months away.

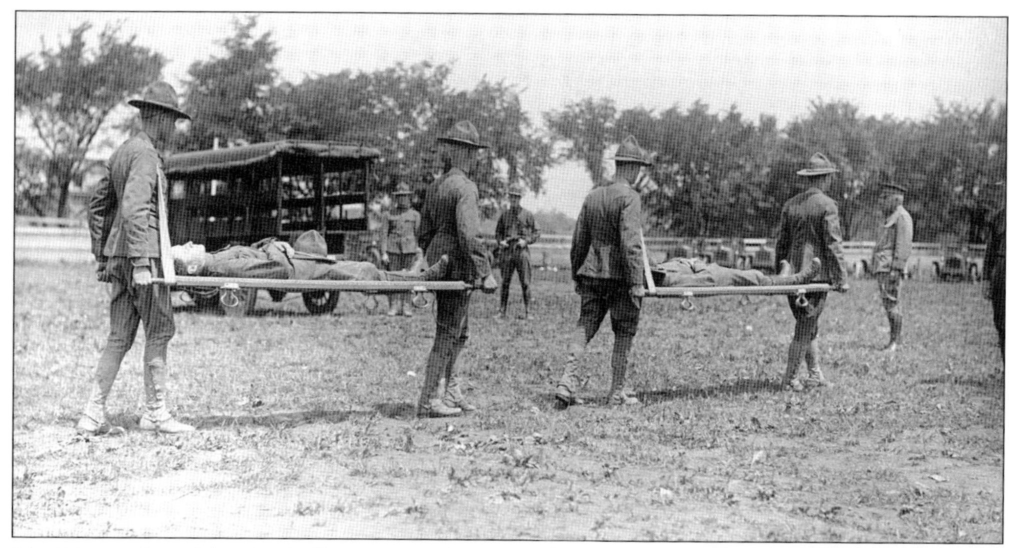

The fair continued despite challenges over the years. The time it was cancelled at its present grounds was from 1917 to 1919 due to the encampment officially known as Camp Crane. Soldiers trained at the camp to provide medical help to those on the front lines of World War I. Here, soldiers complete their "litter training" on the former fair midway. (Courtesy of Library of Congress, Prints & Photographs Division, LC-DIG-npcc-27822.)

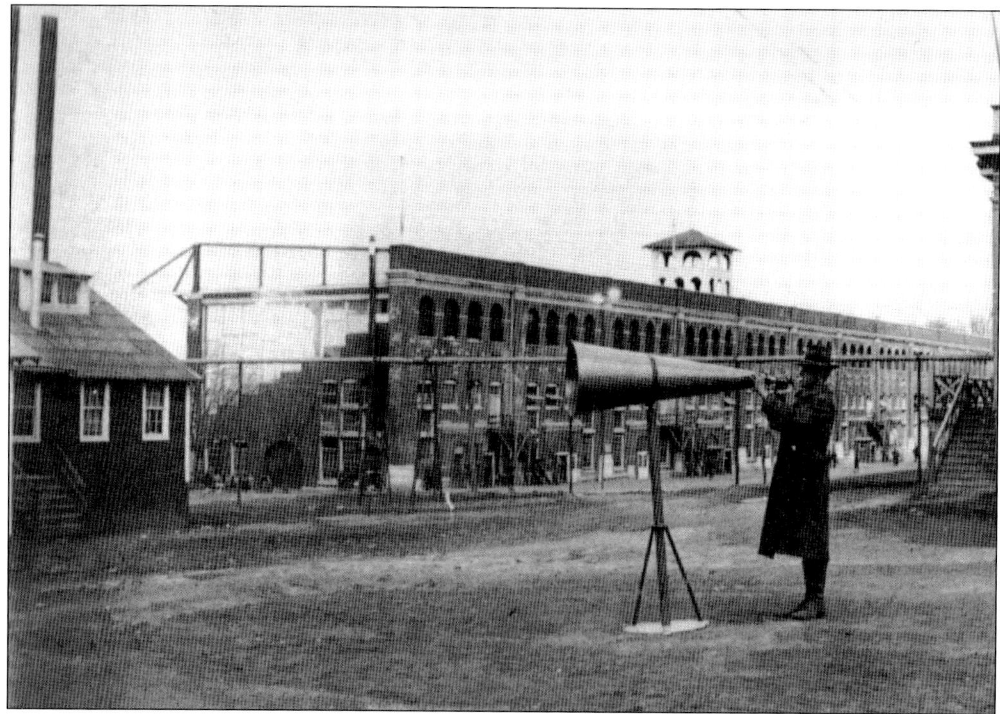

A recruit gets the attention of the camp with his bugle. Behind him, a steam pipe can be seen leading to the Horticultural Hall building. While camped there, the corps made improvements to the grounds by constructing a large steam plant with pipes that connected to the buildings on the grounds, adding heat that had not been necessary for an end-of-summer fair. (Courtesy of David Bausch.)

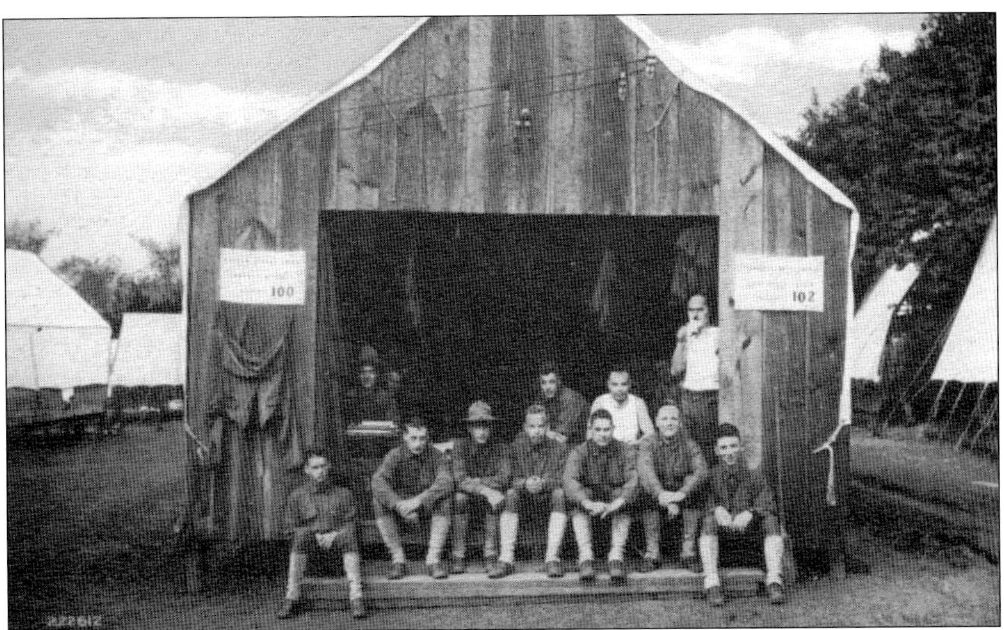

When Camp Crane was designed, it was intended to house 2,500 soldiers. However, before the camp was completed, it was housing 7,500 soldiers in cramped spaces. Many tents and wooden barracks like these were built on the grounds for the soldiers. Others slept in the animal barns or under the roof of the grandstand. (Courtesy of Kelly Ann Butterbaugh.)

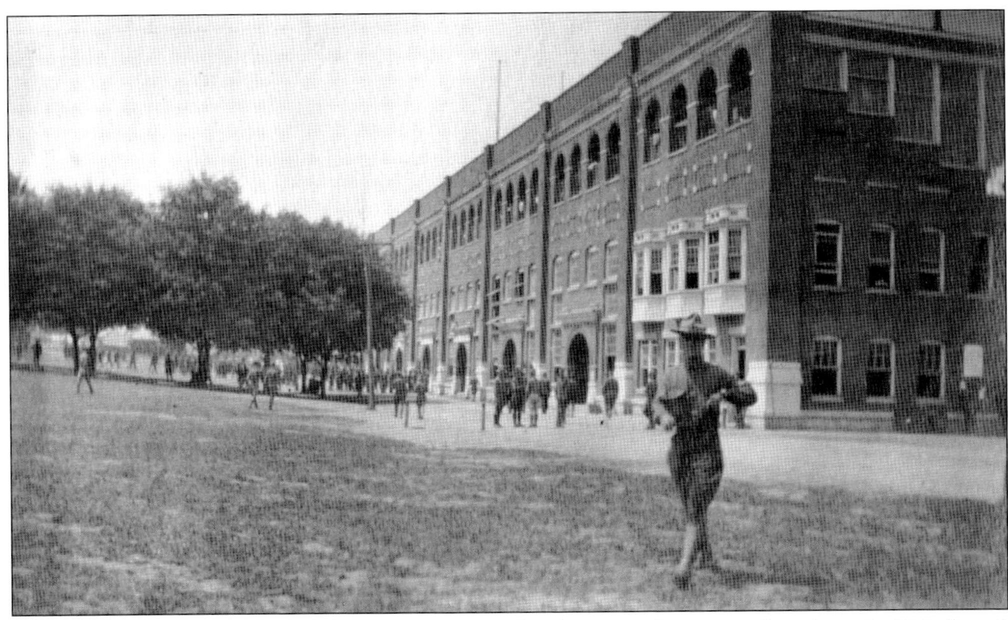

What originally drew the Army's attention to the fairgrounds was its "modern facilities" and the brick and steel-framed grandstand. Those who planned the encampment noted the multiple buildings on site as well as the 100 flushing toilets and restaurant-quality kitchens. While this helped to establish the camp, the wide open space offered little shelter from the winds. The winters were tough for those camped there.

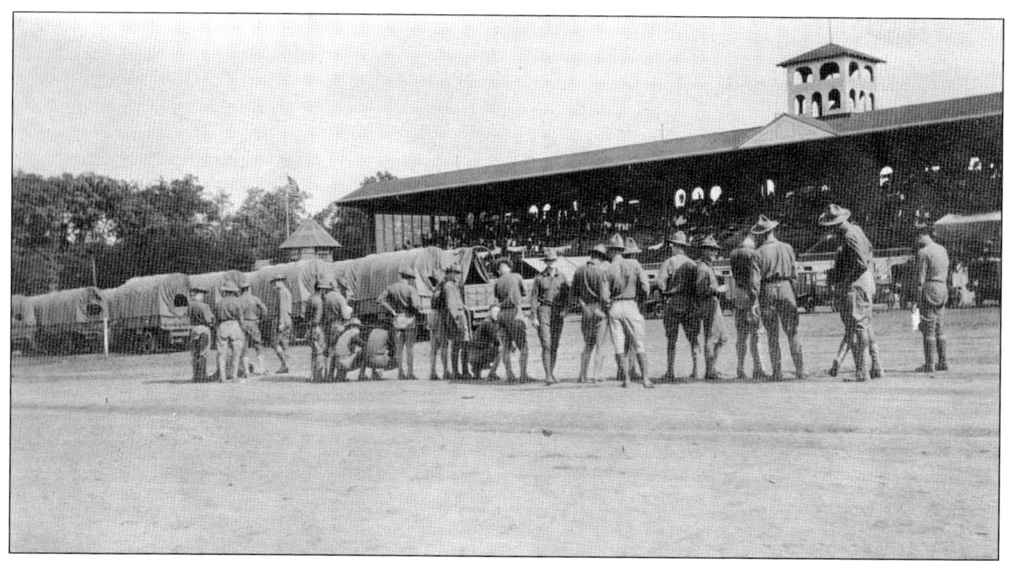

Camp Crane converted what it could to prepare the recruits for war. The grandstand was converted into barracks, the racetrack into a marching field, and exhibition halls into service and entertainment buildings. Several models of Ford motor vehicles were converted for use in war, and Mack AC trucks were designed in 1916 for use in World War I. (Courtesy of David Bausch.)

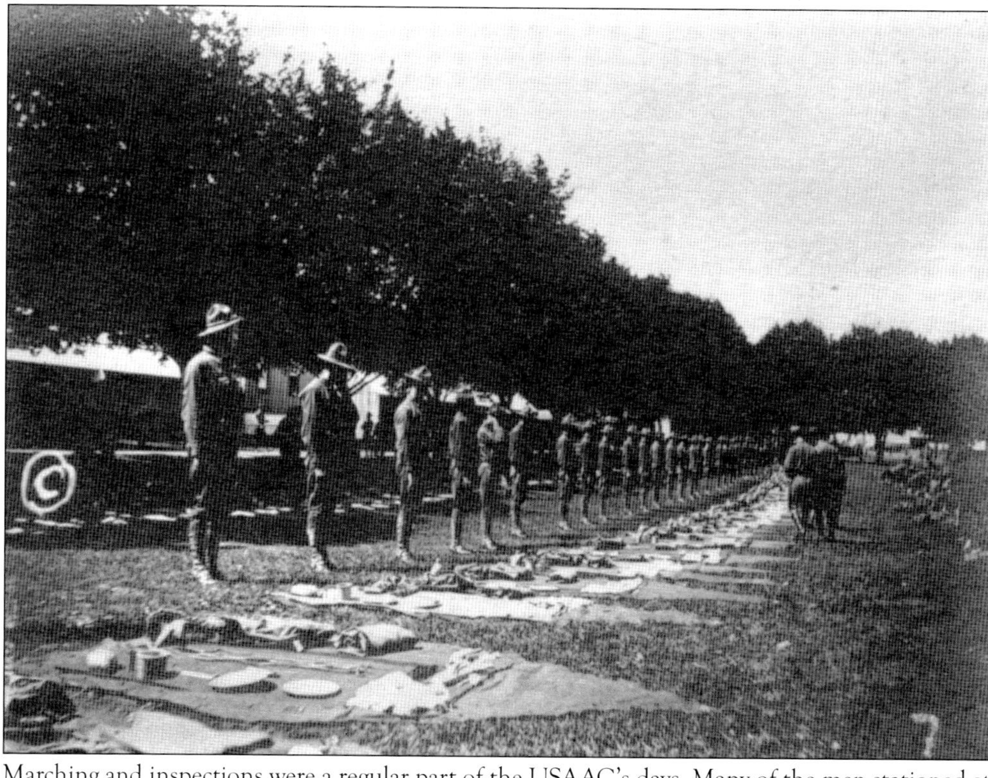

Marching and inspections were a regular part of the USAAC's days. Many of the men stationed at Camp Crane grew weary of the constant marching drills conducted across the fairgrounds. Anxious to be deployed to France, where their medical training was requested, they practiced for their deployment by marching through several different terrains in the area. (Courtesy of David Bausch.)

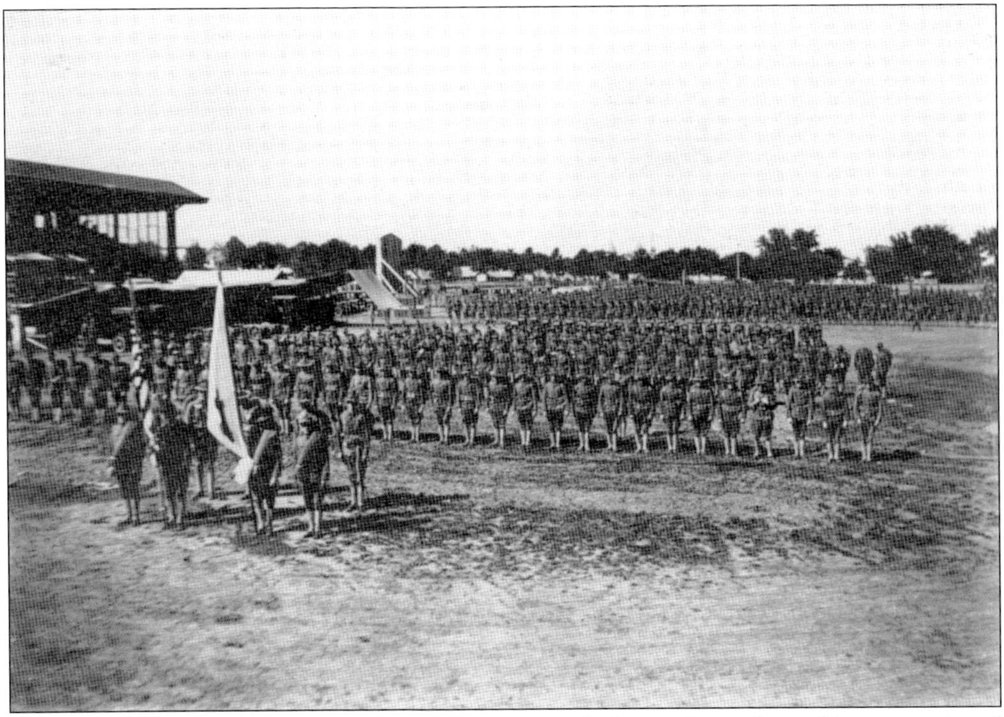

John Philip Sousa was a guest conductor at the fairgrounds during Camp Crane. He was convinced by the camp's commander, Colonel Persons, to write a march in honor of the USAAC. The result was the "USAAC March" written by Sousa in 1919. The bandleader was seen in several performances in the city during World War I. (Courtesy of David Bausch.)

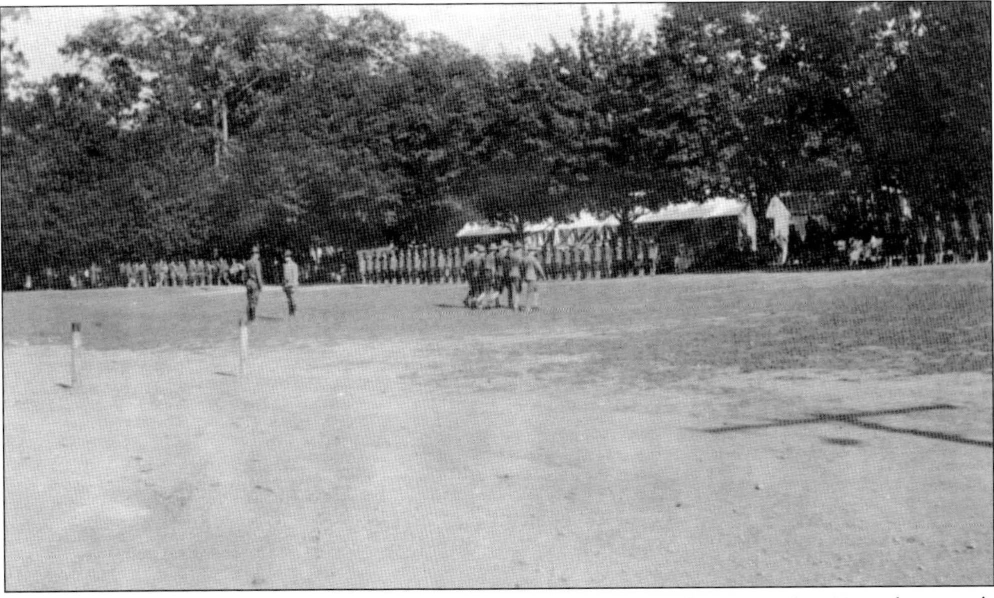

When the war ended, the focus of Camp Crane shifted. From the last part of 1918 to the camp's close on April 10, 1919, the focus of training at Camp Crane was to battle the growing influenza epidemic in the states. During those months, men were sent from the camp to central-eastern Pennsylvania to help with the outbreak. (Courtesy of David Bausch.)

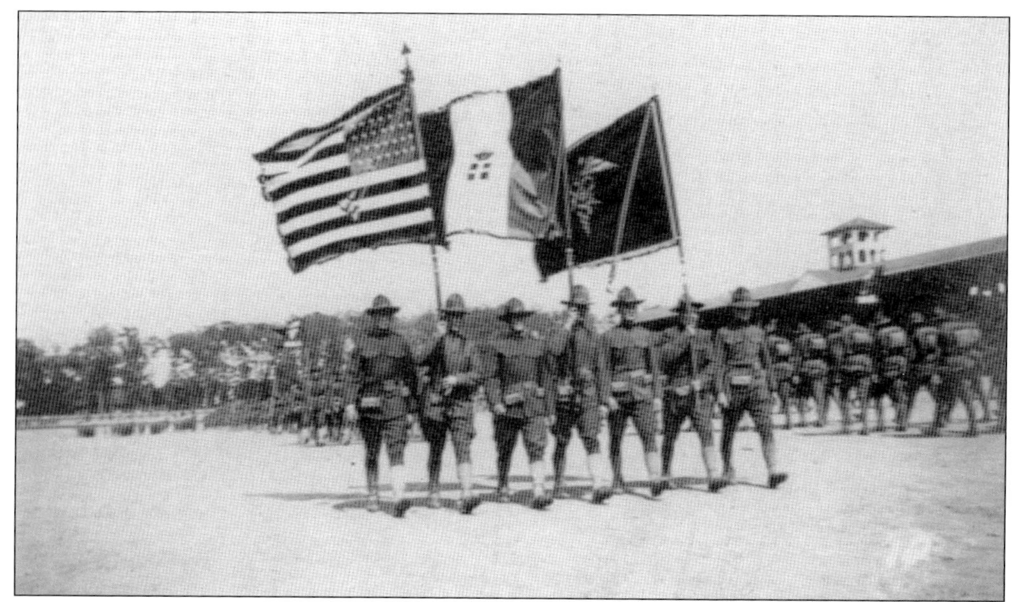

Those enlisted at Camp Crane were embraced by the locals in Allentown and often welcomed into homes for meals. A Big Brother program was even proposed for residents to take in soldiers from the camp. Recruits went into town during their recreational time, and many met their future wives there. West End Park was a popular place for a soldier to walk with a sweetheart. (Courtesy of David Bausch.)

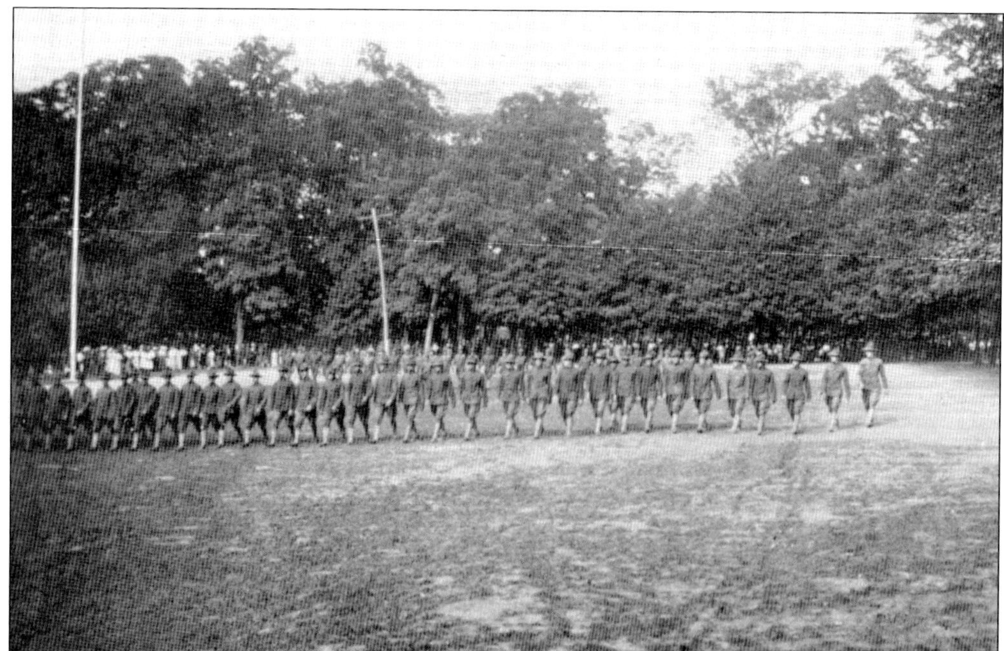

Camp Crane soon became a part of the community. Food for the camp was purchased from local farms, soldiers patronized local theaters, and supplies were purchased from stores in Allentown. One story remembered is when soldiers procured a piano from downtown Allentown and transported it to the fairgrounds on the back of an Army truck while a soldier played a tune on the ivories. (Courtesy of David Bausch.)

When recruits were deployed to either France or Italy from Camp Crane, they were sent in sections known as a Sanitary Squad Unit (SSU). Each SSU included 45 recruits, 20 ambulances, a touring car, a truck, and a portable kitchen trailer. The unit would become attached to a division of infantry once it arrived in Europe. Divisions included thousands of men for whom these SSUs would provide medical care.

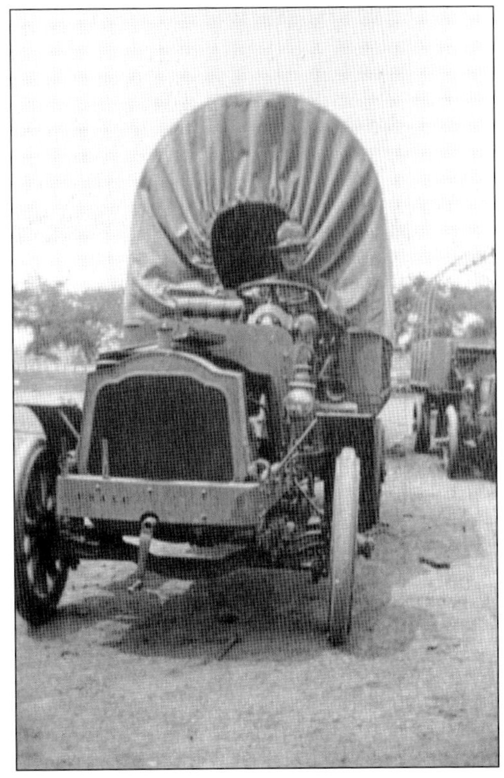

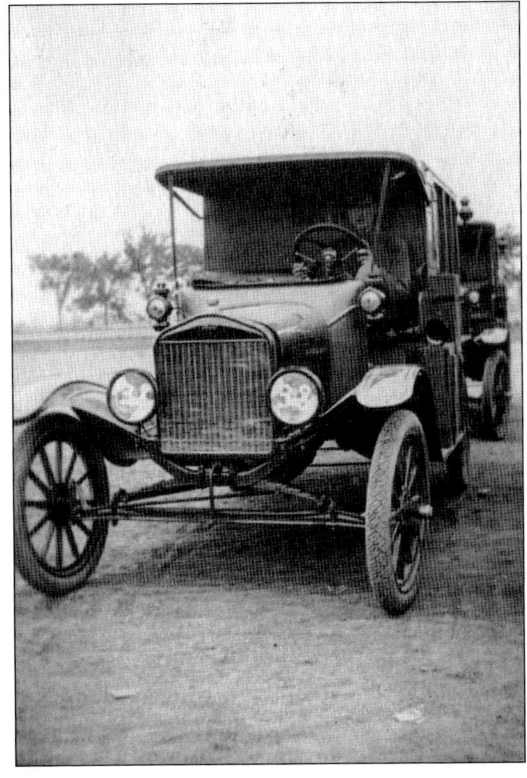

In 1917, the racetrack that had seen horses only a few months ago was used as a driver's training track for the trucks and ambulances of Camp Crane. Meanwhile, the infield was used to store the vehicles that would be shipped out with the soldiers. During their occupation of the grounds, officials at Camp Crane built 12 two-story barracks, two officers' quarters, and an infirmary.

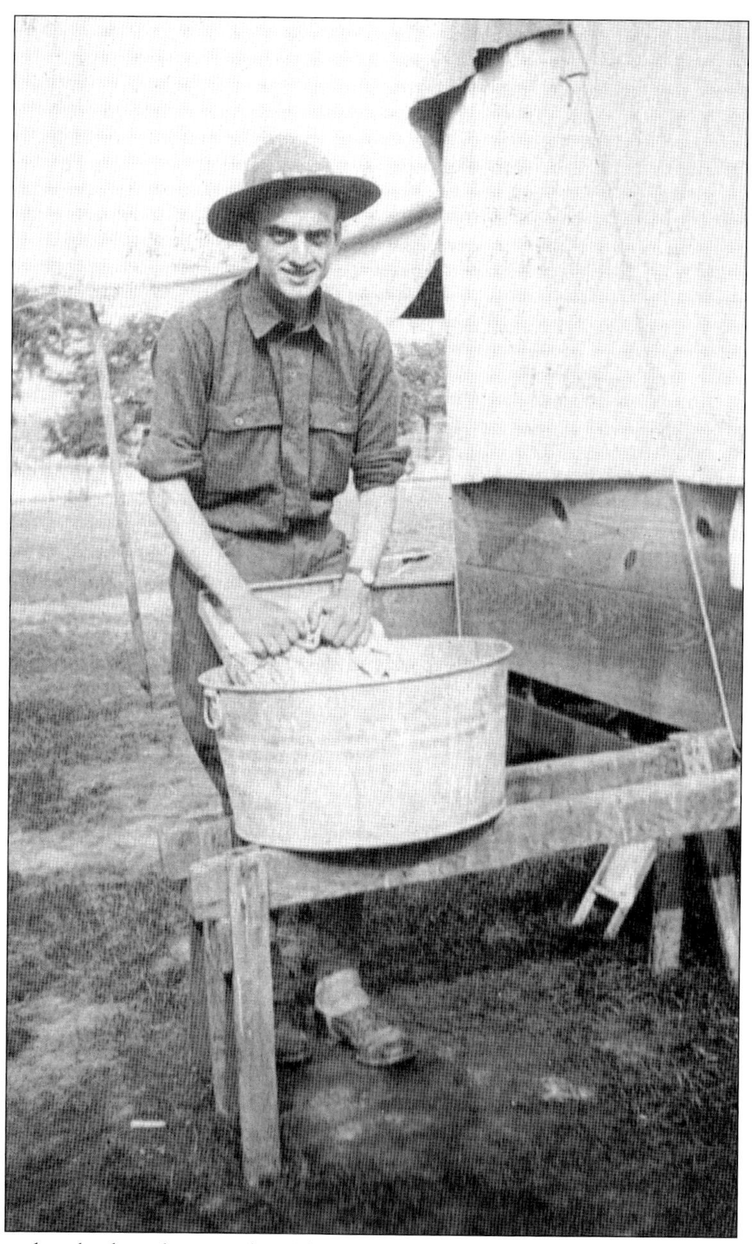

This volunteer does his laundry outside of the wooden tent he called home for a few months. Those stationed at Camp Crane often wrote of the drudgery of endless marching drills and boredom. Some of the monotony was relieved by the organization of a football team that competed against other service football teams and three college teams. Initially, 120 men came out for the team in 1917, with 45 making the cut and receiving uniforms. Within the group of men who made the team, 40 colleges and universities were represented by the athletes, some being All-American designated players. The first game was played on nearby Muhlenberg College's field, and the team continued on to a successful season playing other service organization teams after that. Three colleges were on their schedule that first year: Penn State, Fordham, and Georgetown. All three college matchups resulted in a loss for the team from Camp Crane. The USACC team then traveled to Philadelphia on November 10, 1917, to play the undefeated Marine Corps; the USACCs won.

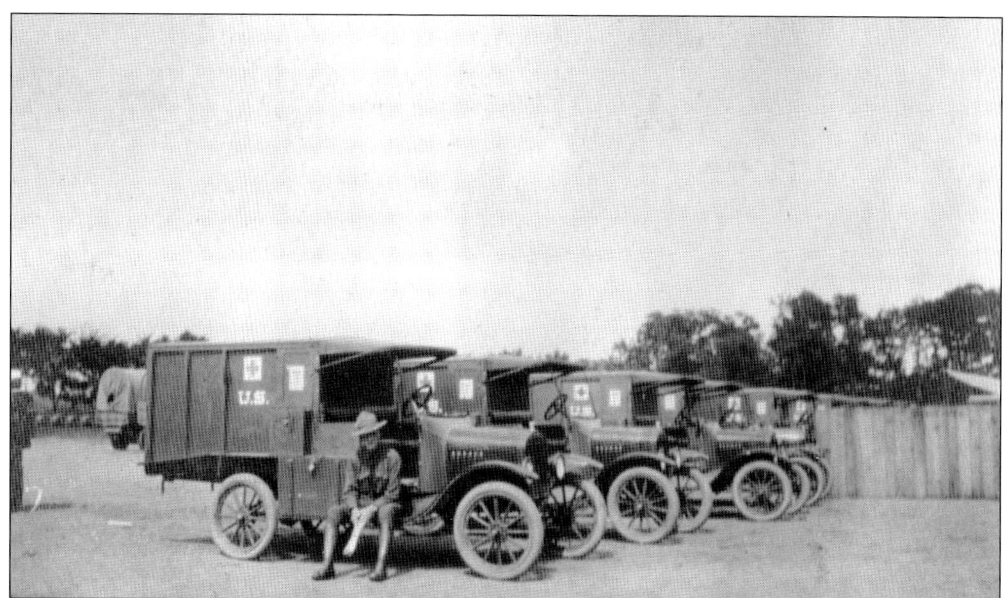

The US Surgeon General ordered Fords to be converted into ambulances for the war. Existing models of trucks were modified into ambulances that could carry several injured patients at a time. Part of the USAAC recruits' training was not only medical; they were also required to learn mechanical skills needed to fix the trucks in the battlefield.

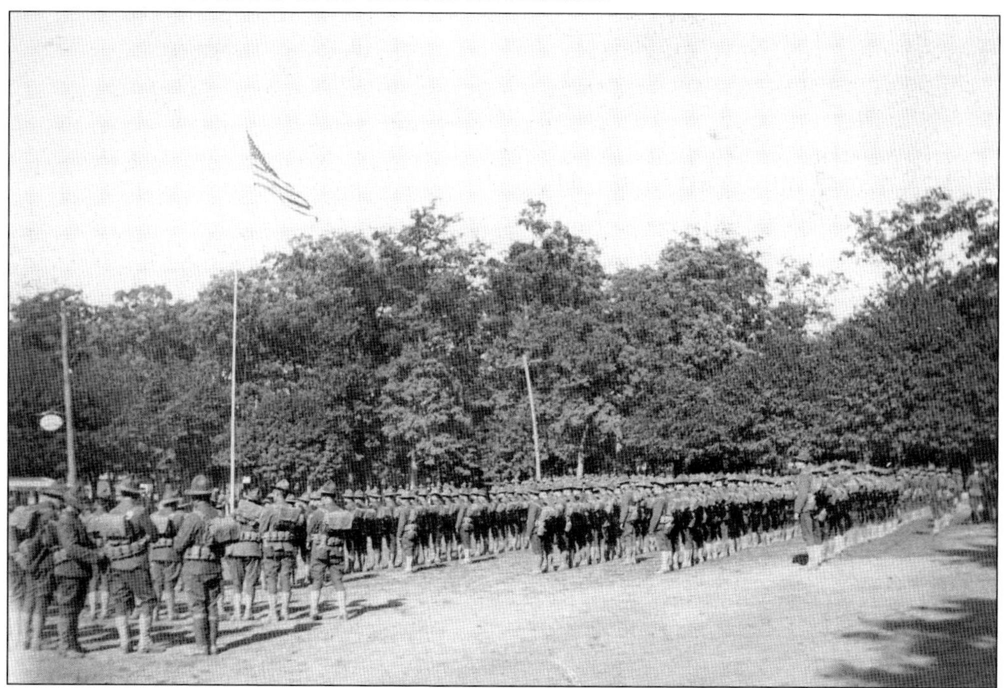

During its operation, Camp Crane housed 18,310 enlistees and 2,085 officers. The average daily population was between 4,000 and 5,000 men. Some were "adopted" by locals who welcomed the soldiers to join them for dinners and church services. Many young ladies fell in love with soldiers as they walked along the trails of West Park, and a few were married before deployment. (Courtesy of David Bausch.)

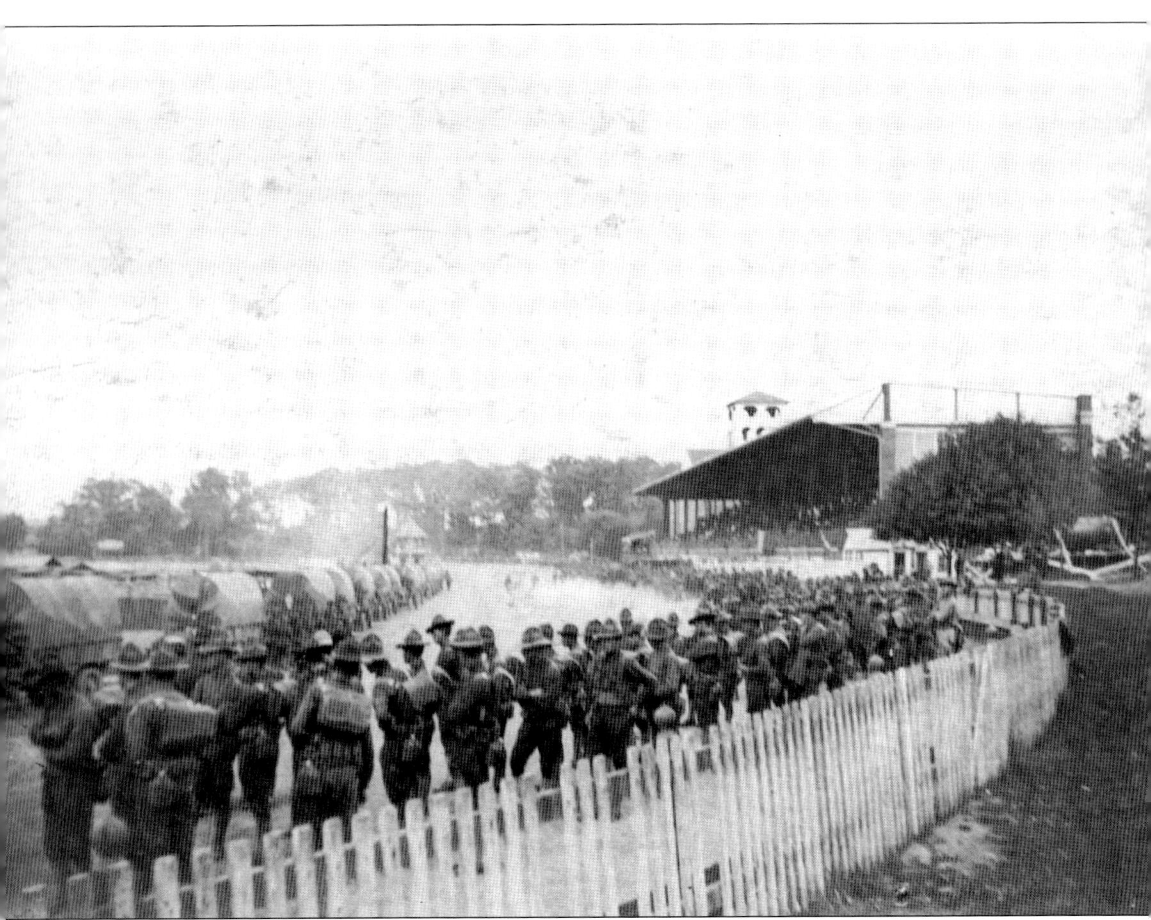

As more soldiers reported to Camp Crane, space became limited, and the camp grew crowded. The grandstand was a large draw when planning the camp because it offered a large area for serving food and operational offices. The dining room allowed 2,500 soldiers to sit at one time while serving food from kitchens on either end of the space. Those who chose the site for the military occupation ranked the kitchens on the same scale as those found in fine hotels. On June 10, 1917, two units of soldiers arrived at the camp: one from Bucknell College and another from the University of South Carolina. The new arrivals were set up to bunk in the seating area of the grandstand before heading to the Grove for Sunday services. Afterward, a chicken dinner was served to 1,248 men from the kitchen beneath the grandstand. The meal was efficiently served within seven minutes. (Courtesy of David Bausch.)

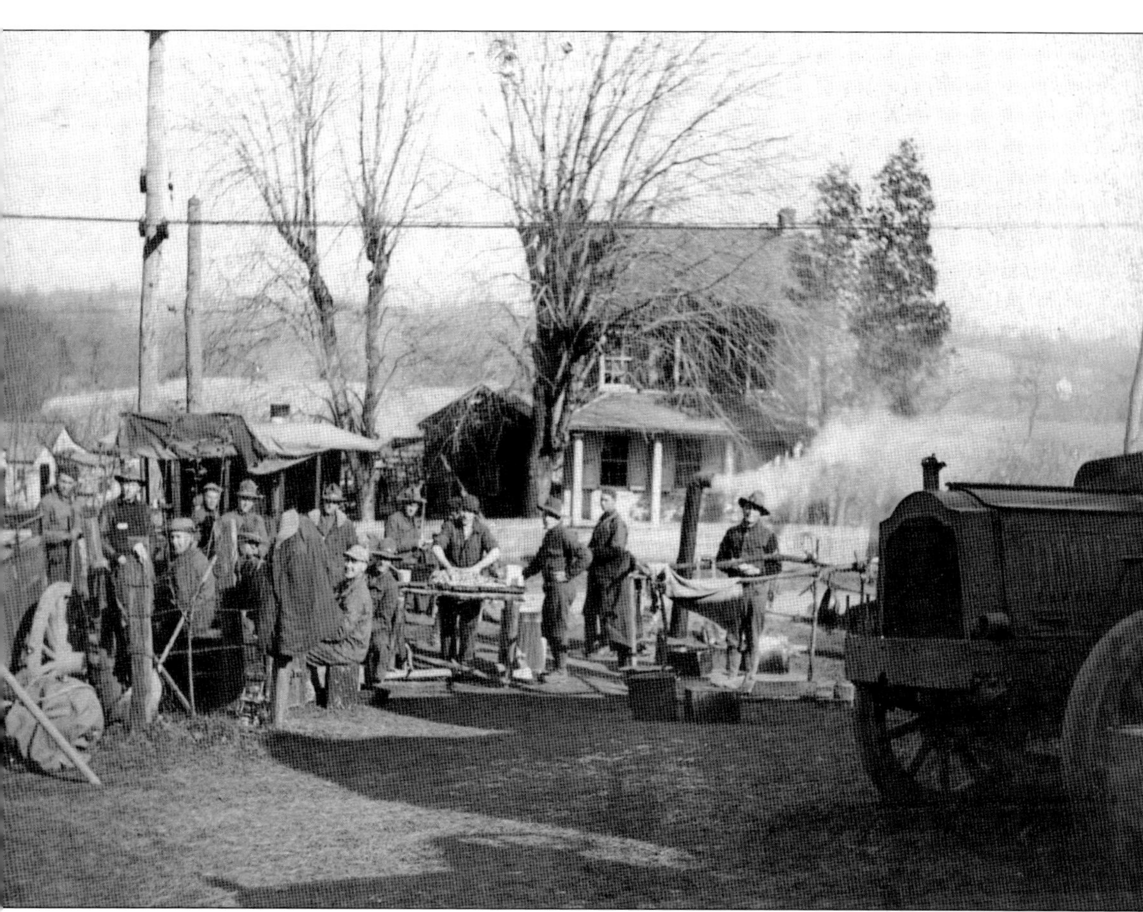

To alleviate crowding at the fairgrounds, a few outpost stations were constructed in the area in 1917. At these outposts, trenches were dug eight feet into the dirt and into the sides of hills where soldiers built small shacks with stoves like the one seen here for cooking and washing. This setup provided a good glimpse of what life would be like on the western front when the men arrived in Europe. Camps like this were set up in Kern's Mill near Slatington, Belzwood near Norristown, and Guth's Station in South Whitehall Township. Soldiers also took hikes over various terrains to prepare themselves for what was to come once they were overseas. Marching units led treks to Tobyhanna in the Pocono Mountains, and they marched to the outpost at Guth's Station to practice walking in muddy ground. (Courtesy of David Bausch.)

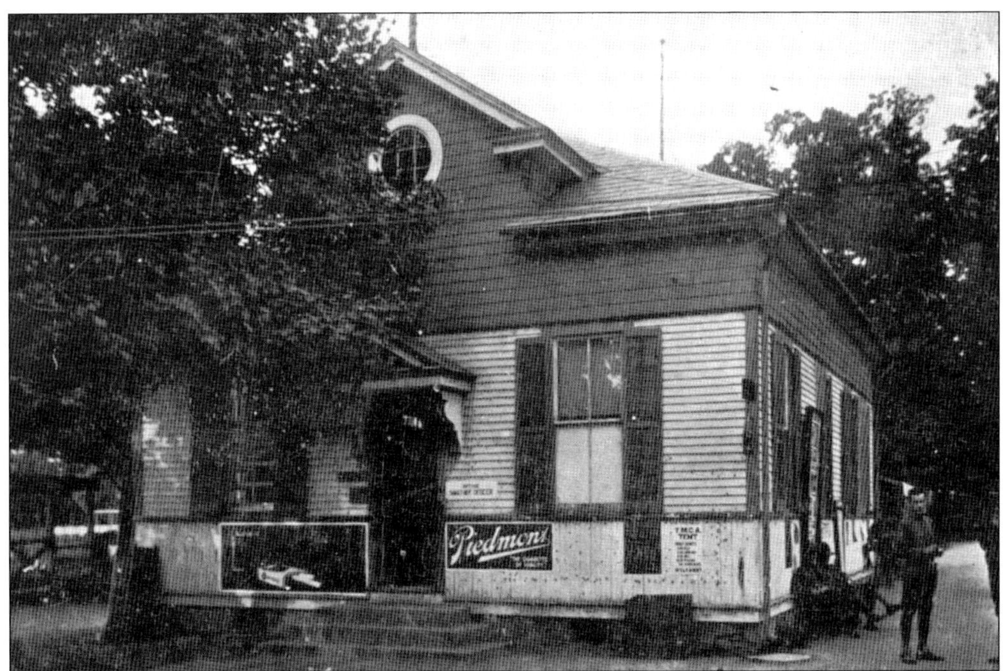

The Executive Building was used as the post office for Camp Crane. When the camp closed, the LCAS had work to do if there was going to be a fair that year. With $100,000 in reparations paid to LCAS for rent and damage to the property, the USAAC left behind structures and supplies that needed to be removed. By the end of August, LCAS scrapped more than $120,000 of materials.

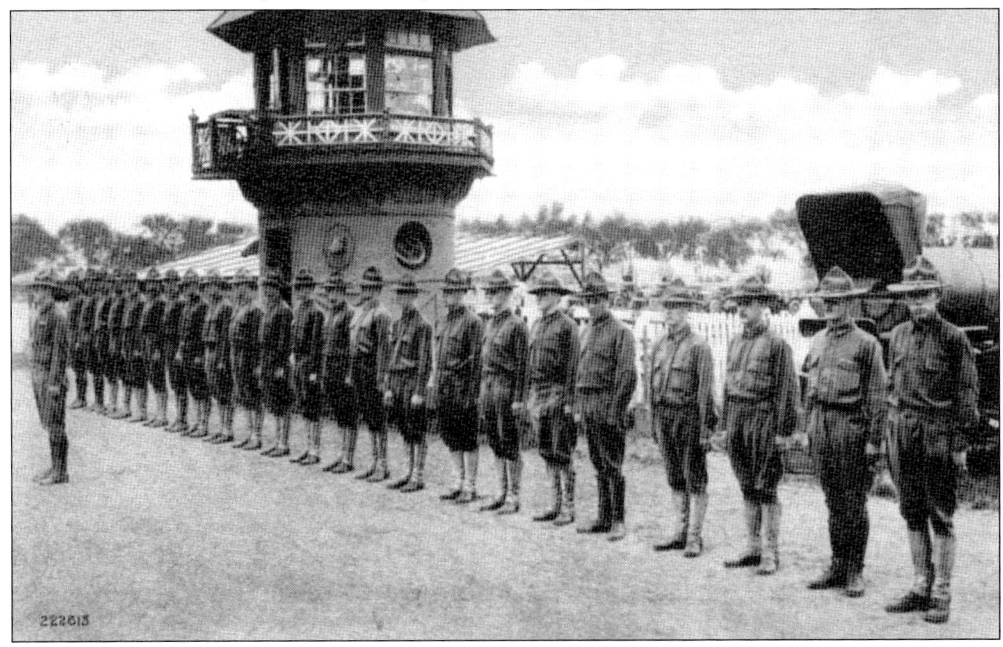

The exact number of soldiers present at Camp Crane at any time is difficult to calculate. Soldiers arrived unannounced and deployed regularly. This made housing difficult and, at times, crowded. Meanwhile, troops like these would hike to destinations around the area, freeing up space on the camp while they were out. (Courtesy of David Bausch.)

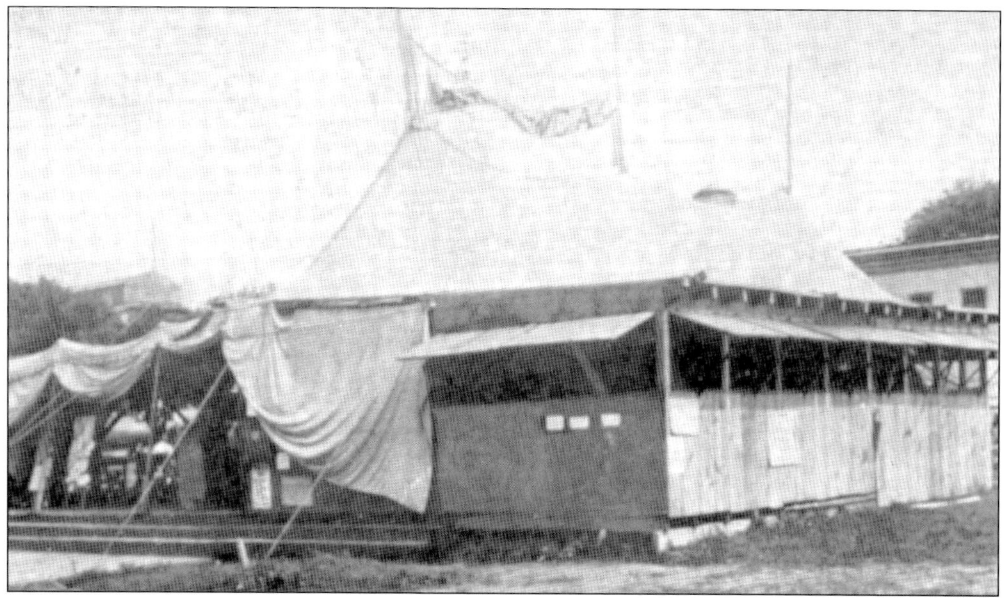

The Army YMCA sought to boost the morale of the recruits at Camp Crane by constructing this building, where it offered entertainment in the form of books, magazines, and records. The Army YMCA and the post exchange also converted the main exhibition hall to a recreational building with gym equipment for the soldiers to use until a fire destroyed the building on June 20, 1918. (Courtesy of David Bausch.)

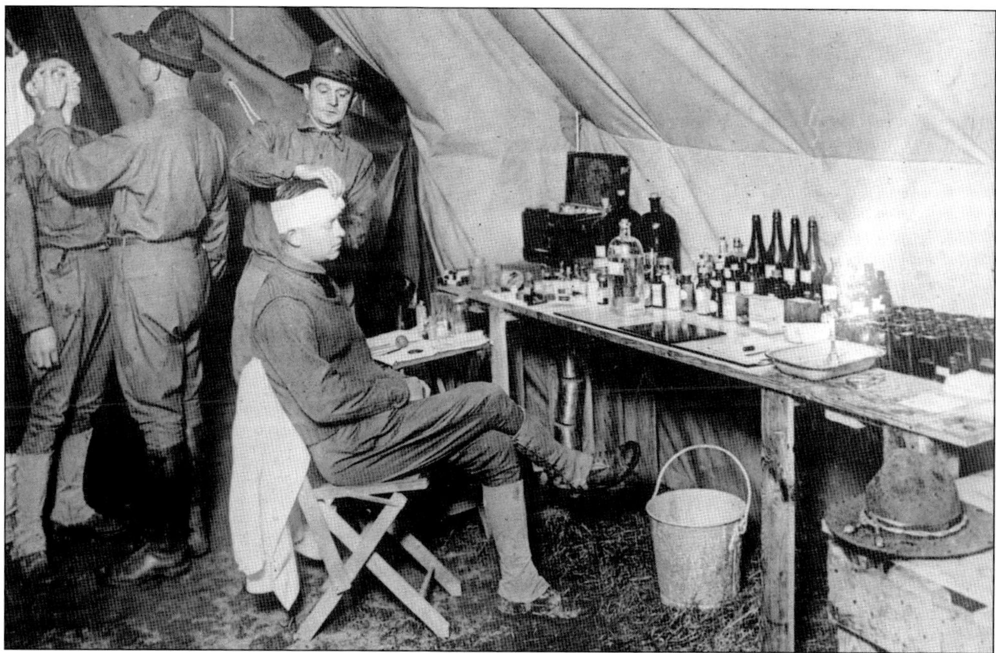

Soldiers demonstrate their knowledge of first aid in the first aid tent. While their first job was to find wounded soldiers in battle, they would then need to transport the wounded to the base unit, where they would continue the injured soldiers' care in a safer environment. (Courtesy of Library of Congress, Prints & Photographs Division, American National Red Cross Collection, LC-DIG-anrc-06203.)

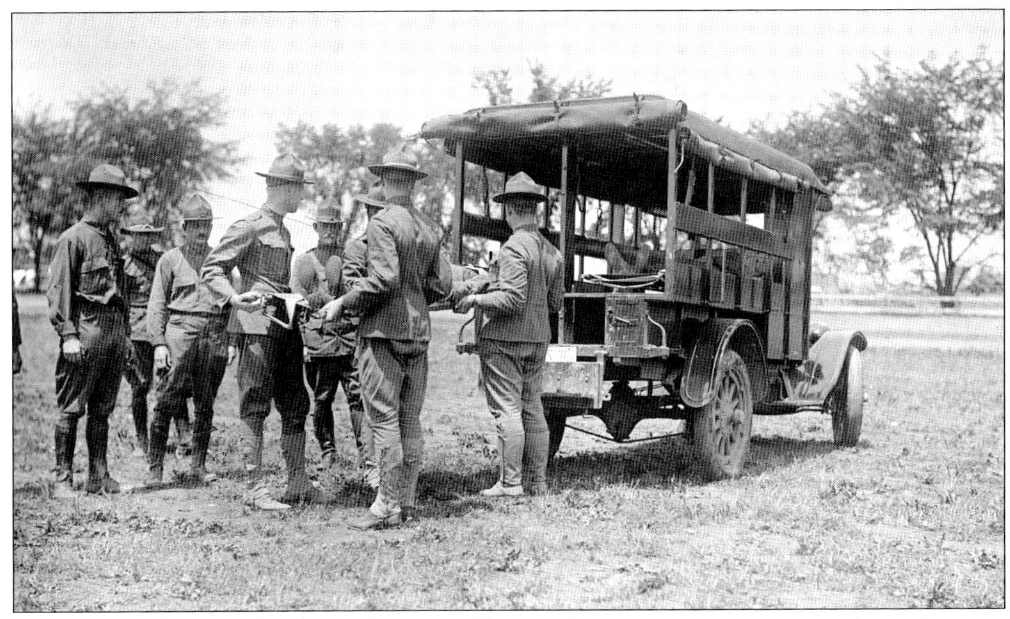

The recruits who trained at Camp Crane would enter dangerous territory and care for and remove the injured as quickly as possible. The training at the camp taught recruits to evacuate the injured from the front line using ambulances to take patients to hospitals located at base units. Here, recruits practice just that. (Courtesy of Library of Congress, Prints & Photographs Division, LC-DIG-npcc-27824.)

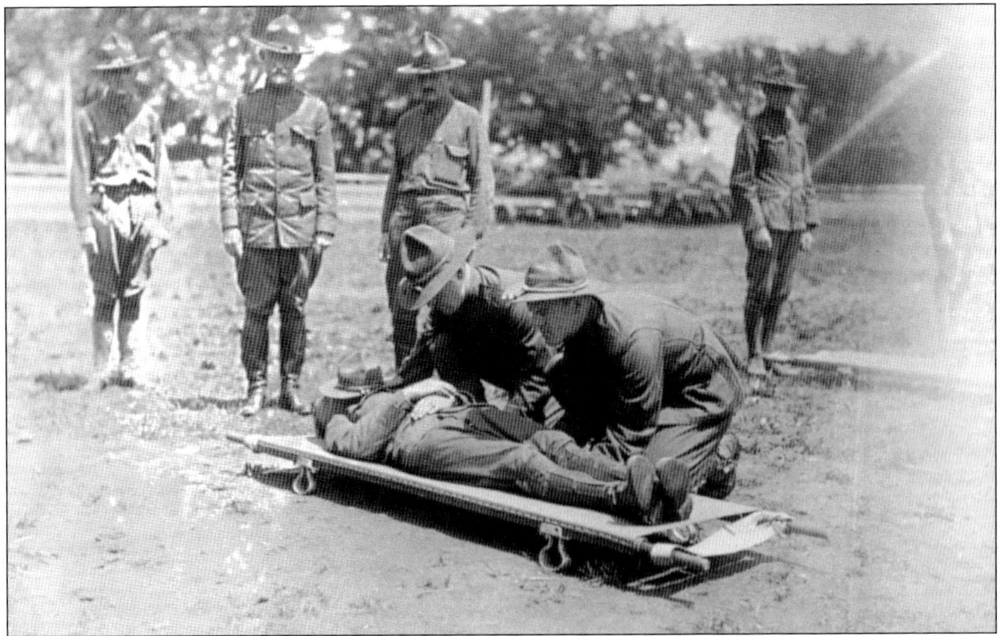

It was dangerous being a member of the USAAC. As recorded by Lawrence Flick Jr. in June 1917, an ambulance driver worked long hours, got little sleep, and had to make quick decisions. While many opted to train at Camp Crane in order to avoid combat, many of them found themselves on the dangerous front anyway. (Courtesy of Library of Congress, Prints & Photographs Division, LC-DIG-npcc-27826.)

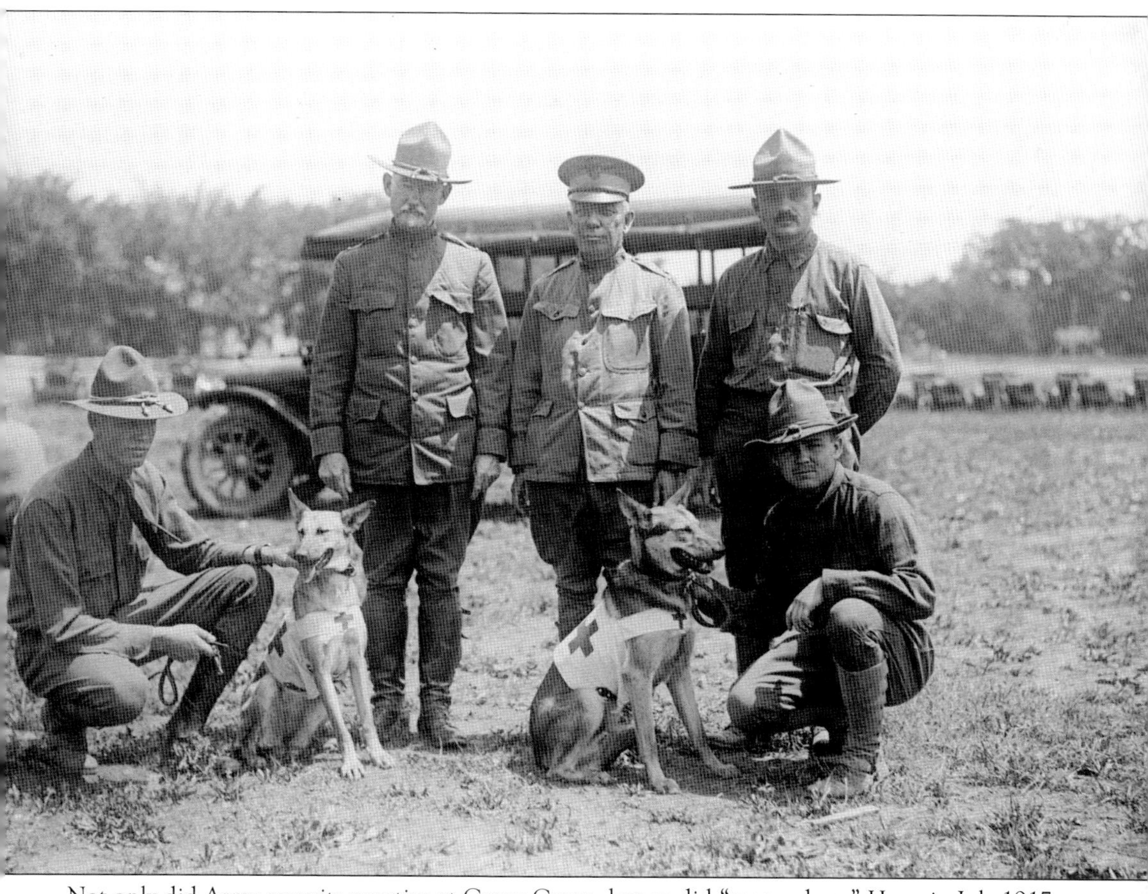

Not only did Army recruits practice at Camp Crane, but so did "mercy dogs." Here, in July 1917, dogs are trained to find wounded soldiers in the mud and to bring them emergency supplies and rations. The dogs were trained to provide comfort in a variety of ways. One was to bring emergency supplies to the soldiers. Another was to get help for a wounded soldier and to alert the medics about his location. Not wanting to alert the enemy to his whereabouts, instead of barking, the dogs would find the wounded soldier and bring an item of his back to the medical unit. Then, the dog would lead the way to where it was needed. Some of the dogs were also trained in triage skills. If the soldier they found was beyond help, they would sit beside him and offer companionship in his last moments. (Courtesy of Library of Congress, Prints & Photographs Division, LC-DIG-npcc-27825.)

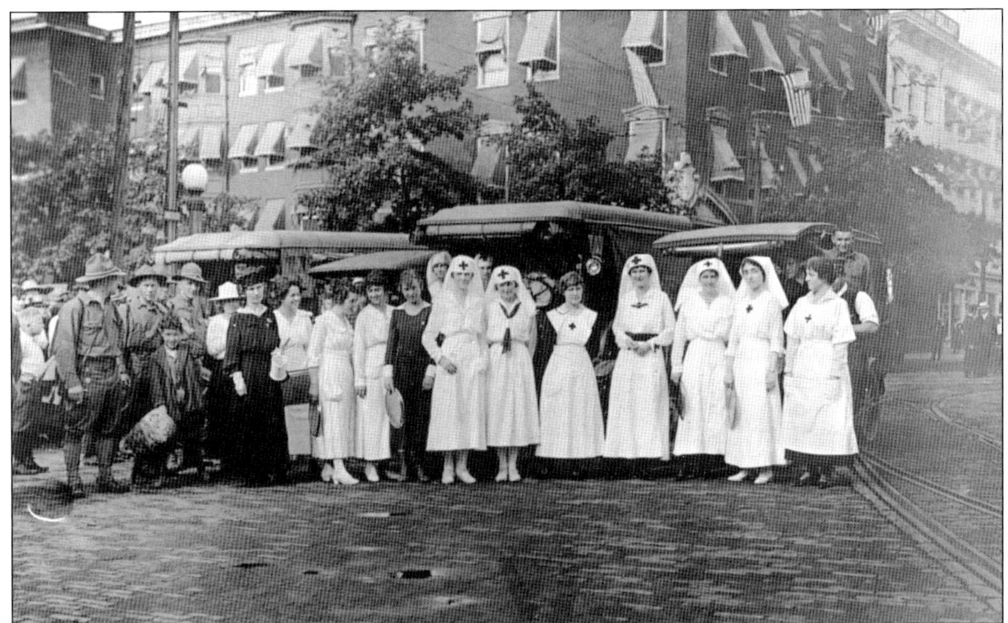

Here, some USAACs pose with nurses from the Allentown Hospital School of Nursing next door to the fairgrounds. The ambulance corps claimed one of the highest percentages of both casualties and honors of the American Expeditionary Forces. USAACs earned 1,653 awards, including 55 Distinguished Service Crosses and 1,118 Cros de Guerres. (Courtesy of Library of Congress, Prints & Photographs Division, LC-DIG-ppmsca-40767.)

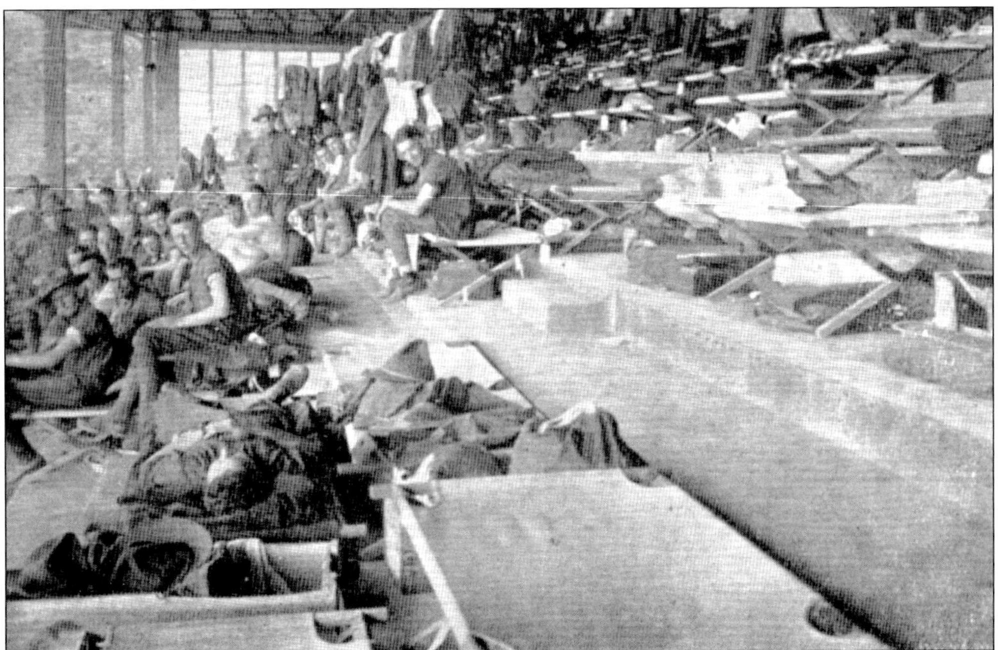

When Camp Crane opened in 1917, soldiers slept in the buildings that were already on the ground. Cots were added to the sheep barns, hog barns, and poultry building. When those buildings were filled, grandstand seating was removed from the upper levels, and cots were added to that area. This is the sleeping area seen in this photograph. (Courtesy of David Bausch.)

Five

Grandstand Events

The grandstand has always been the center of the fair. The track, complete with an underpass leading from the infield to Liberty Street, was built for the initial purpose of hosting harness horse races. Crowds lined the track and filled the seats to see the competitions. Eventually, horse racing transitioned to automobile racing and would attract the same large crowds. Over time, even those races would be upstaged by nationally known entertainers who graced the stage. Once again, the crowds filled the grandstand.

The largest event to draw visitors to the grandstand was in 1905, when the famous harness racing horse Dan Patch made an appearance. Fair attendance was boosted to a record 80,000 visitors, with 22,000 gathering around the track to see the star. Spectators even climbed the trees in the Grove to catch a glimpse of the horse as he set a world record during the visit to Allentown. Racers were known to withdraw from competition when they saw they were up against the pacer Dan Patch, leading to a career of exhibition performances like the one at the fair that year.

Like the rest of the fairgrounds in the 1950s, the grandstand saw a change. The transition began in 1956 when Guy Lombardo and his orchestra performed on stage. As the first national singing star to perform at the fair, he kick-started the type of show that replaced the vaudeville and dancing shows. By 1958, night performances featuring television personalities were added to the stage. Television stars and performers continued to fill the marquis each year during fair week, drawing lines at the box office. So important were the shows that the 1964 fair moved from its late fall dates to early August just to accommodate the Hollywood filming schedule. Then, in 1965, Herb Alpert and the Tijuana Brass filled the seats to the point of standing-room only. The "Home of the Stars" was born.

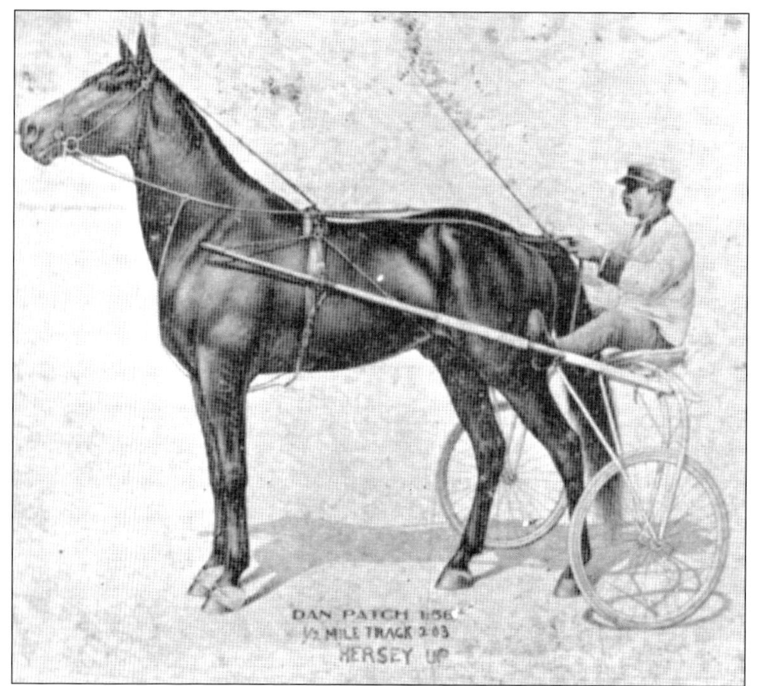

Dan Patch visited the fairgrounds track in 1905. In this exhibition performance, he beat the long-standing record for two-wheel harness racing by running a mile in 2.01 minutes. He followed it by setting the world record for four-wheel racing, one set by his sire, by running a mile in 2.05 minutes; this record has never been broken. (Courtesy of David Bausch.)

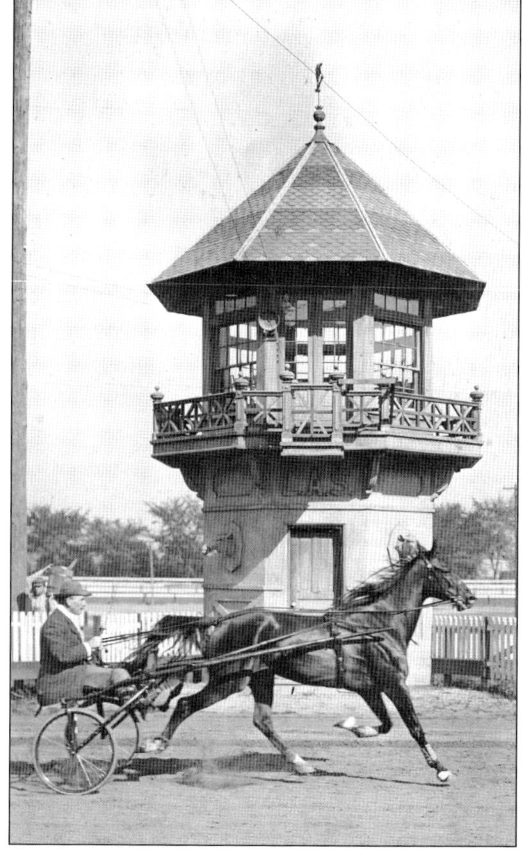

Harness racing was a main draw from the fair's beginning at the original fairgrounds. It was the reason the current fairgrounds was purchased, and the construction of a track and stands was the priority in 1889. In the earliest races, only local horses competed for fans who lined the track for a good view. The races could last for as long as four hours each day. (Courtesy of David Bausch.)

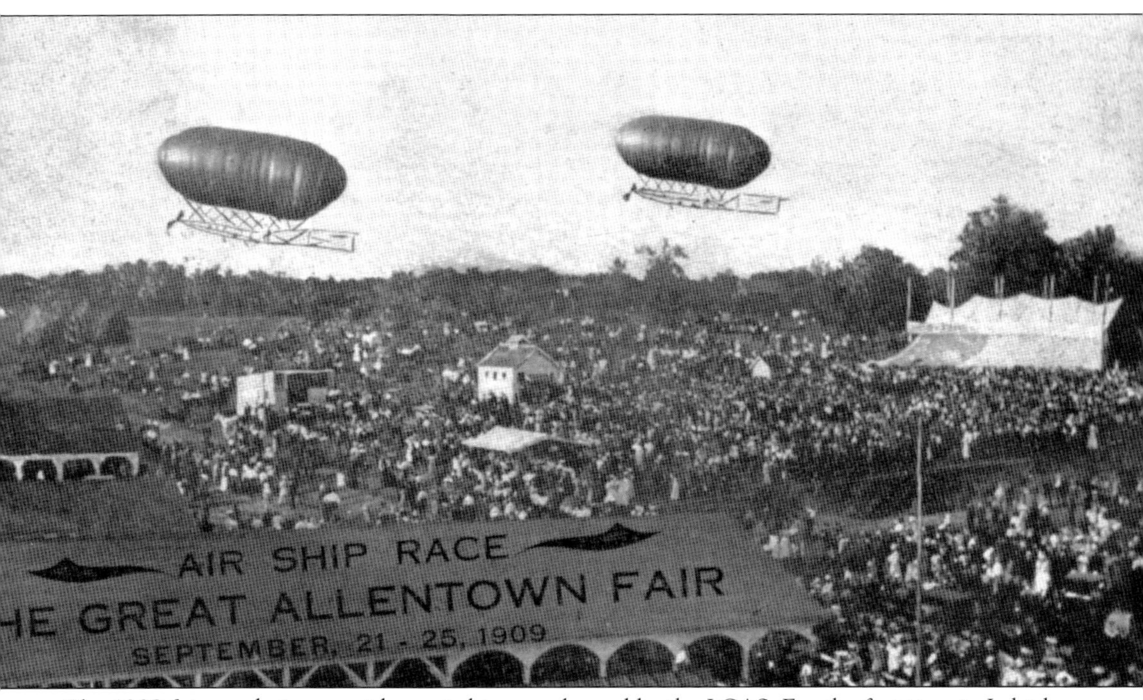

The 1909 fair awed viewers with an airship race, hosted by the LCAS. For the first time in Lehigh County, a race pitted one 54-by-15.5-foot dirigible against another 58-by-12.5-foot ship. Each airship had a 7.5-horsepower engine and a skin made of Japanese silk coated in eight layers of linseed oil. The balloon-like structures held 6,500 cubic feet of hydrogen gas that took nine hours to fill. One ship was given an American flag to fly, and the other was given a German flag in honor of the heavy German heritage of the region. Commanding the ship that flew the American flag was Capt. R.C. Millman with pilot Frank W. Goodale, and the other ship flying the German flag was staffed by Capt. Charles D. Brown and pilot Fred Owens. Weather put a damper on the planned event, though they did manage to fly two races, allowing each ship to win one. (Courtesy of Kelly Ann Butterbaugh.)

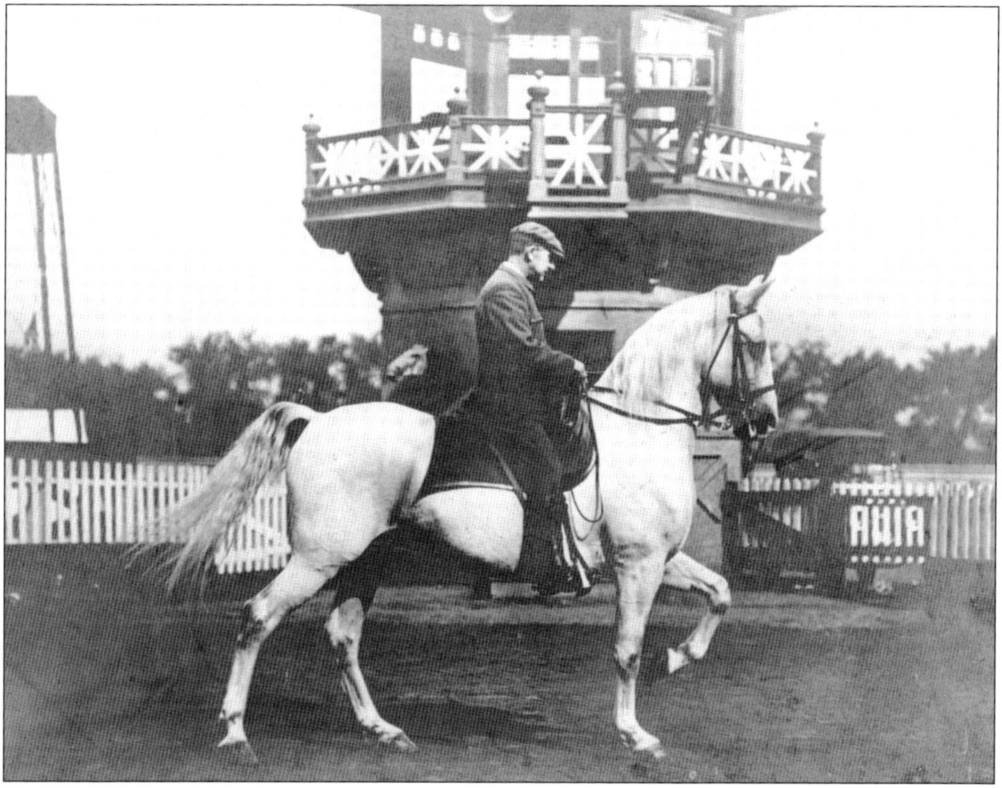

The judges' stand was an ornate addition to the infield. It served as an elevated viewing platform to determine race winners. In 1914, the upcoming horse races were announced from this structure by bugler Bernard McNulty. McNulty's fanfare would call the riders to bring their horses from the stables that lined Liberty Street. This man shows his steed in competition in front of the stand.

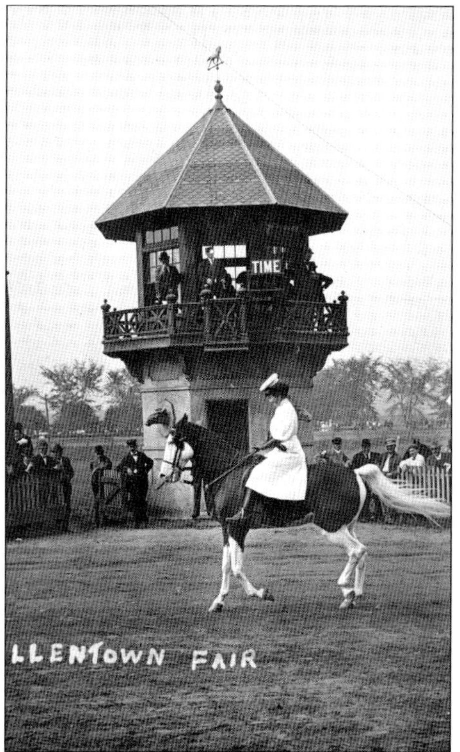

It was said in 1920 that the horse was "the king of the fair." That same year, Gen. Harry C. Trexler won $200 and Best in Show for his team of 16 Percherons. Harness races continued to dominate the afternoons each year, and this rider performed in 1929 as part of an exhibition of female riders. Indeed, the horse was the king of the fair. (Courtesy of David Bausch.)

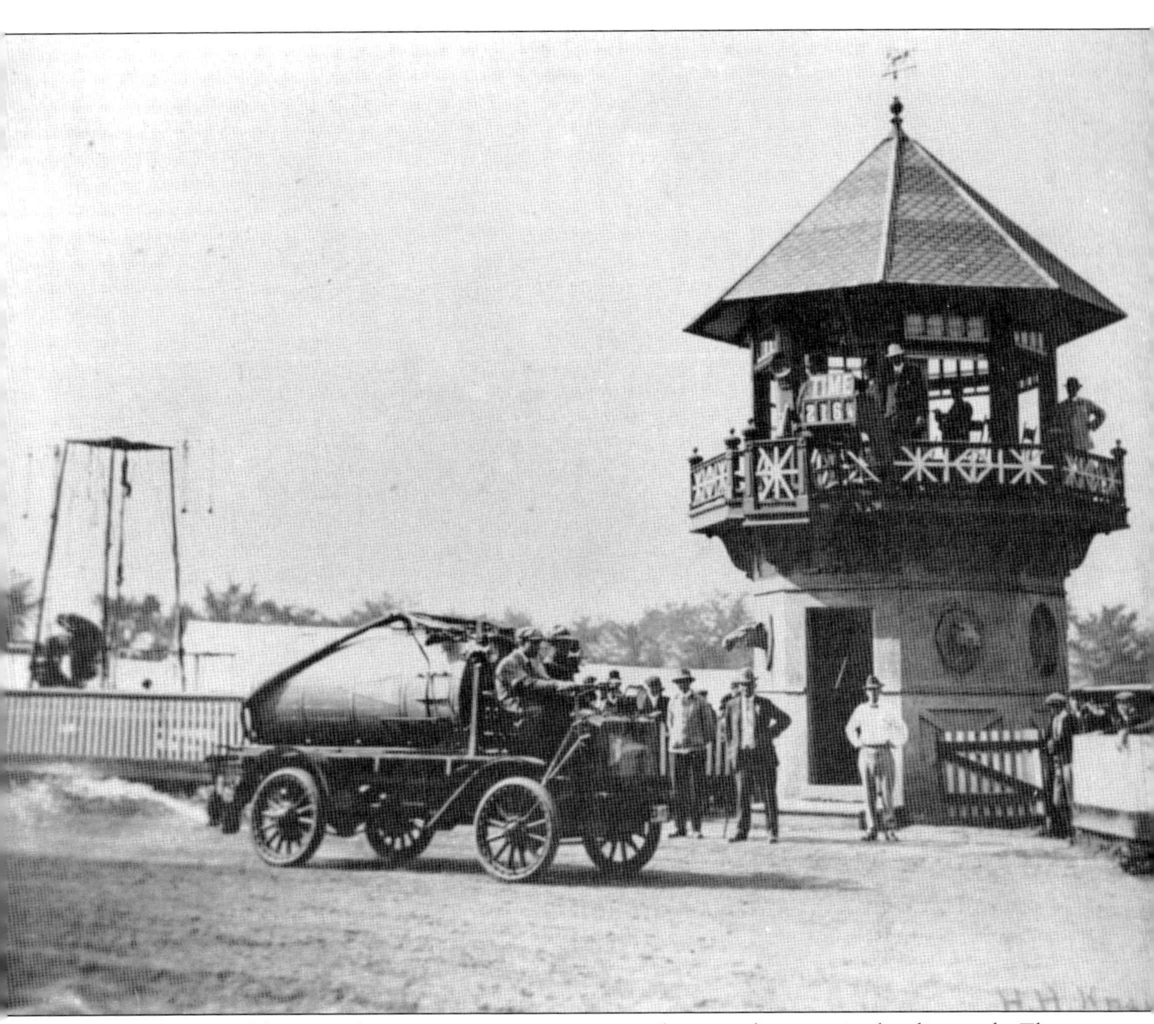

A break is needed between horse racing events to water down and maintain the dirt track. The truck sprays down the dirt to reduce dust and to create a better track for the next race. The half-mile dirt racetrack was considered one of the fastest tracks, and records were set on it over the years. The most notable was when Dan Patch, possibly the most famous harness race horse, set a record during an exhibition at the 1905 fair. Spectators were entertained during these breaks by vaudeville performances, acrobatic routines, and dancers on the small stage in front of the grandstand and track. Aside of the stage was the judge's stand, a Victorian structure with horse head reliefs on the lower level and a time display on the top balcony. This Victorian structure reflected the style of many of the original buildings on the fairgrounds.

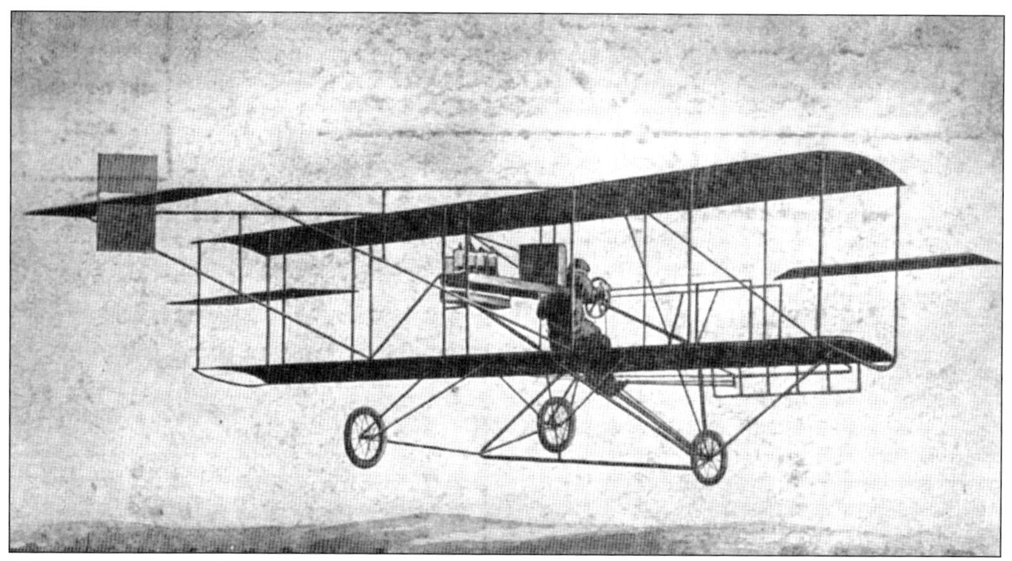

Glen Curtis was paid to fly his biplane around the racetrack for the 1910 fair. He used Nineteenth Street as his runway and circled the fair each day that week. This was the first documented flight of a heavier-than-air craft flying over the ground in the Lehigh Valley. In 1914, the fair hosted an airplane show as part of its entertainment lineup. (Courtesy of David Bausch.)

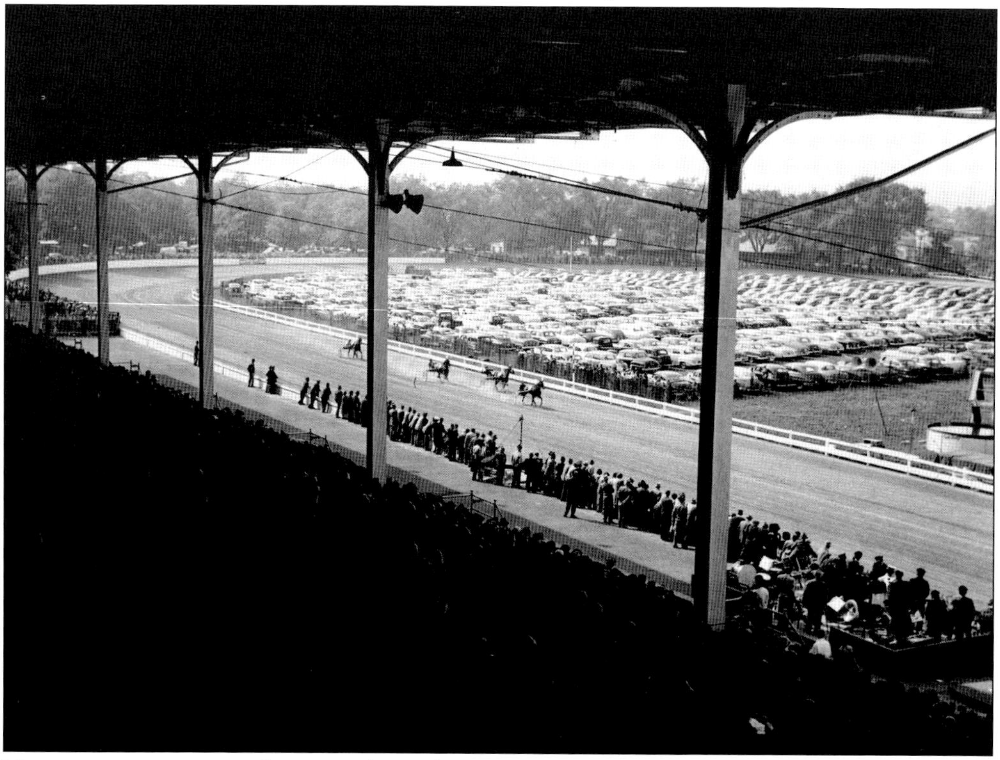

Upon moving to its new location, the fair's focus was to build a racetrack for harness racing. In these earliest days, the entertainment acts on the stage were used as intermissions between the races, not as independent shows themselves. The purses for winners were high, with the 1900 races offering a $300 purse for the winner.

The Hawaiian Islands always inspired creative dance routines for Hamid's revues. In 1945, his "Song of Victory" review featured the popular Hawaiian dance routine. It ended with a climactic dive into a volcano to represent a Hawaiian princess sacrificing herself into a live volcano. The result was not a spewing of lava but of fireworks on the stage.

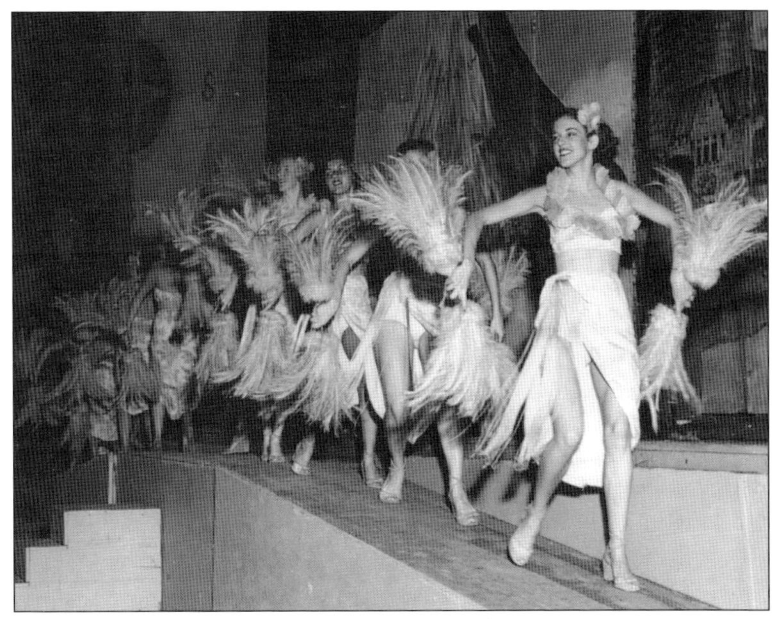

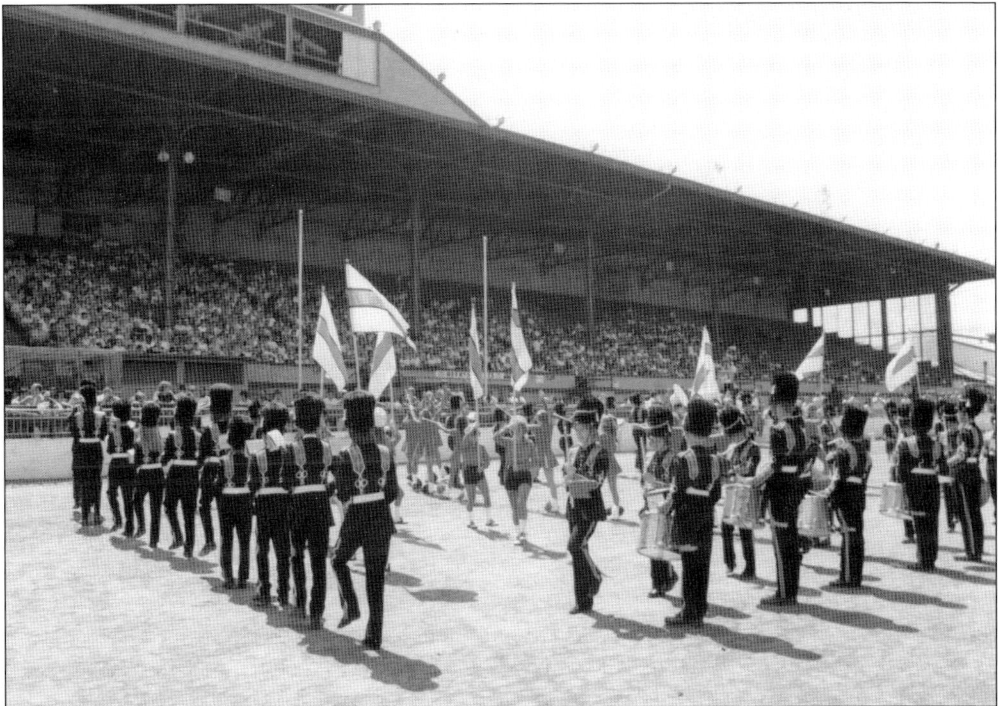

A local high school band performs for the audience. Since the 1920s, bands have performed in front of the grandstand, often opening the cavalcade parade. On September 18, 1946, Albert P. Marchetto and his Marine Band did just this by playing the march he composed entitled "The Allentown Fair." Fair president Edmund Scholl was presented with the original manuscript of the march afterward.

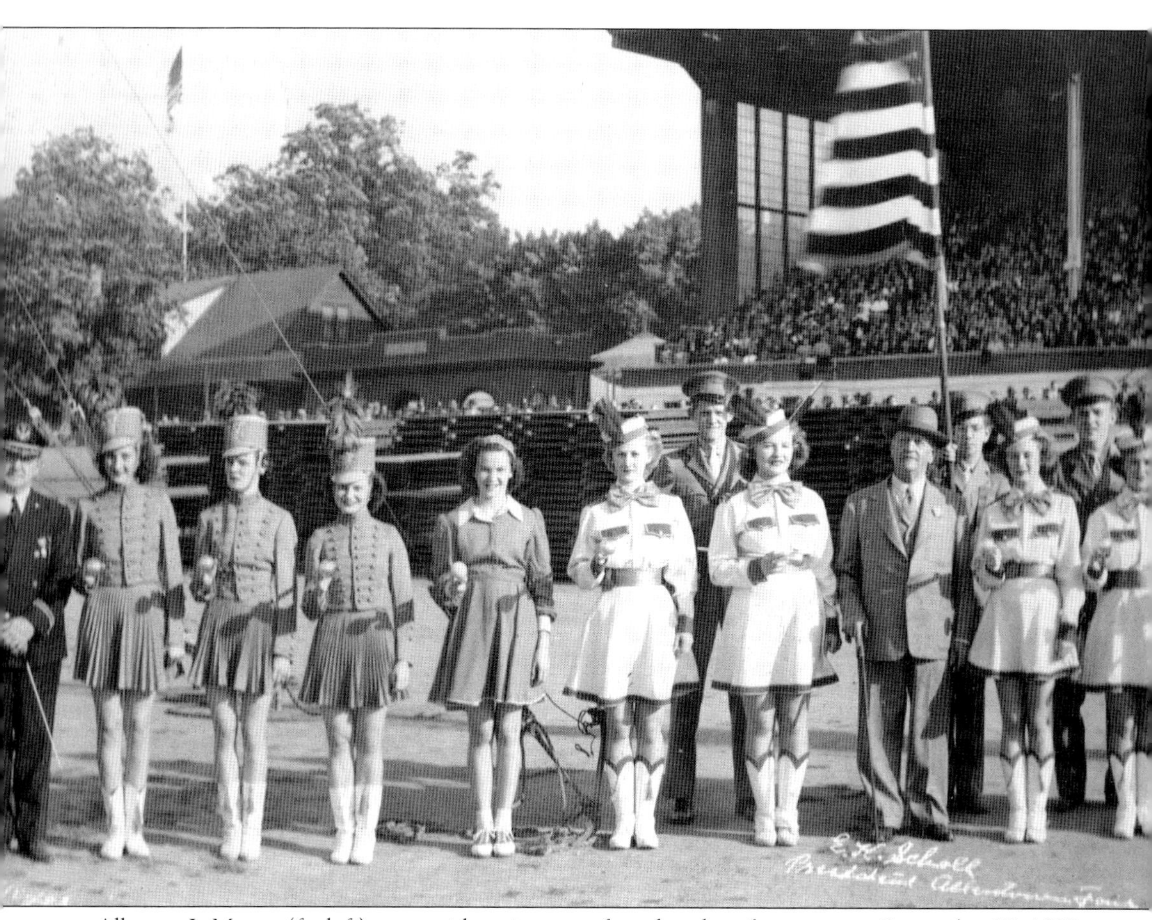

Albertus L. Meyers (far left) poses with majorettes after a band performance on September 27, 1928, at the fair. Meyers was the bandleader for the Allentown Band from 1926 to 1972, after starting as a cornet player in John Philip Sousa's band. Sousa and Meyers were close friends throughout their careers, so close that Meyers was the last person to talk to Sousa before his sudden death. Over the years, Sousa, known as the March King for his rousing parade marches, recruited at least 20 musicians from the Allentown Band for his own band. While playing with Sousa, the musicians learned his personal style and brought it back to the Allentown Band. This is where Meyers finetuned his skills before returning to conduct the Allentown Band. In this picture, the man standing beneath the flag is LCAS president Edmund H. Scholl.

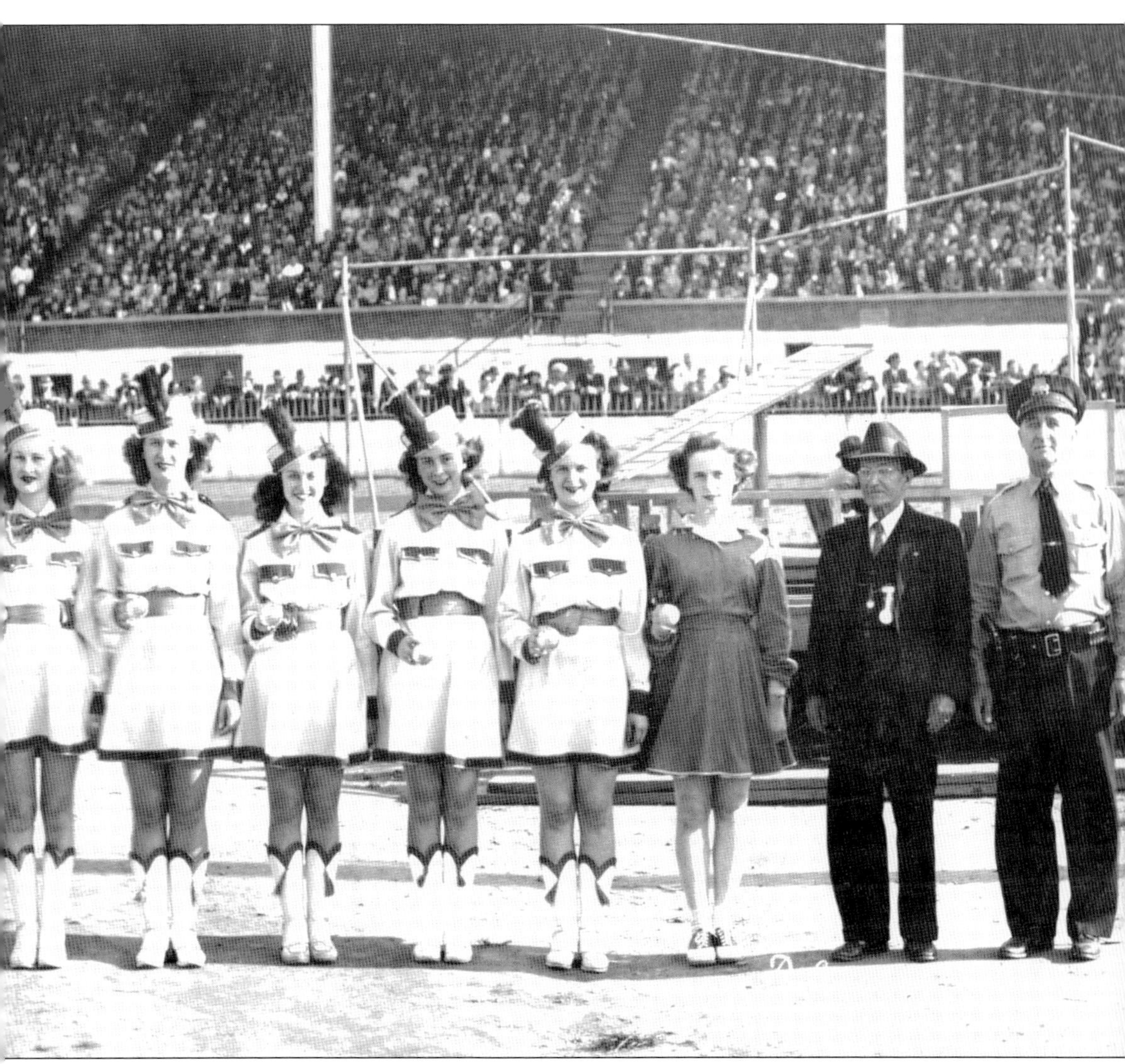

More of the majorettes from Albertus L. Meyers's band pose in front of the grandstand with the stage manager of the fair (second from right) on September 27, 1928. Both the Allentown Band and the Pioneer Band led the daily cavalcade of prizewinning animals at the start of the 20th century. Meyers was a large musical presence in Allentown. Besides leading the Allentown Band, he directed the band at Muhlenberg College from 1957 to 1965 and was the director of instrumental music at Allentown High School, his alma mater from 1940 to 1956. He was also a guest conductor for several large bands, including the Marine, Navy, Army, and Military Academy Band at West Point. In 1974, the Eighth Street bridge was renamed the Albertus L. Meyers Bridge in his honor. Meyers led the Allentown Band when it played at the original dedication to the bridge in 1913.

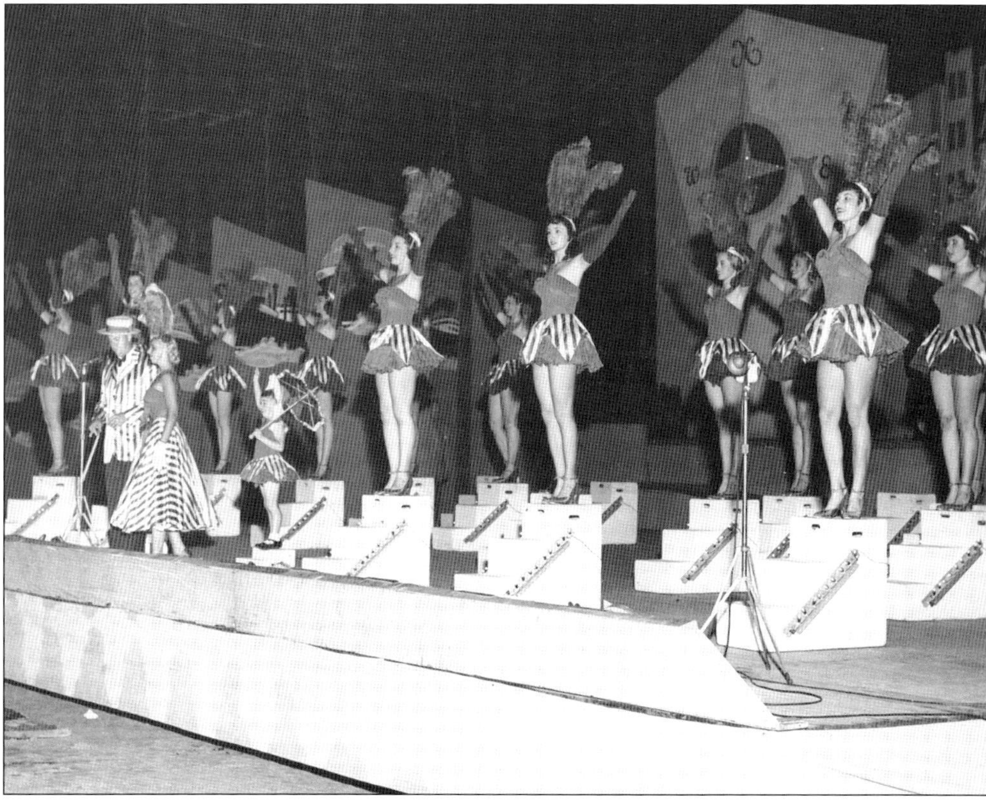

The Hamid dancers were known as the Roxyettes, and they mimicked New York City's Rockettes in their chorus girl performances. The dancers were billed as coming from the Roxy Theater in New York City. Their name's appearance on a ticket or on a marquee sounded like New York City had come to the Allentown Fair. A little bit vaudeville and a little bit Broadway, the dancers delighted their audiences.

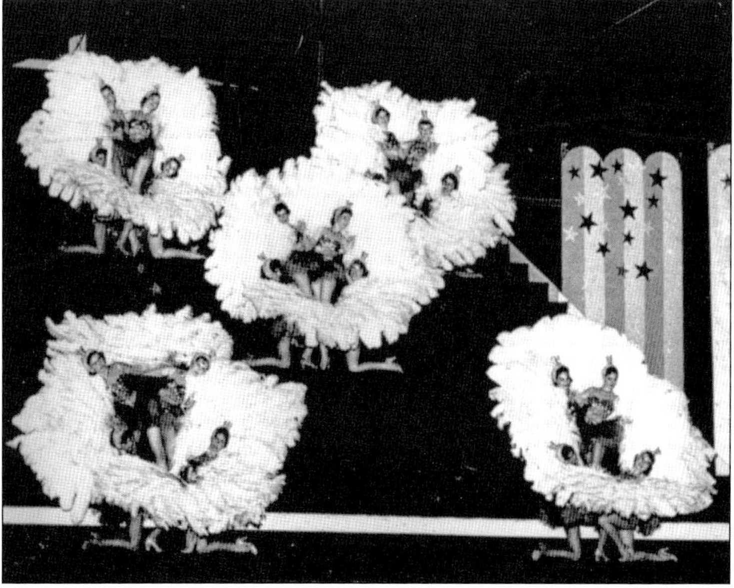

George Hamid's productions were known for their over-the-top costumes and chorus girls from New York City. Many of the shows' fashions were straight from Paris, offering an exotic flair to the productions. Hamid himself had a fashion flair with his colorful shirts and sports coats. (Courtesy of the Danner family.)

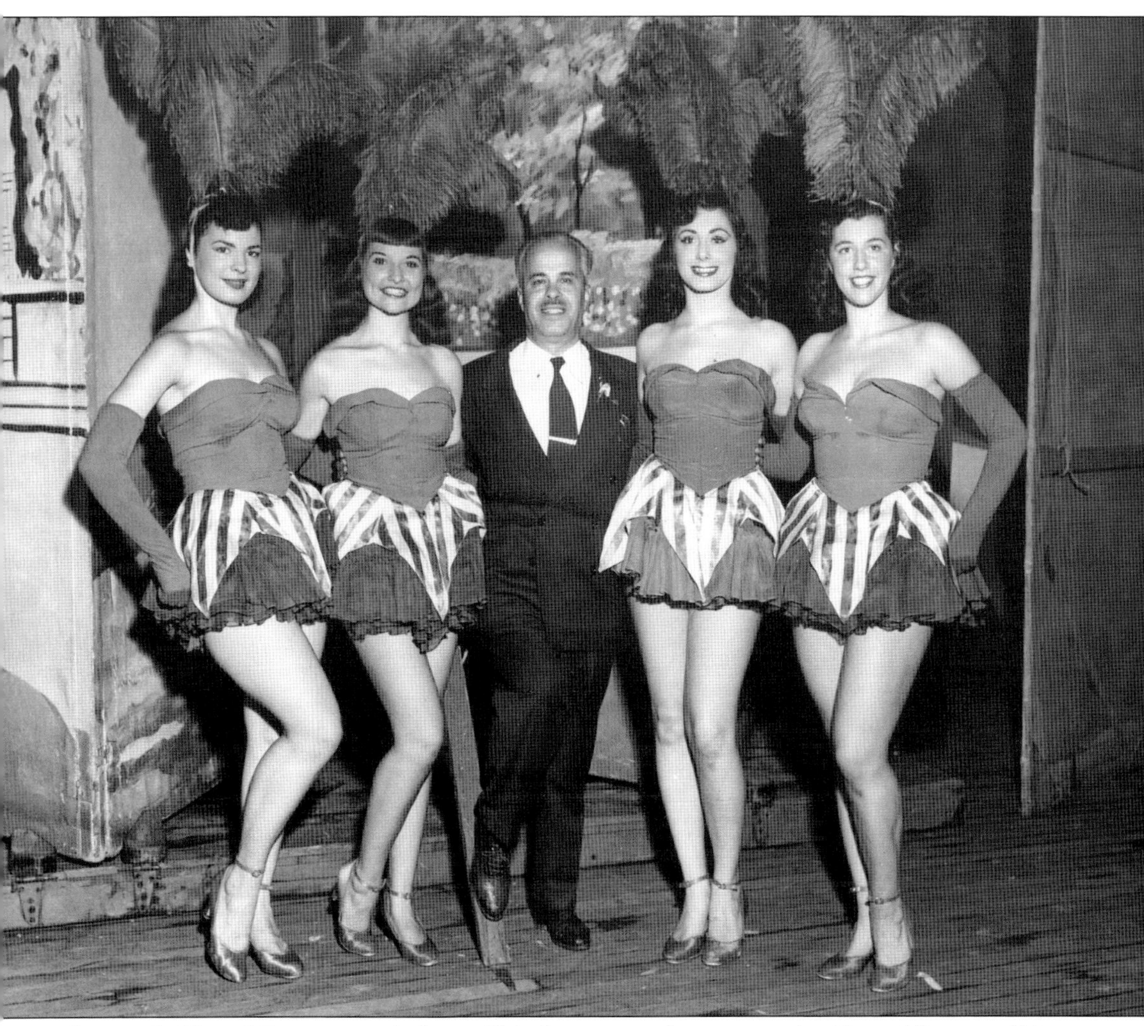

George A. Hamid Sr. poses with four of his dancers on the stage at the Great Allentown Fair. Hamid first performed in Allentown on the trapeze in 1914 after immigrating to America from Lebanon as part of an acrobatic troupe. In 1923, Hamid returned to the stage at the Allentown Fairgrounds, but this time, he was a promoter rather than a performer. He brought with him that year the fair's first vaudeville show. Hamid became known as the premier outdoor entertainment booking agent throughout his decades-long career. He continued to bring aerialists to the Great Allentown Fair's midway and grandstand stage each year, even after he purchased the New Jersey State Fair in 1936 and the Steel Pier in Atlantic City in 1945. When interests turned away from themed dancing shows, the fair booked its last Hamid performance for the grandstand in 1955.

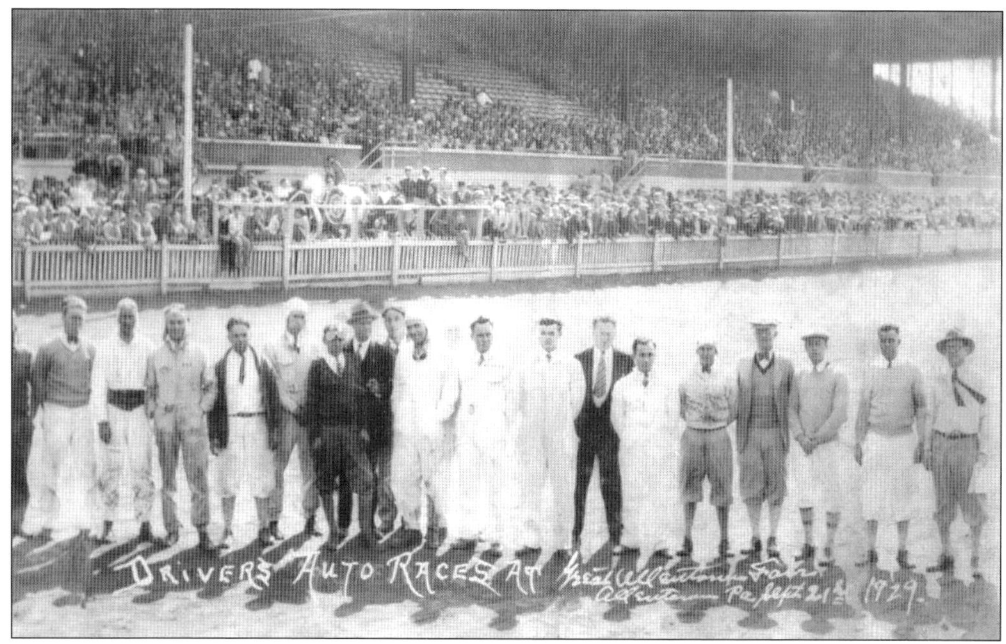

The automobile races on September 21, 1929, were the closing event of the fair that year. It was a professional, sanctioned American Automobile Association race. Drivers looked forward to the race because of the track's reputation for being "fast." Hopes were high for setting new records. Because of the sanction, the race promised the spectators a race with professional drivers.

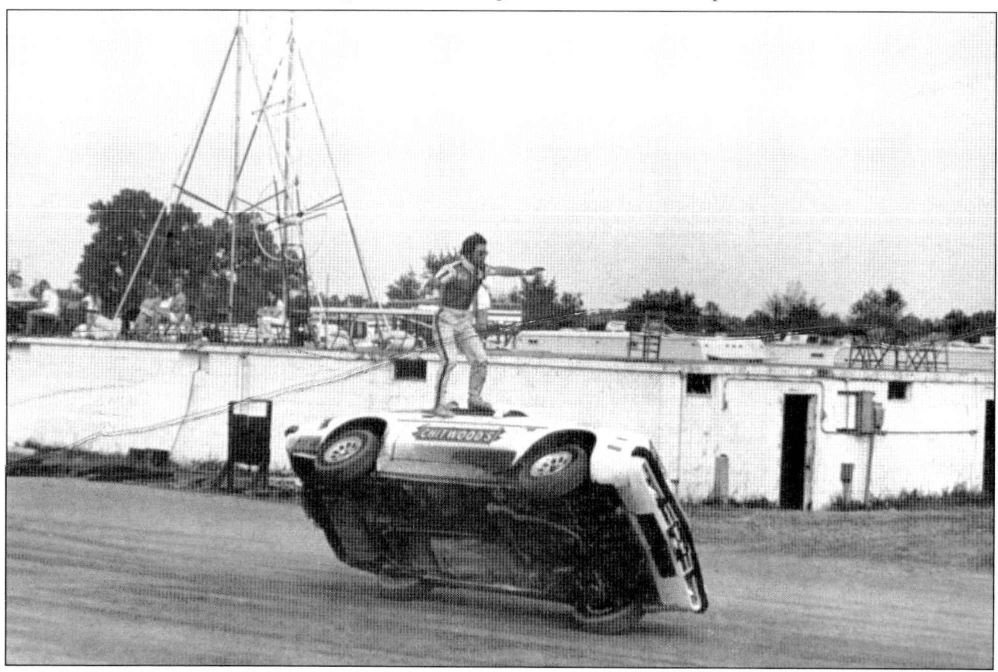

Joie Chitwood's show Hell on Wheels was modeled after the original Lucky Teter show, though Chitwood claimed that his was more spectacular. The danger of these stunt shows was realized as early as 1939, when the Allentown Fire Department stood alongside the track with the newest foaming firefighting equipment ready for any accidents.

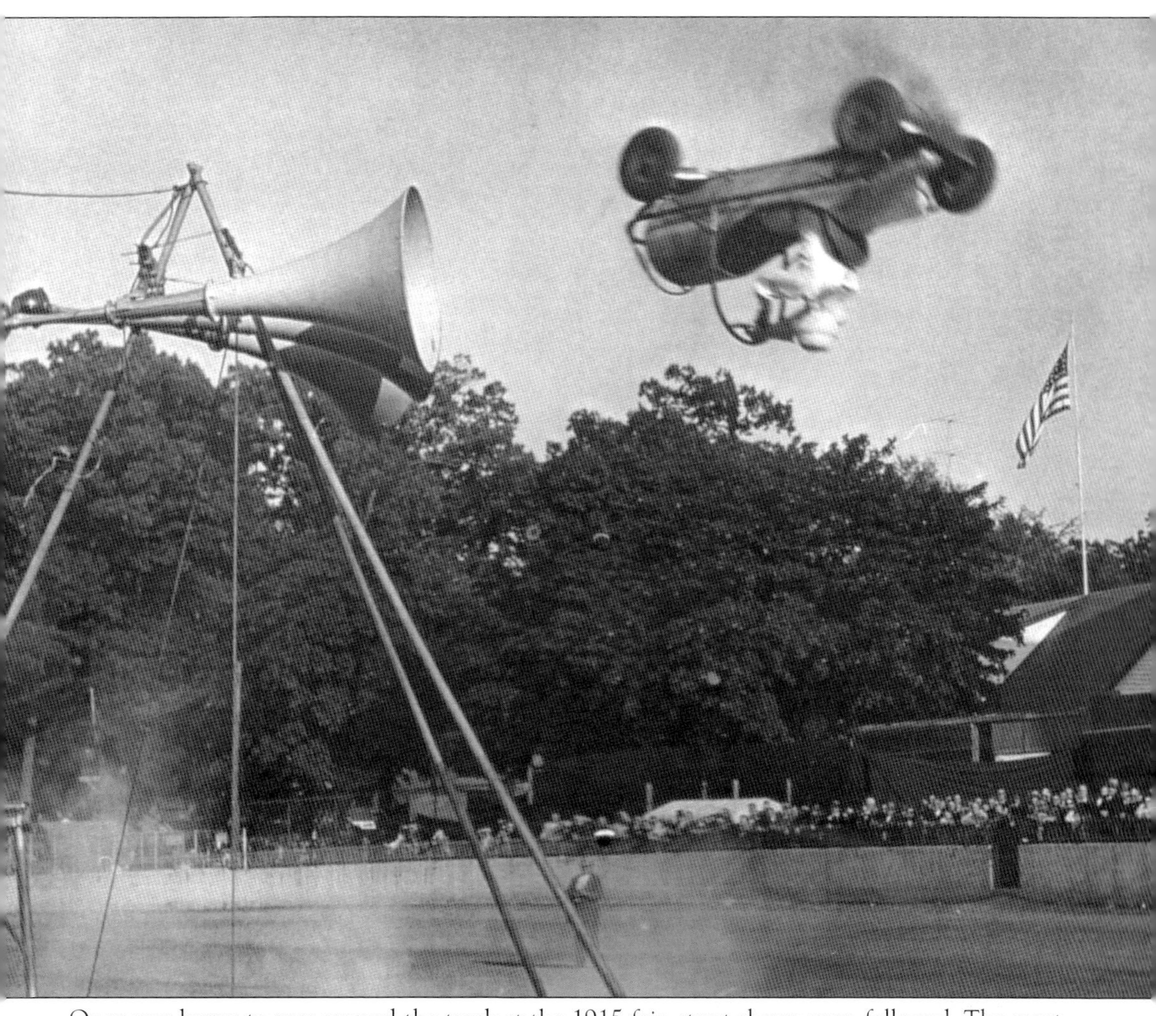

Once cars began to race around the track at the 1915 fair, stunt shows soon followed. The most popular were the Hell Drivers, established by Lucky Teter. The Hell Drivers' show of jumping cars and daredevil driving visited the Allentown Fair several times before Teter's death as well as after his death in the rebranded show run by Jack Kochman. Despite the effects of World War II that canceled most automobile events, the 1943 fair closed with the daredevil show called a Thrill Cavalcade. Due to the rationing of rubber and gasoline, automobile races and shows seemed impossible. The daredevil drivers, however, found a way to perform by altering their cars. They replaced rubber tires with cleated tire rims and created a synthetic fuel to use instead of gasoline. With these modifications, the show could go on. The following year, automobile races capitalized on these ideas to return to the track after a three-year hiatus.

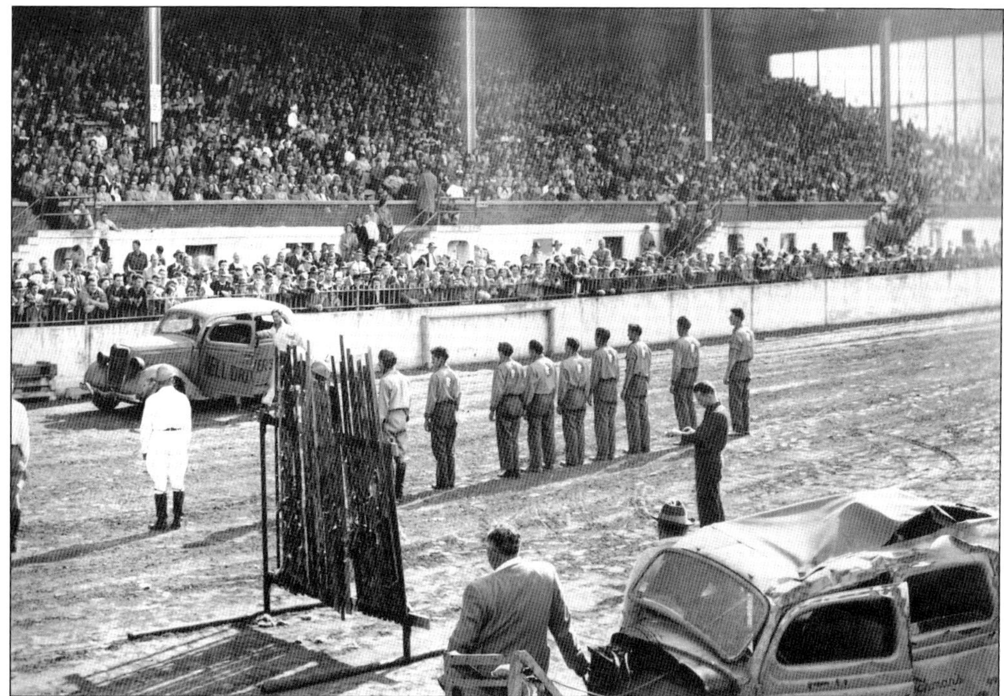

Lucky Teeter's Hell Drivers line up after their performance on the racetrack. They were known to crash into brick and wooden walls as well as to sail through the air and over obstacles. Their driving skills were lauded as being the best in the world. As the interest in automobile shows grew, the harness races started to see themselves pushed out of the forefront.

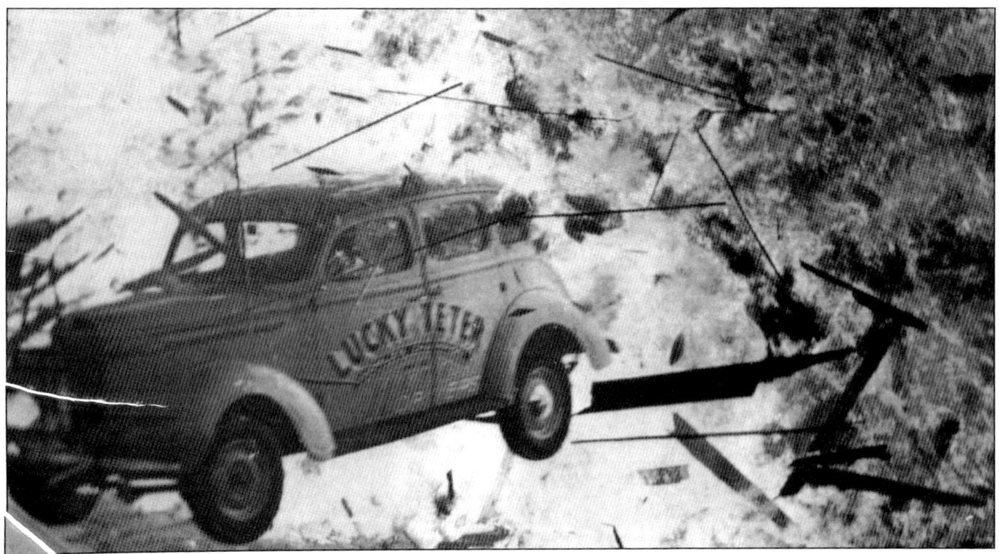

Earl "Lucky" Teter and Robert "Spooly" Hutchinson started Lucky Teter Hell Drivers in 1934. With a crew of 60 drivers, they sent out teams to perform stunts at fairs across the country. Teter died during a stunt in 1942, and Jack Kochman purchased the show, continuing to tour under the name World Champion Hell Drivers.

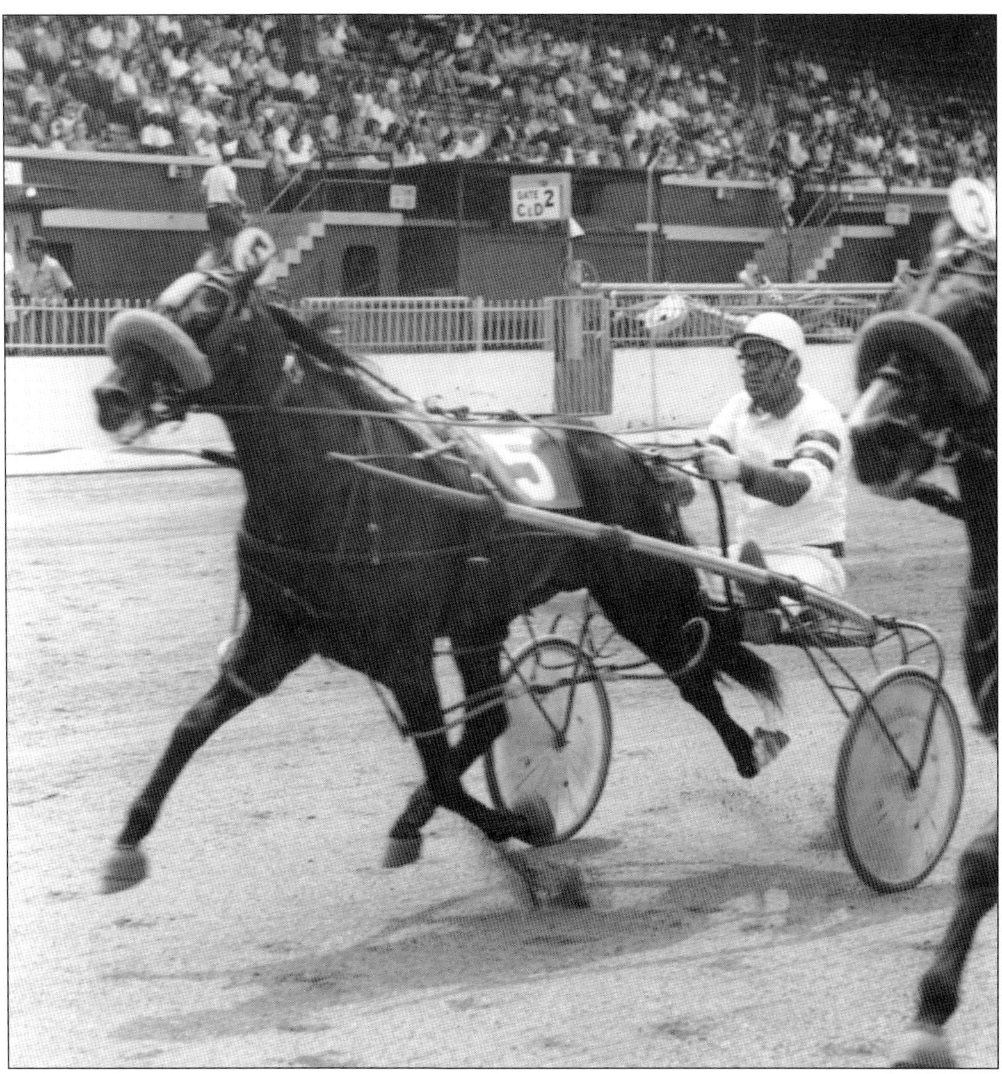

Harness racing began at the Allentown Fair in 1853 and was the catalyst for the LCAS to purchase a larger property and to build a larger racetrack. It, too, was the reason for the construction of the larger grandstand. Several star horses raced at the present fairgrounds, including Prince Albert in 1901. Visitors in the grandstand hoped to see the horse break the world record set in 1896. Unfortunately, he did not. The world champion trotter Cresceus appeared in 1902, along with Major Wellington, who won three heats in a row in 1903. In 1905, spectators saw the world record broken at the fair. The world's most famous harness racer, Dan Patch, ran exhibition races at the fair that year and broke the standing world record. Unofficially, he broke his own record the following year at an unofficially timed event. His record stood until 1960, the same year that harness racing stopped at the Great Allentown Fair.

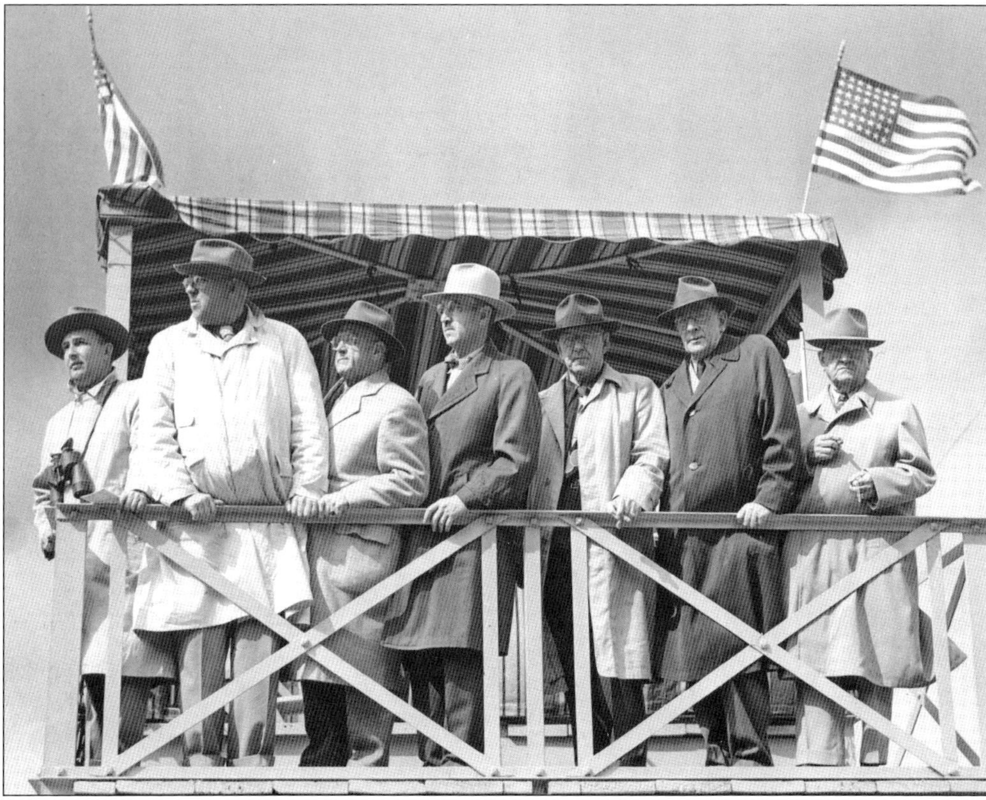

Judges and fair executives crowd the old timing and judges' booth during a harness race. Once this infield structure was removed, the prime location for viewing the track events became the cupola on top of the grandstand. Now used as a press box, only a few are invited to climb the extremely narrow staircase to the cupola's perch.

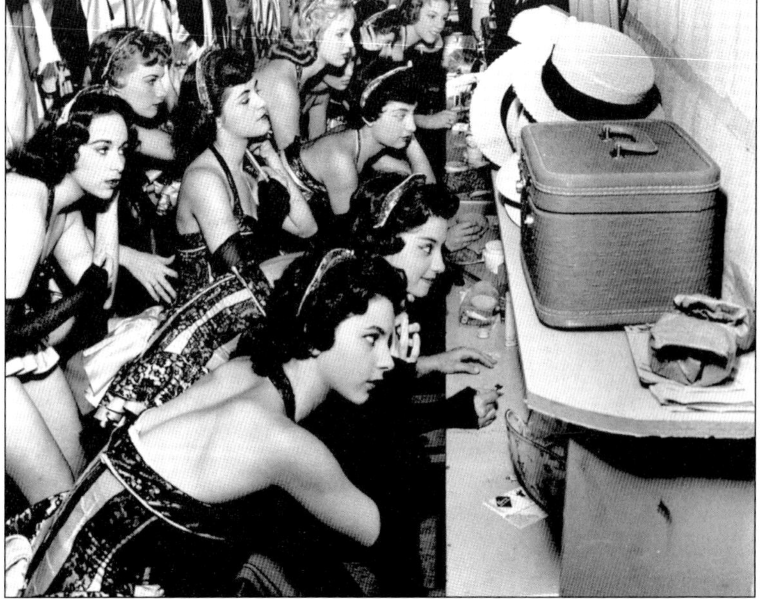

The June Taylor Dancers performed several years at the fair during the 1950s and 1960s. The group of 16 dancers, famous for their tap dancing and high kicks that were seen on *The Jackie Gleason Show*, is backstage getting ready for a performance. In 1958, the dancers performed at the fair for four nights with entertainers Red Buttons and Jonathan Winters.

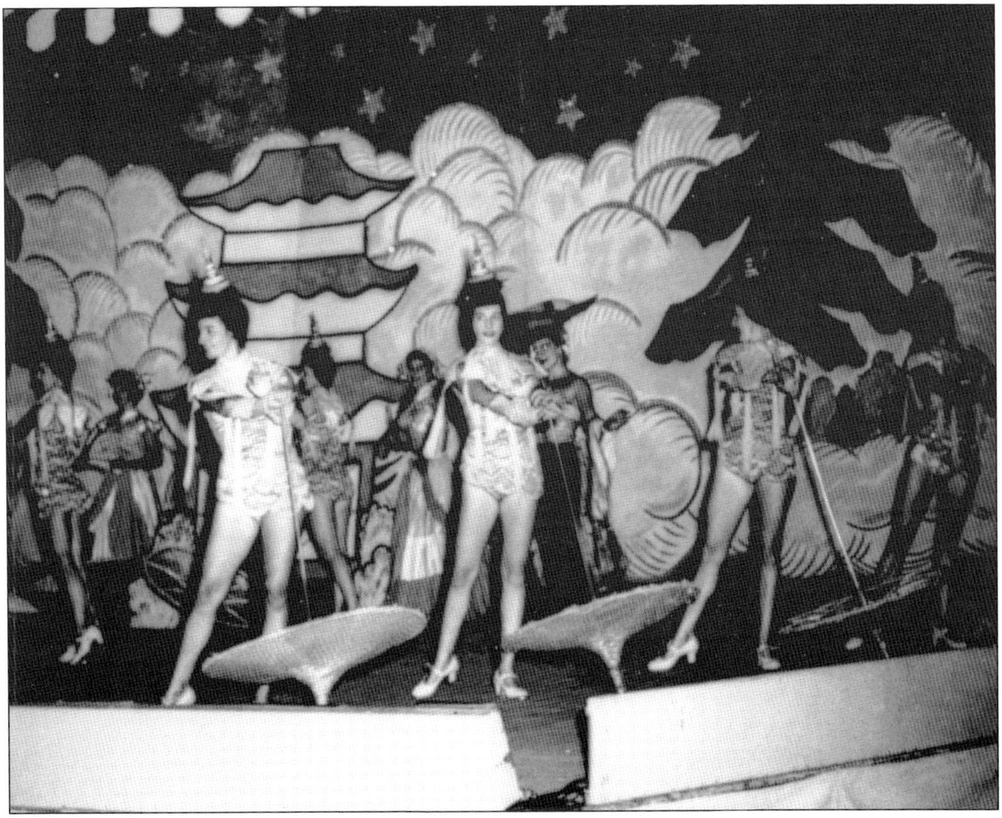

The 1954 George Hamid grandstand show "The Grandstand Follies" was performed despite a day of rain that soaked the stage. Workers used a tarp to create a roof over the stage while the dancers performed in heavy rain. One Japanese dance routine featured a dance titled "Lotus Land." (Courtesy of the Danner family.)

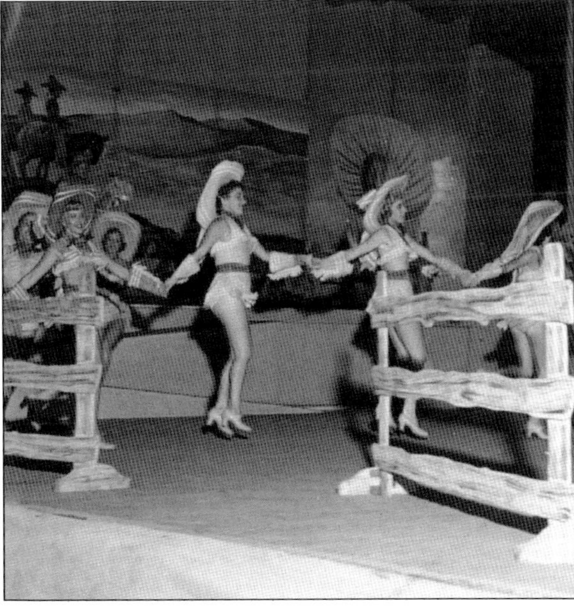

Each year, George Hamid gave a theme to his grandstand show. Some years, they performed novelty routines on roller skates or performed water ballets. Their music reflected the popular choices of the year, and they drew crowds to the stands every year. Wild western shows were always popular. (Courtesy of the Danner family.)

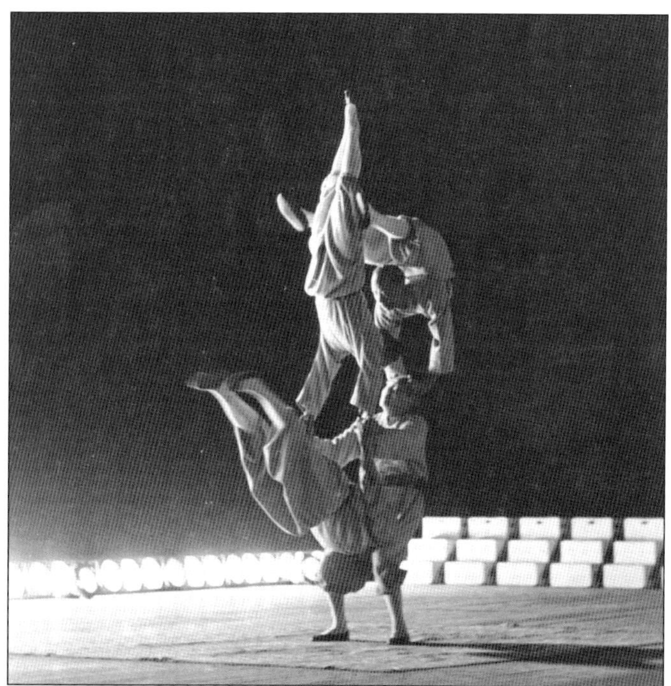

The fair had always closed its gates at 6:00 p.m., but when Edmund Scholl became LCAS president in 1925, he introduced the idea of the "night fair." That year, the fair remained open in the evening with plenty of entertainment thanks to George Hamid and his shows like these hand-balancers. (Courtesy of the Danner family.)

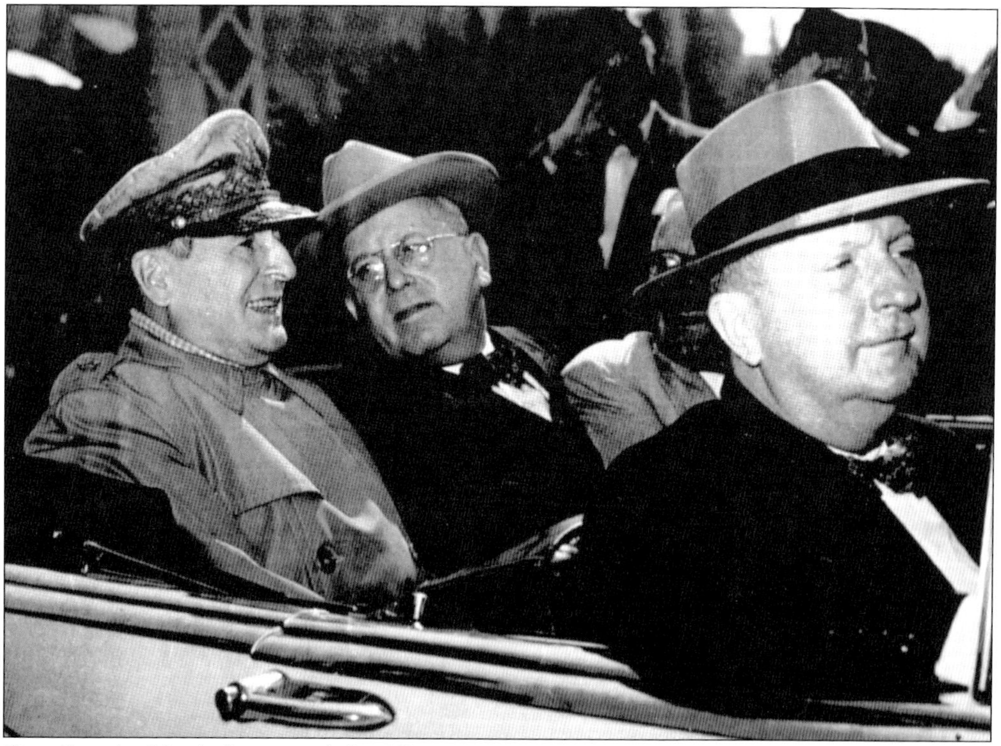

Gen. Douglas MacArthur visited the Allentown Fair on September 21, 1951, along with his wife, Jean, and 14-year-old son Arthur. The event was initiated by Howard Singmaster, LCAS president, who invited the World War II general to visit the fair for Father and Son Day. MacArthur accepted, stating that he wanted his son to see a real American fair after spending most of his life abroad.

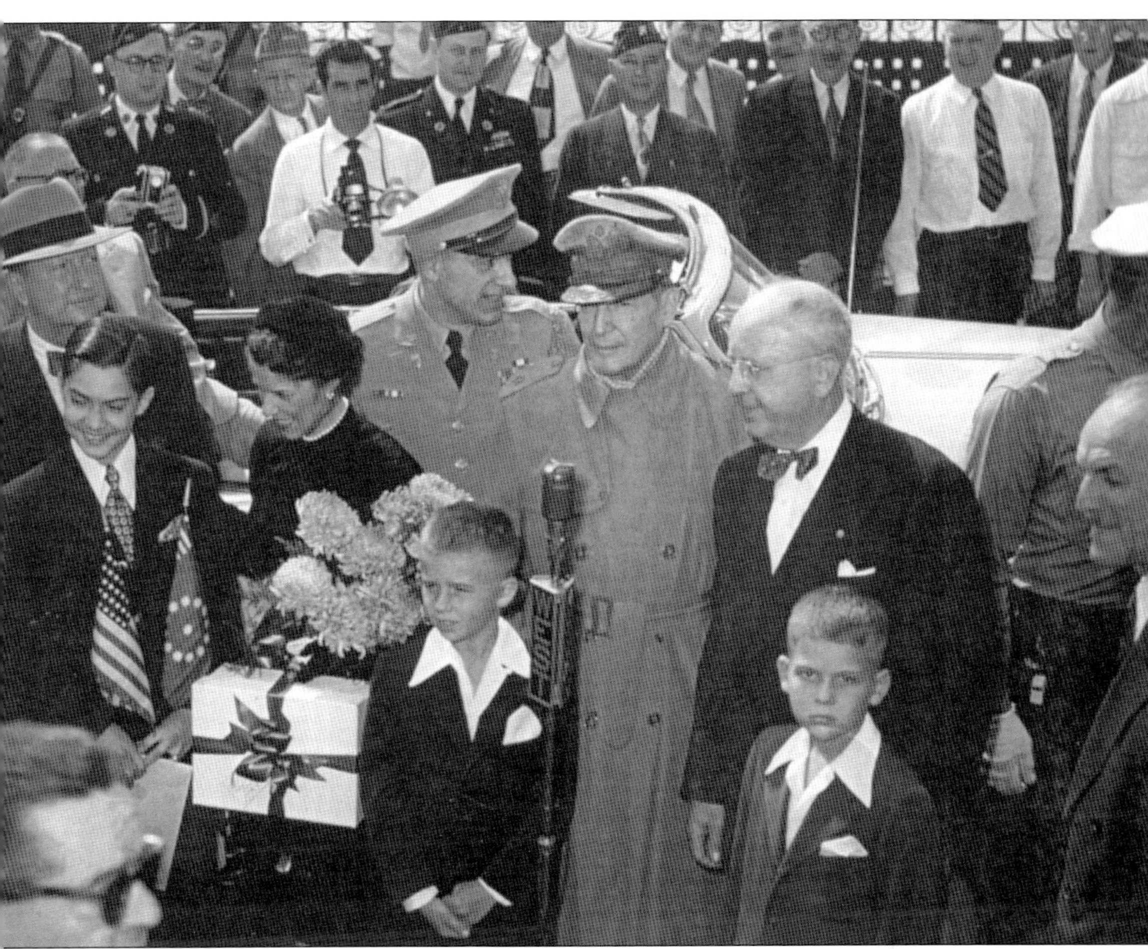

Gen. Douglas MacArthur's visit to Allentown was a noteworthy event to those who resided within the town. The general's family was escorted to the Allentown Fairgrounds, where they dined on a sauerkraut dinner in the fair president's office. Afterward, amid a packed crowd of onlookers, they entered the grandstand where they enjoyed an afternoon of vaudeville acts and harness racing. The general had plans to walk the midway of the fair, but the plans were cancelled due to the overly enthusiastic crowds who pressed tightly against his entourage. Toured through the fairgrounds by LCAS president Howard Singmaster and his wife, MacArthur was impressed with the grounds. Some believed that the fairgrounds had paid for MacArthur's visit as a publicity stunt, but it was made clear that the trip was paid for by the general himself or by local businesses who donated items such as his touring car. While visiting the fair, Gen. Douglas MacArthur was given a bust sculpted by local artist Mike Iacocca, and later, a street in the city was named after him.

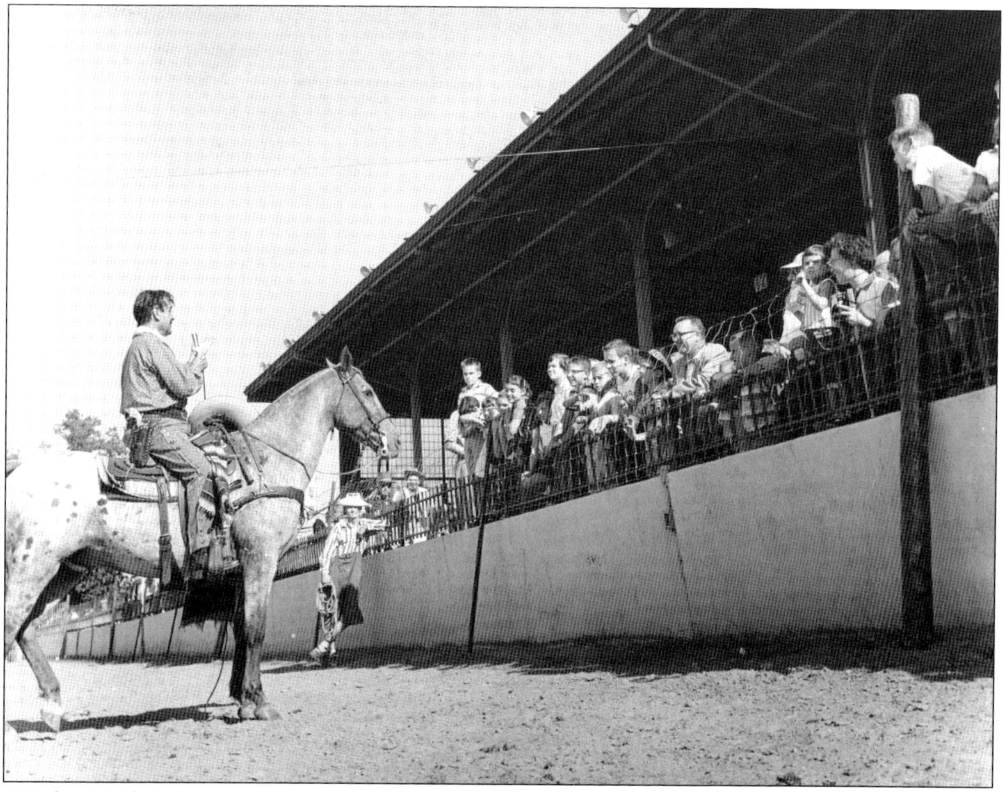

Candy Candido appears in his cowboy garb to introduce a performance at the grandstand. Candido had some experience as a cowboy when he appeared in the movie *Cowboy from Brooklyn* with actors Ronald Reagan and Dick Powell. Candido has numerous movies to his credit, mostly as a voice actor with a four-octave range. As the fair's goodwill ambassador, Candido introduced shows at the grandstand and Farmerama stages.

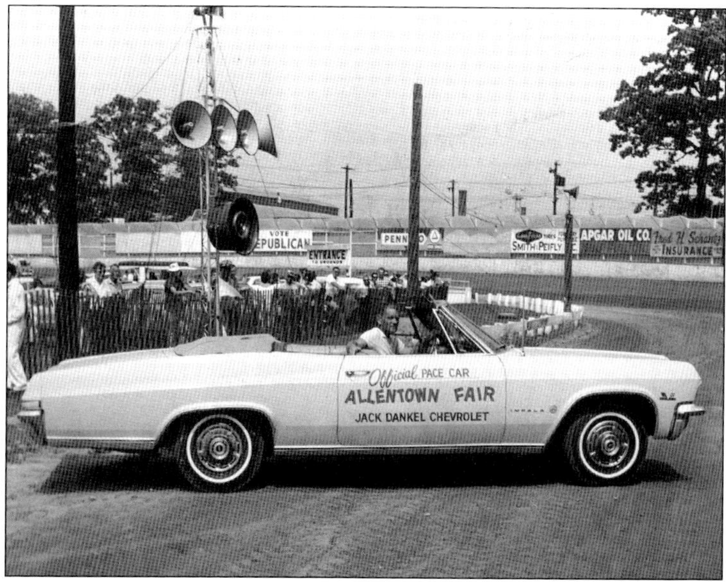

The official pace car of the auto races in the mid-1960s was a Chevrolet Impala from Jack Dankel's showroom in Allentown. Dankel even ran a 1967 newspaper advertisement telling readers to "set the pace" with a new Chevy from his sales lot. Dankel began selling Chevrolets on Tilghman Street in 1933 and branched out to multiple service and sale locations by the 1960s.

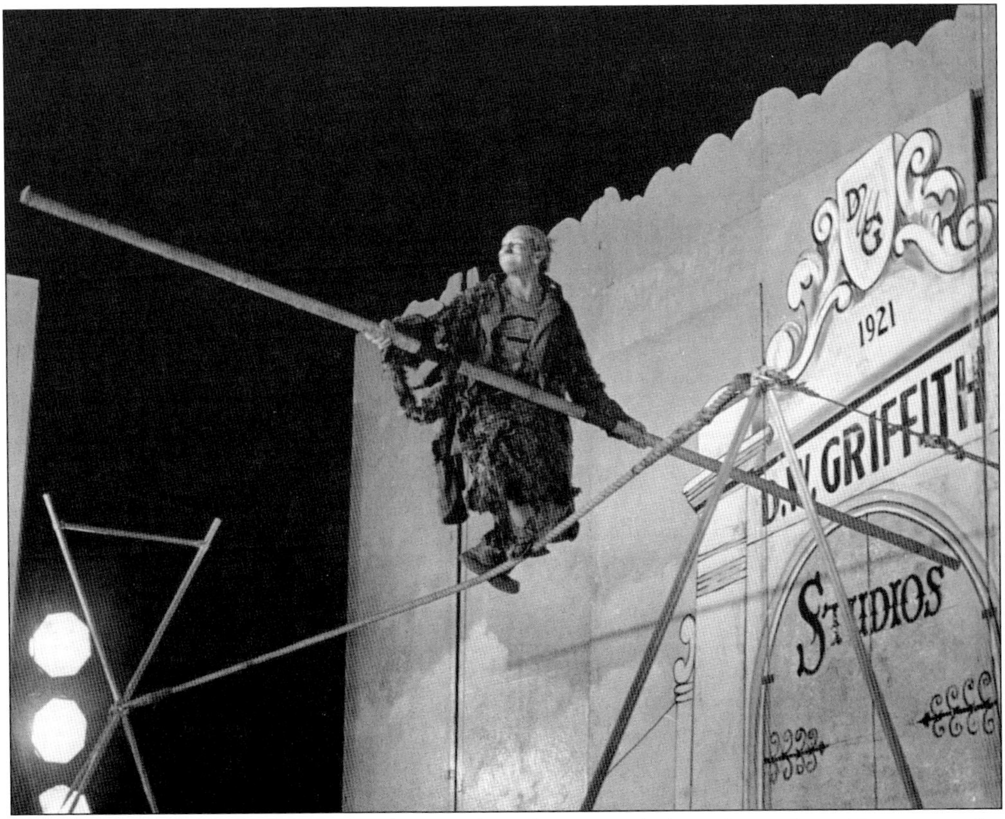

For decades, the performances on the grandstand stage and throughout the midway were the work of George Hamid. Each year, he booked daring aerialists, gymnasts, novelty performers, and dancers. Hamid borrowed acts from other larger fairs and tried to bring some of the New York performances to Allentown. Hamid was a nationally known promoter of outdoor performances. (Courtesy of the Danner family.)

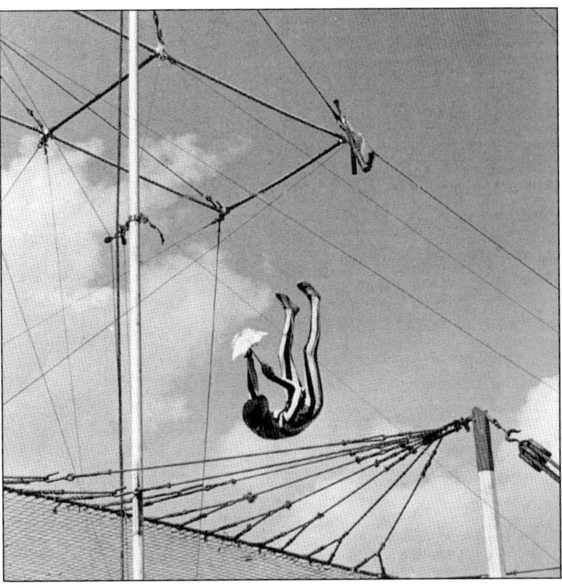

Death-defying tricks and humor made the aerialist routines popular with visitors each year. This artist adds humor to his heart-stopping but planned fall as he tries to use a tiny umbrella as a parachute. Other acts had performers riding bicycles across tightropes or balancing on poles high above the stage. (Courtesy of the Danner family.)

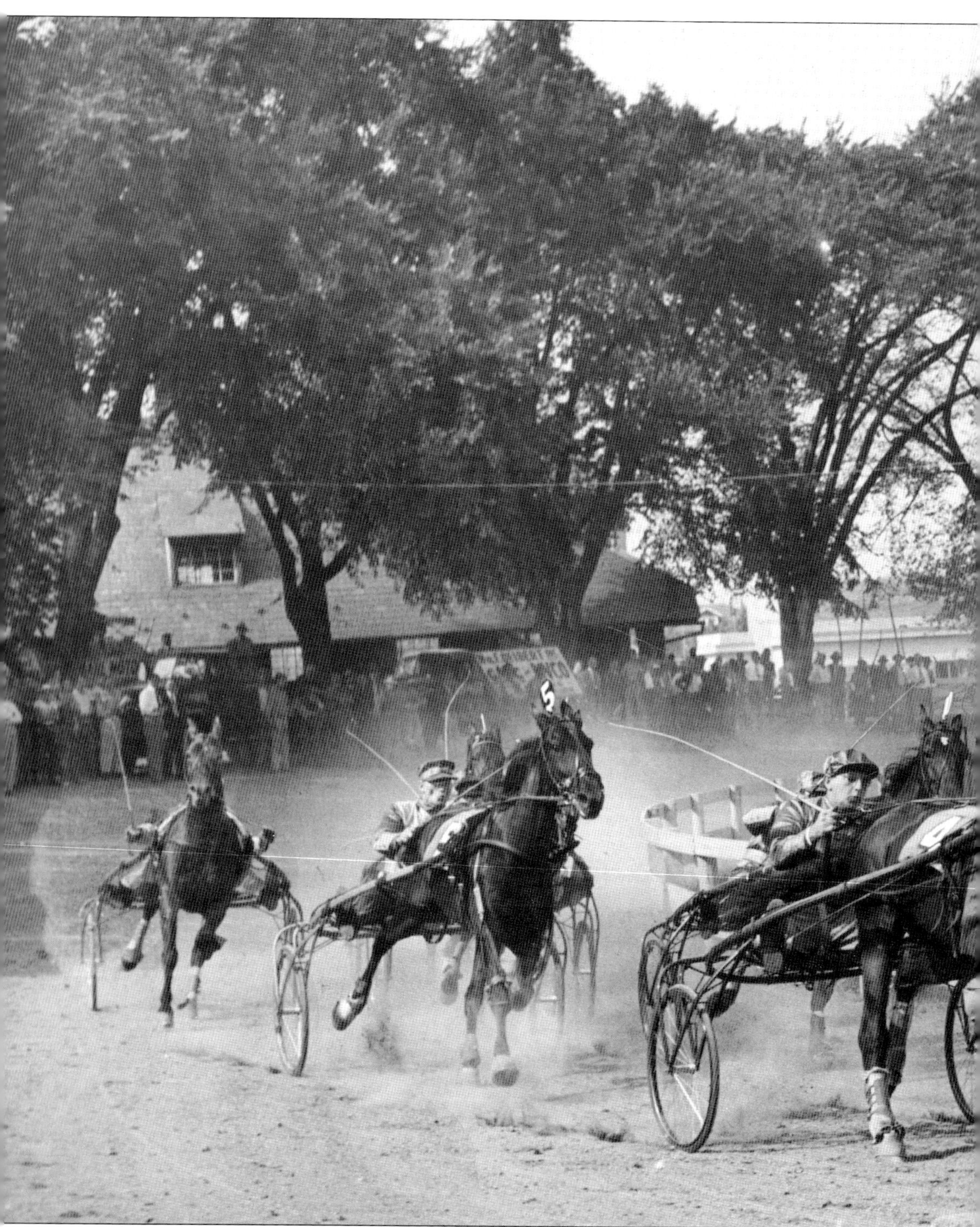

The horses take a turn on the track at this 1951 race. Note the spectators standing nearly on the track and the wooden snow fence around the infield. The outside wall of the track was built in later decades at the height of the automobile races. During the second harness race, a large pile-up occurred. Five carts piled up on top of one another in the crash. Miraculously, only one driver was

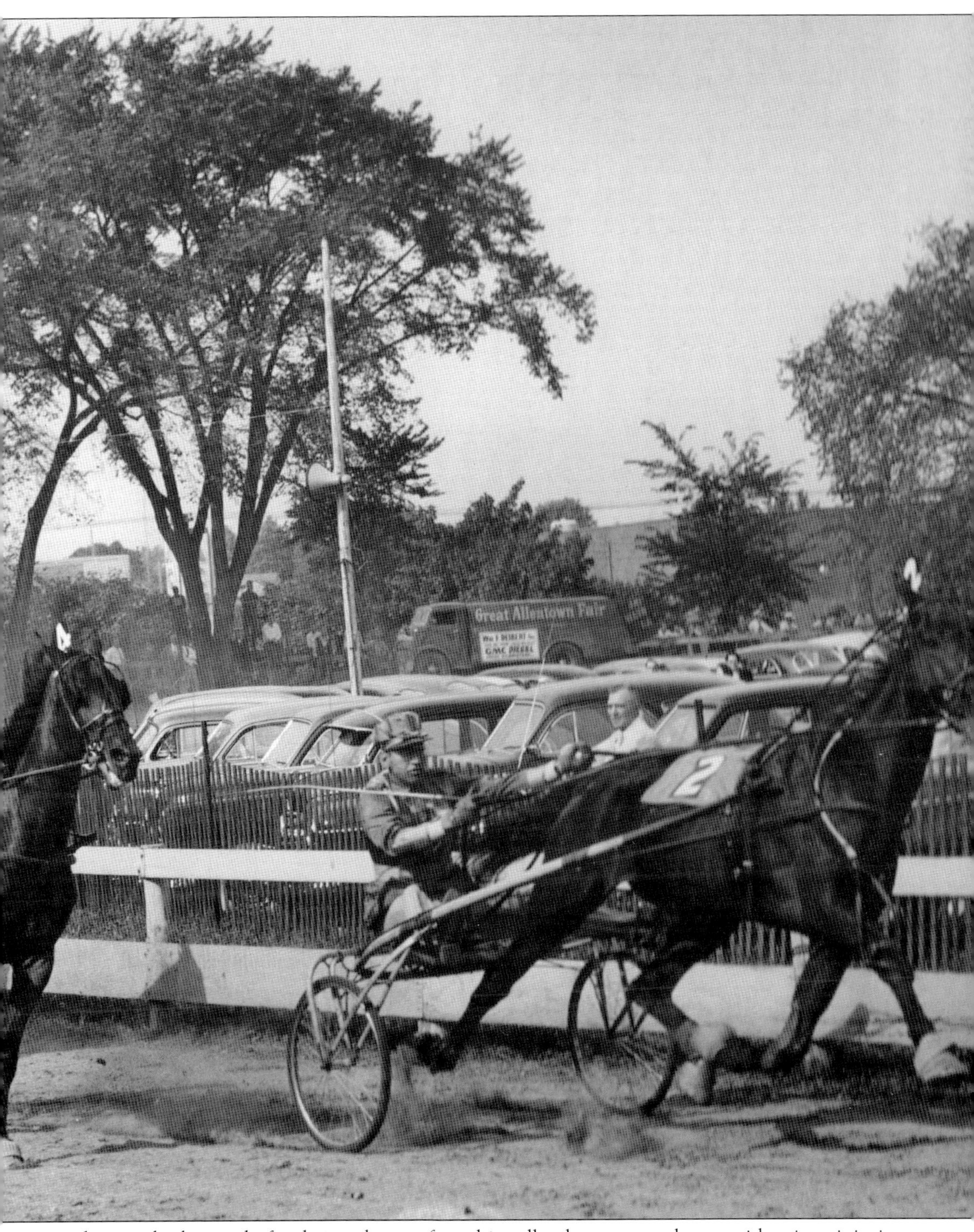

taken to the hospital after being thrown from his sulky; he was sent home with minor injuries. Later that week, General MacArthur toured the fairgrounds and sat front-row center for that day's harness race.

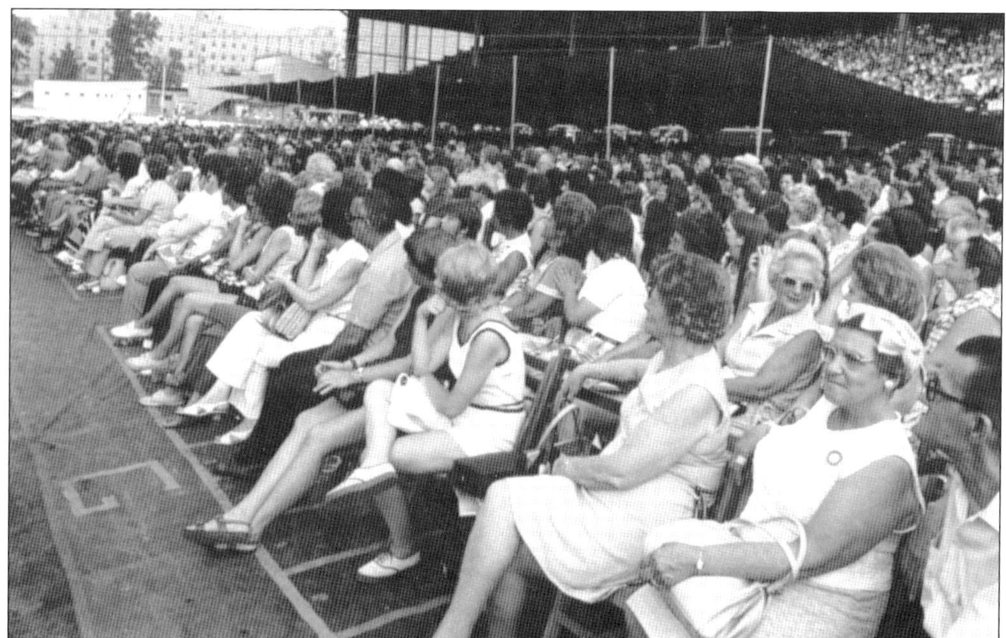

When crowds got too large in the 1960s and 1970s, tickets for events could be purchased as grandstand seating, covered track seating, or uncovered track seating. Large tarps were laid out on the track, with the assigned seating spaces painted on them. These prime, front-row seats offered little protection from the sun or rain but offered great views of the shows.

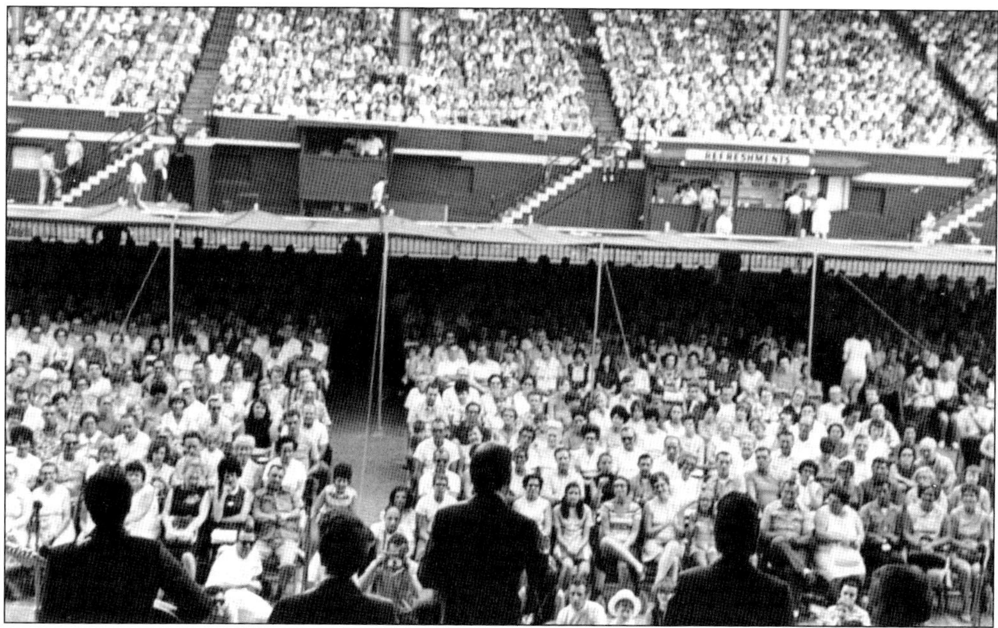

In 1956, the grandstand stage stopped its annual bookings with George Hamid and instead opted to book well-known performers. In 1966, Herb Alpert and the Tijuana Brass filled the grandstand beyond capacity in a standing-room-only performance. A photograph similar to this one, featuring the band performing to the sold-out crowd, was featured on their next album titled *SRO*, with credit given to the Allentown Fair.

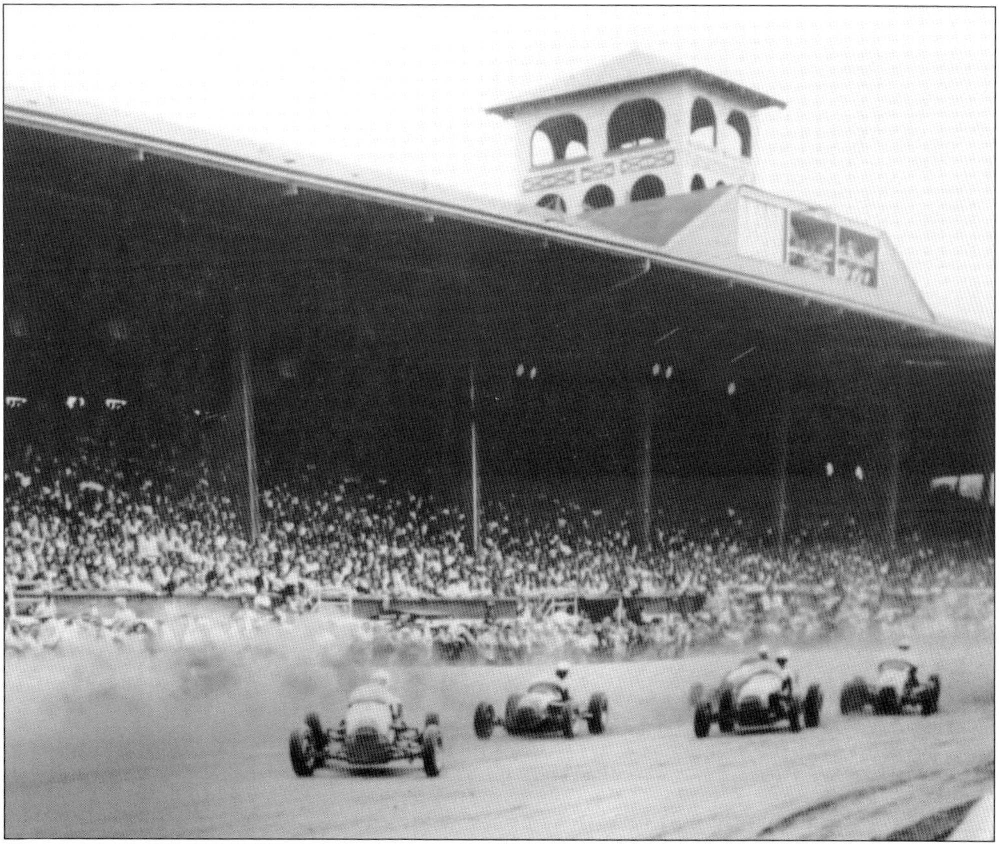

Automobile racing joined the fair lineup in 1919. Workers rushed to convert the track from the Friday horse races to Saturday automobile races by oiling the track and lining the curves with hay bale barriers. Racing are, from left to right, Jiggs Peters, Tommy Hinnershitz, Jimmy Musselman, and Mike McGill. (Courtesy of Stuart Lathrop and the LCAS.)

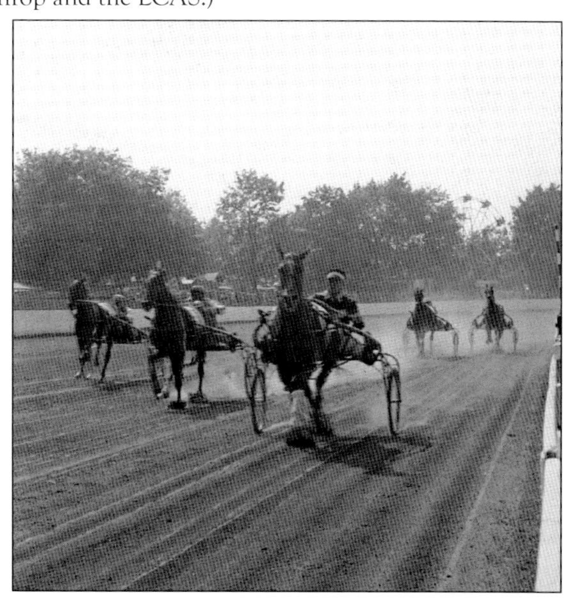

Known as the "farmer's sport," harness racing was a workaround to avoid the 1820 ban on racing and gambling. Since the horses and carts originally used in harness races were also used for farming, the races were exempted from the ban on betting events. This created a path for harness races to become the main draw at fairs and dirt tracks in Pennsylvania. (Courtesy of the Danner family.)

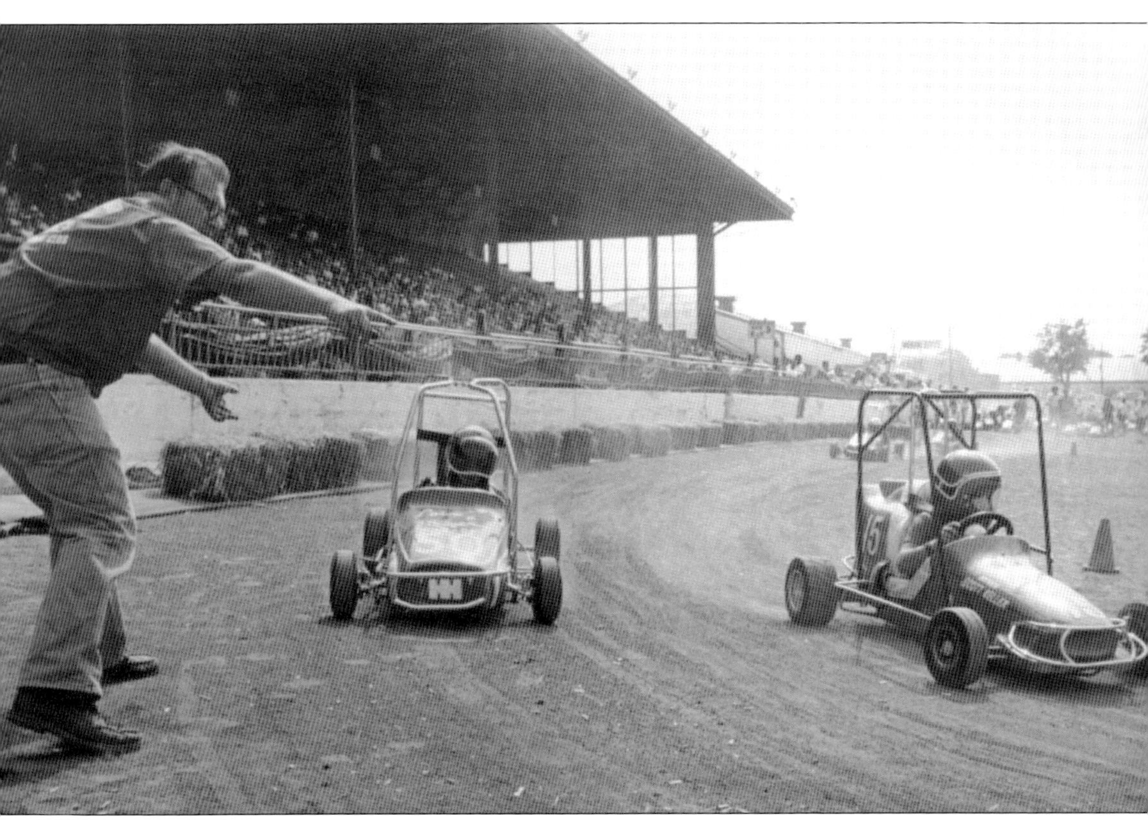

Here, young racers get their first taste of the dirt track as they race their midget cars around the half-mile track. The first automobile race held on the track at the Allentown Fairgrounds was on July 31, 1915. Joe Lambert, No. 11, won the first race while George Jessup, No. 7, won the last two races. All races that year were five miles. Racer Ira Vail won the first race of 1919; he would continue his career in racing and start at the Indianapolis 500 five times. Over the years, 18 more Indianapolis 500 drivers would compete in races at the Allentown Fairgrounds, including locals Mario Andretti and Tommy Hinnershitz, known as the "Flying Dutchman." In addition to the dirt track racing, micro-midget and three-quarter midget cars raced indoors on a concrete oval track set up inside the Agri-Plex over several winters in the 1960s.

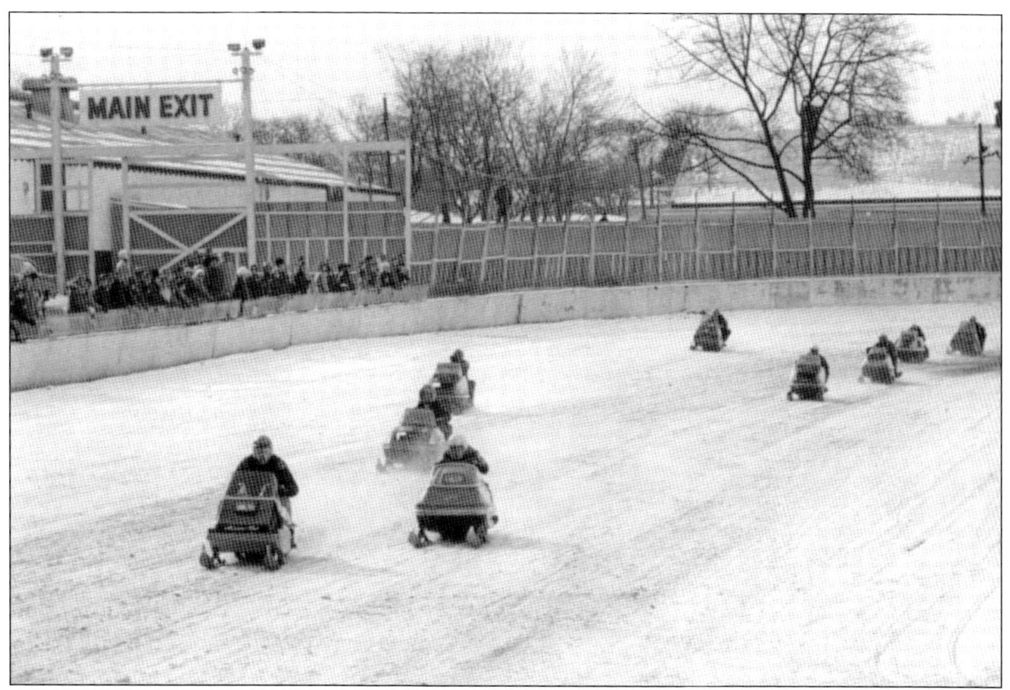

A snowmobile race was to be held at the fairgrounds' racetrack on Sunday, January 16, 1972, but the unseasonably warm weather postponed the event until January 30 (above). Plans had been made to make artificial snow for the event, but the weather in mid-January was too warm for that. Sponsored by the Allentown Kiwanis Club, the Kiwanis Lehigh Valley Snowmobile Races had 250–300 racers from Pennsylvania and neighboring states. Racers circled the track at speeds of 60 miles per hour on the front and back stretches in front of a full grandstand of spectators who paid $2 admission. The races ran again in 1973 (below) with the same uncooperative weather; the original January 28 date was without snow, so the races ran on February 11. (Below, courtesy of the Danner family.)

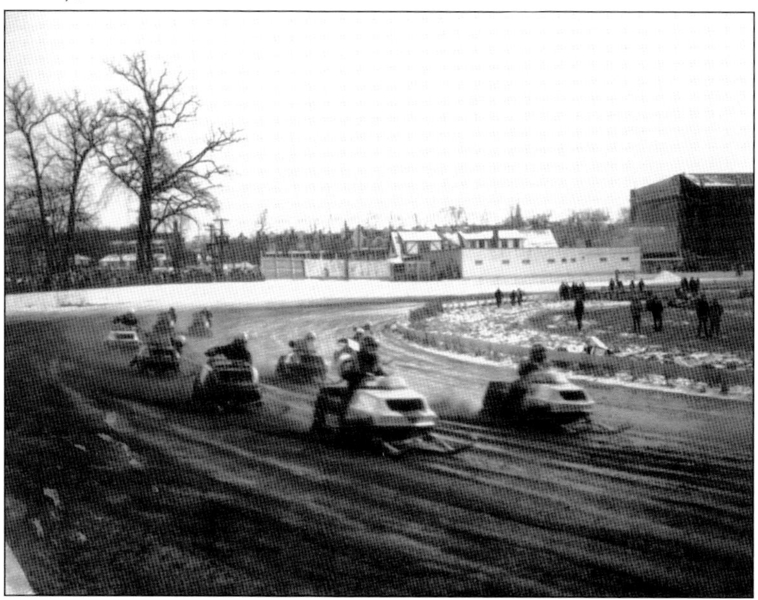

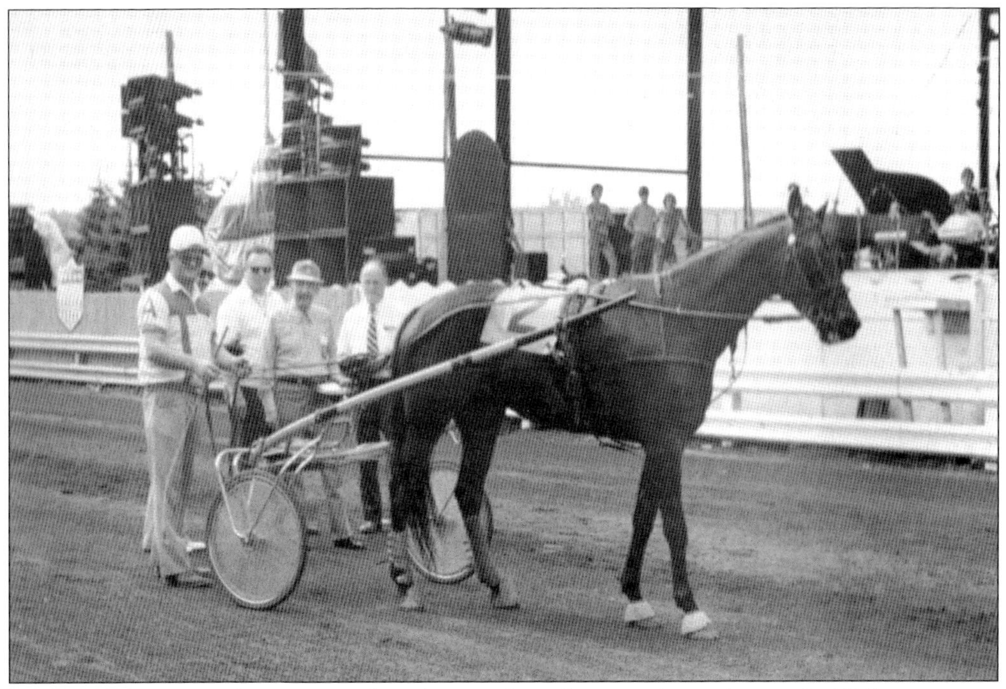

Five-year-old pacer Erik Brian raced at the grandstand racetrack on August 3, 1975, winning a second- and third-place finish. His owner, Alvin M. Lineweaver, was also the driver and trainer. The horse completed a one-mile trot that day in 2:07, the fastest time recorded at any fair that year. Both driver and horse earned awards for their performance. (Courtesy of the Danner family)

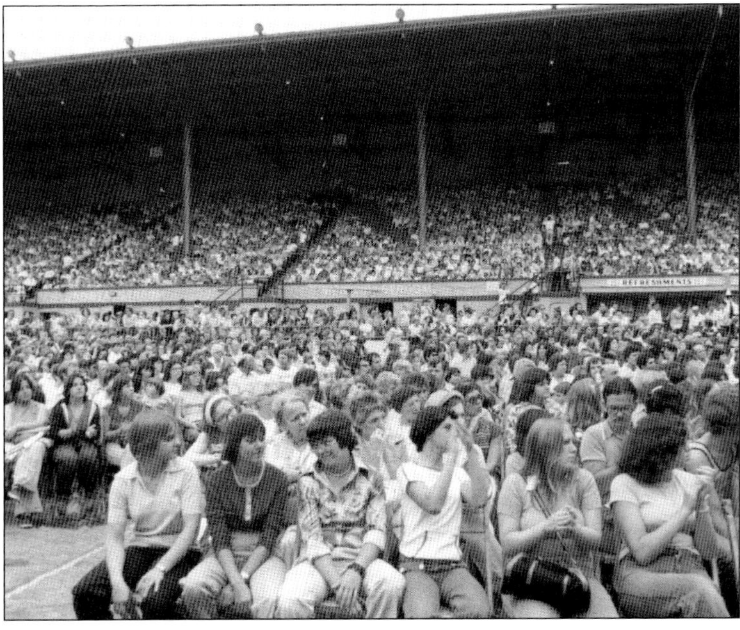

The 1970s brought year after year of big-name performers to the grandstand and stage. Tom Jones appeared in 1971 and 1975. Johnny Cash performed in 1969, 1970, and 1971. Dolly Parton joined the list of performers in 1977 and 1980. Kate Smith and heartthrobs such as Engelbert Humperdinck began to book the venue during the decade as well. These fans await one of the 1977 shows.

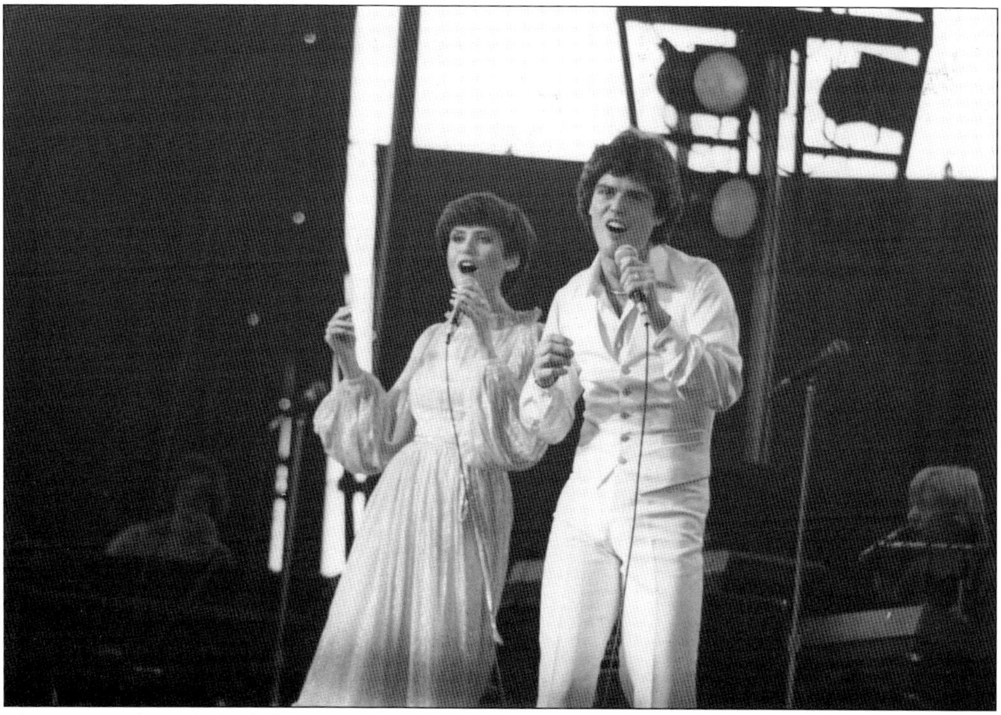

The Osmond family had already visited the fair four times by 1975, but the biggest cheers that year was for the new duo of Donnie and Marie. The brother and sister duo came back in 1976, sold out the grandstand in 1977, and returned for the 1978 show seen here. When they performed again in 1984, they were given a standing ovation just for walking on stage.

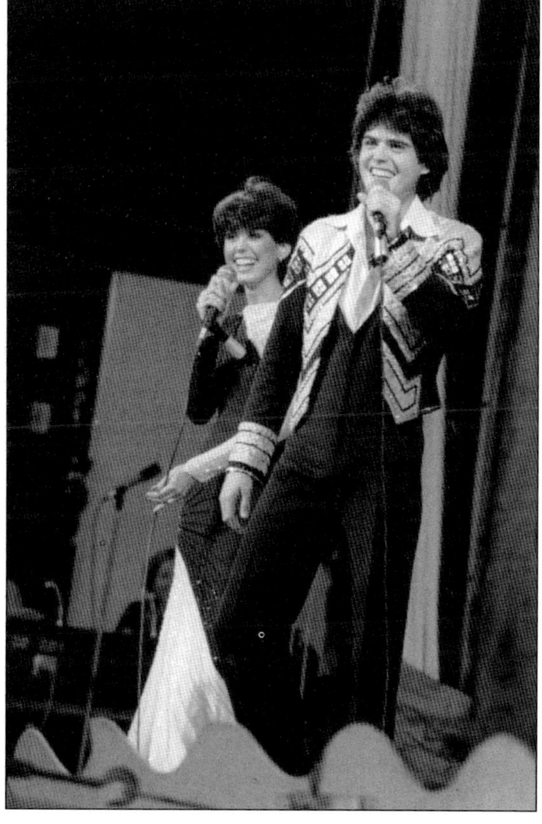

The Osmond family appeared at the fair more than any other performing act, totaling eight years and 28 shows. Given honorary Allentown citizenship, the family declared the Great Allentown Fair as their favorite fair in the country. From the performances of the Osmond brothers in the 1960s to the teen family in the 1970s that included sister Marie, Osmondmania flooded the grandstand for two decades.

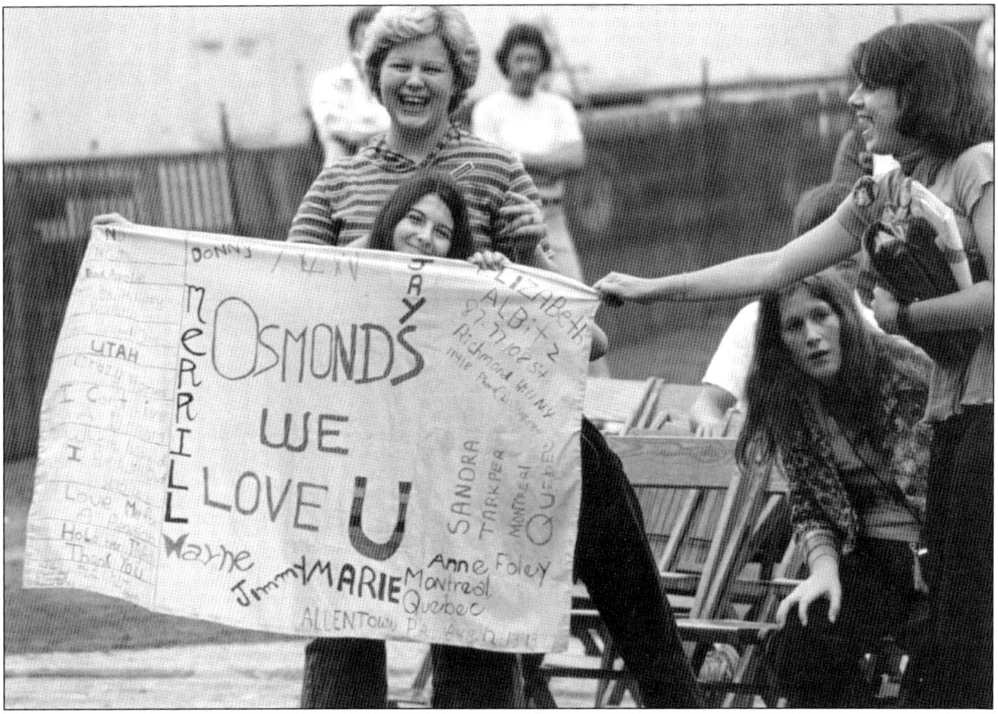

Fans are excited for the upcoming performance of Donnie and Marie Osmond in 1977. That year's performances on August 12 and 13 sold out of tickets, even with the additional track seating seen here that sold for $7. When they appeared on stage, Marie wore a long pink dress, and Donnie wore a white suit with pink sequin details to match his sister's outfit.

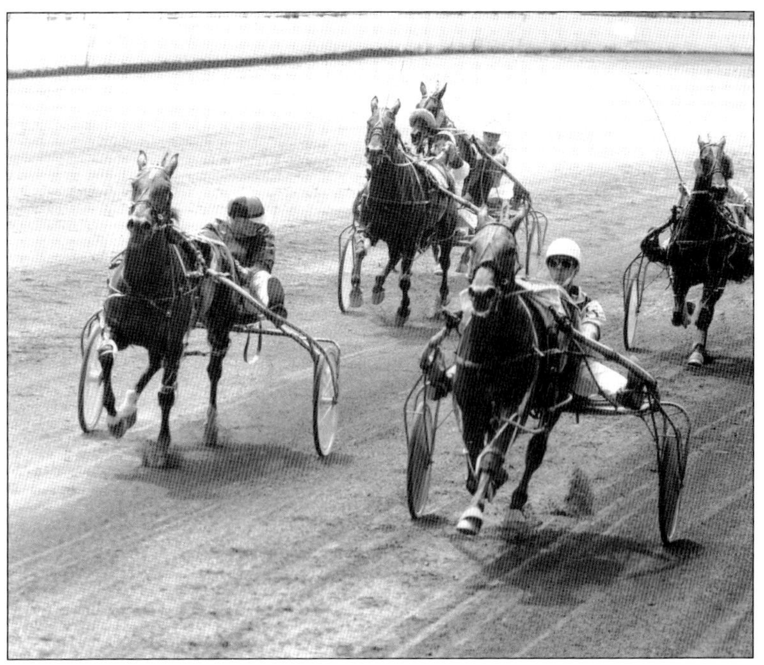

This is the last sulky race ever held at the fairgrounds on July 4, 1976, for America's bicentennial celebration. For more than 60 years, horse racing drew crowds to the fairgrounds track. Regular harness races ended in 1960. Horse racing returned from 1969 to 1975 before ending permanently at the fairgrounds. The interest in horse racing was over.

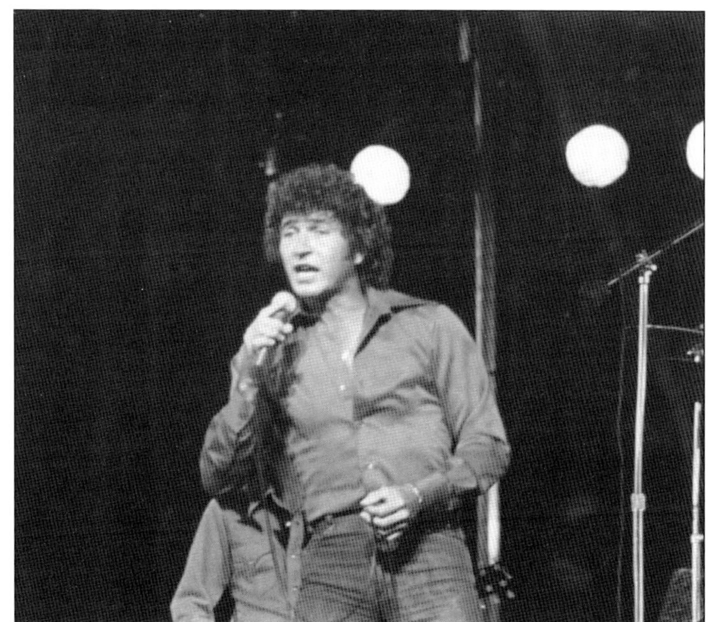

Singer and songwriter Mac Davis performed at the fair in 1972, 1975, and 1978. While in town, he also enjoyed some of the local golf courses, as Davis was an avid golfer. Davis performed his own songs at the fair, but he was known for writing hits for Elvis Presley, Kenny Rogers, and Glen Campbell, to name a few.

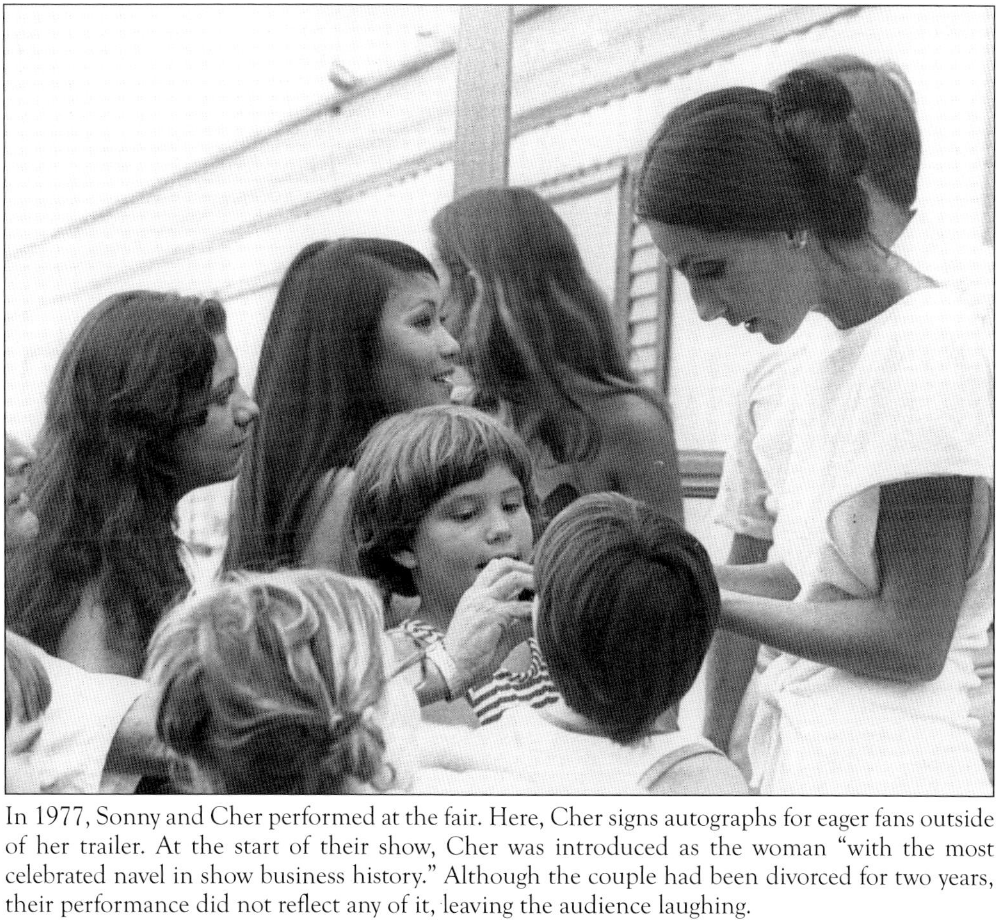

In 1977, Sonny and Cher performed at the fair. Here, Cher signs autographs for eager fans outside of her trailer. At the start of their show, Cher was introduced as the woman "with the most celebrated navel in show business history." Although the couple had been divorced for two years, their performance did not reflect any of it, leaving the audience laughing.

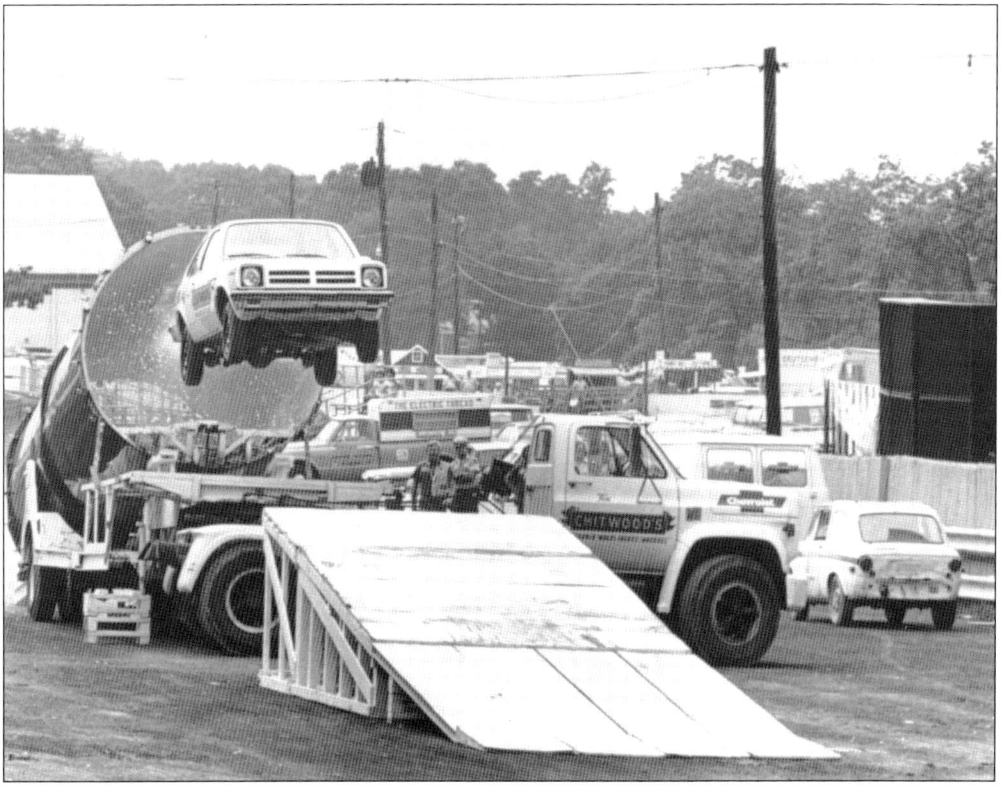

The Joie Chitwood Hell Drivers entertained audiences with death-defying stunts like this Chevy Vega launching into the air in 1978. Earlier on May 13, 1978, Joie Chitwood Jr. set a world record for driving a Chevrolet Chevette on two wheels for 5.6 miles. Stunt-car shows have been appearing at the fair since the 1930s.

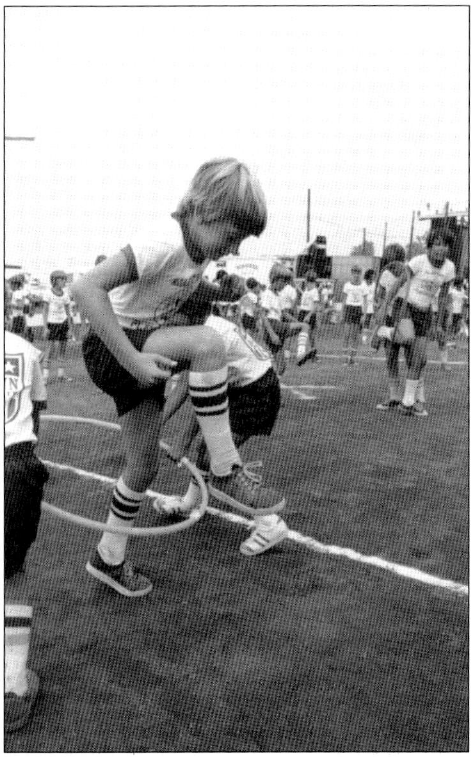

In 1913, Emma Shankweiler, Agnes Gaffney, Marian Ruhe, and Helen Schweyer of the Playground Association organized a competition between the city's playgrounds. This turned into Romper Day, a children's competition focusing on playground activities, dances, and maypoles, held during fair week at the fairgrounds. Here, boys are seen competing in a hoop event on August 4, 1975. The event still runs today but no longer coincides with fair week.

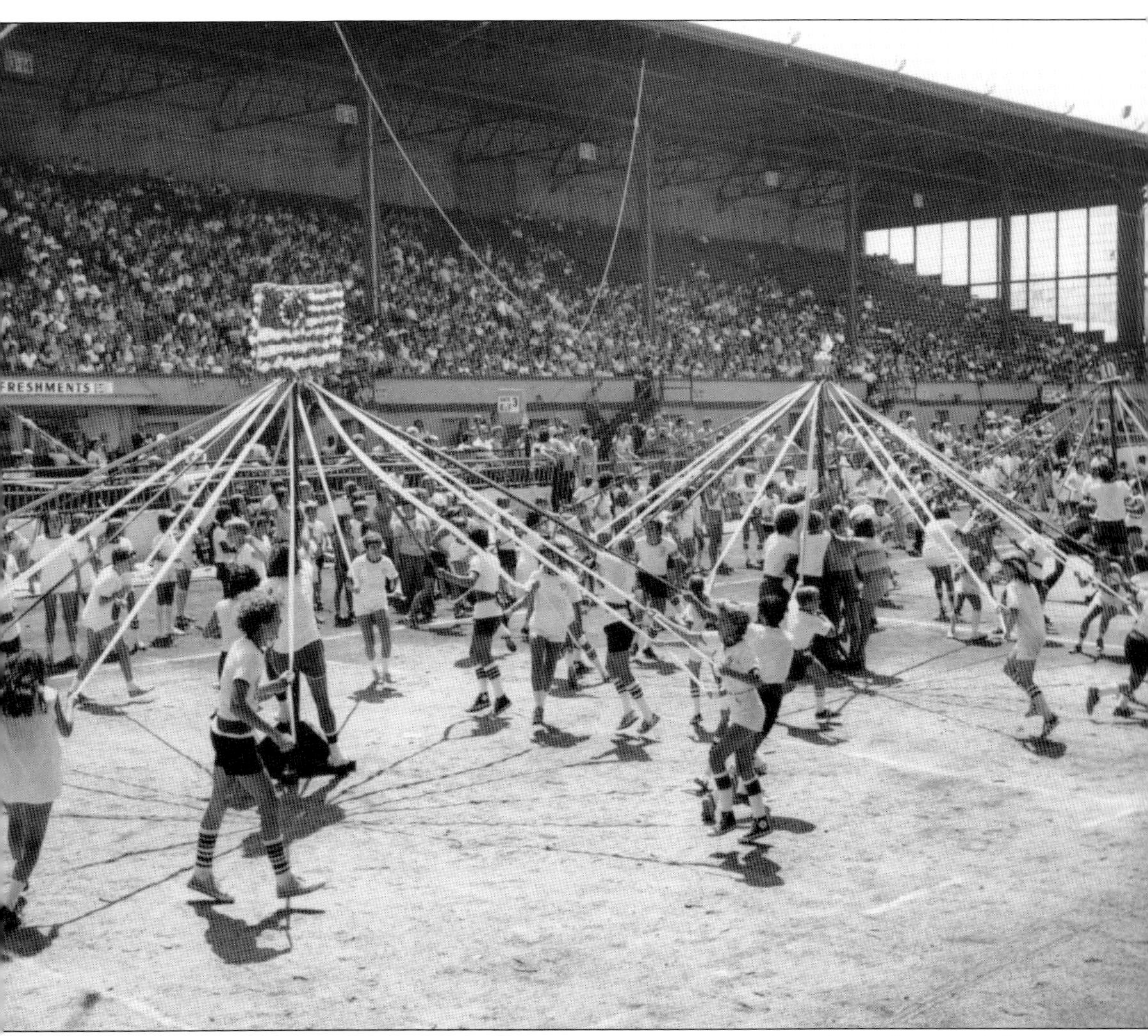

Romper Day participants display their skills in various events and traditional musical dance routines, with the maypole dance and weave as the crowning event. The groups in this photograph weave their maypoles in front of a full grandstand in 1975. Romper Day officially started in 1914 with a smaller preceding event held in 1913. More than 3,000 children participated in the 1914 Romper Day at the fairgrounds, where 4,600 "frankfurter sandwiches"—hot dogs—were distributed at the end of the competition. The event was inspired by the playground competition held the year before. Gen. Harry Trexler and his wife organized the 1914 event and named it Romper Day after the garments called rompers that the children wore. Held at the fairgrounds grandstand for more than 80 years, the program was renamed the Allentown Playground Program in 1993 and later moved to J. Birney Crum Stadium, where it continues today.

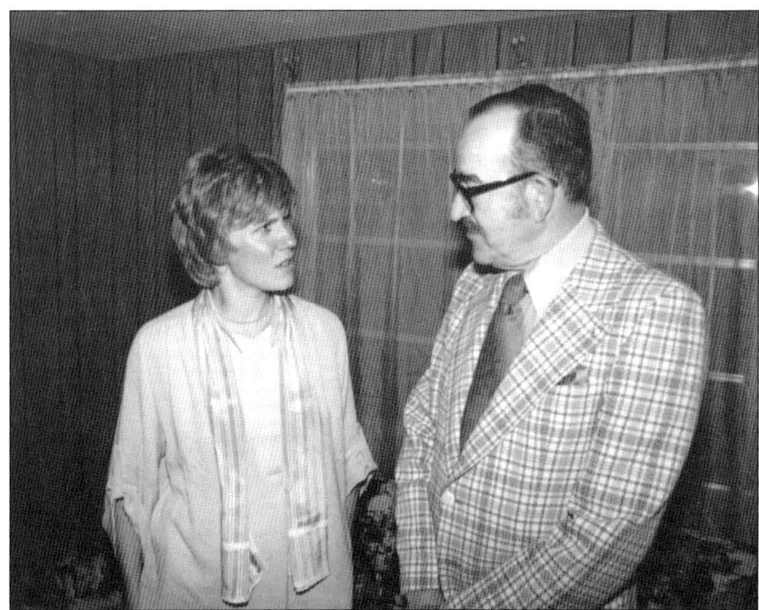

Anne Murray (left) performed at the fair on September 1, 1979. Here, she talks with Martin Ritter (right), the general manager of the fair at that time. Murray won a Grammy that year for Best Female Singer of the Year. She performed two shows that day at the fairgrounds, and sang her 1978 Grammy-winning song "You Needed Me."

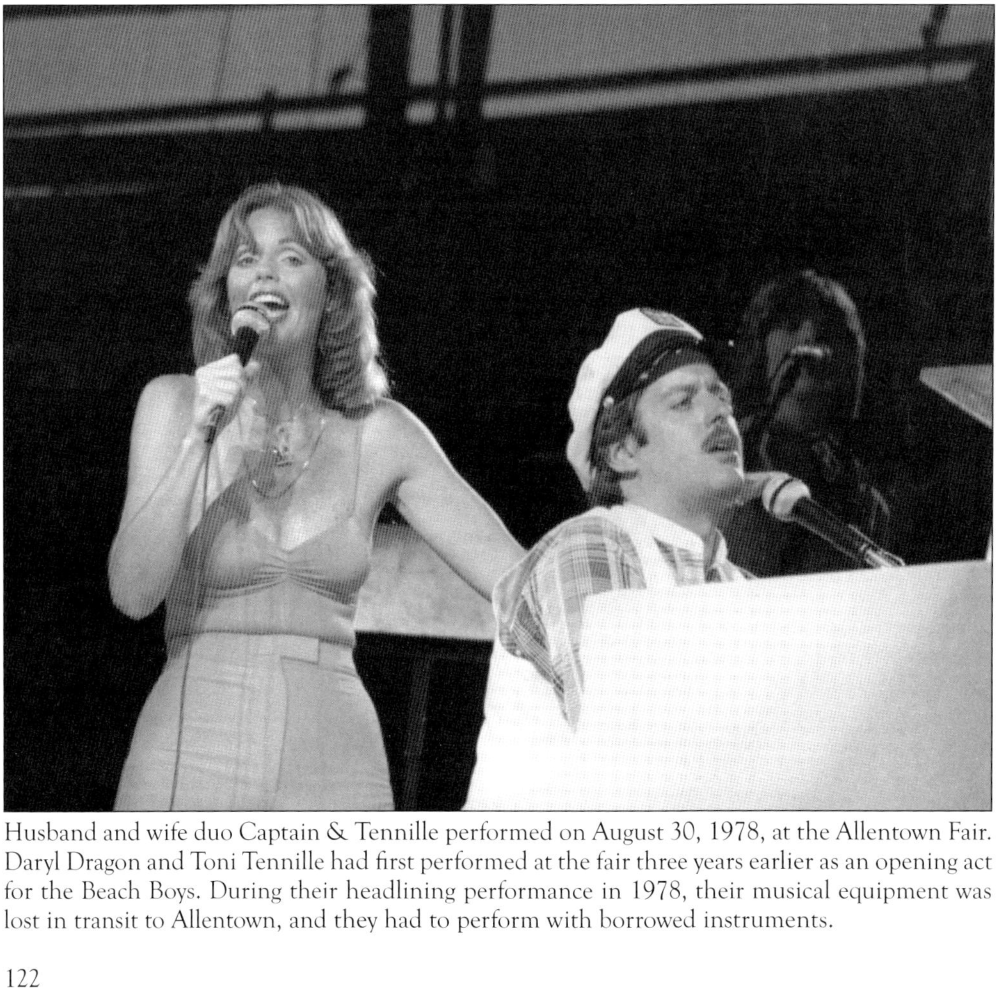

Husband and wife duo Captain & Tennille performed on August 30, 1978, at the Allentown Fair. Daryl Dragon and Toni Tennille had first performed at the fair three years earlier as an opening act for the Beach Boys. During their headlining performance in 1978, their musical equipment was lost in transit to Allentown, and they had to perform with borrowed instruments.

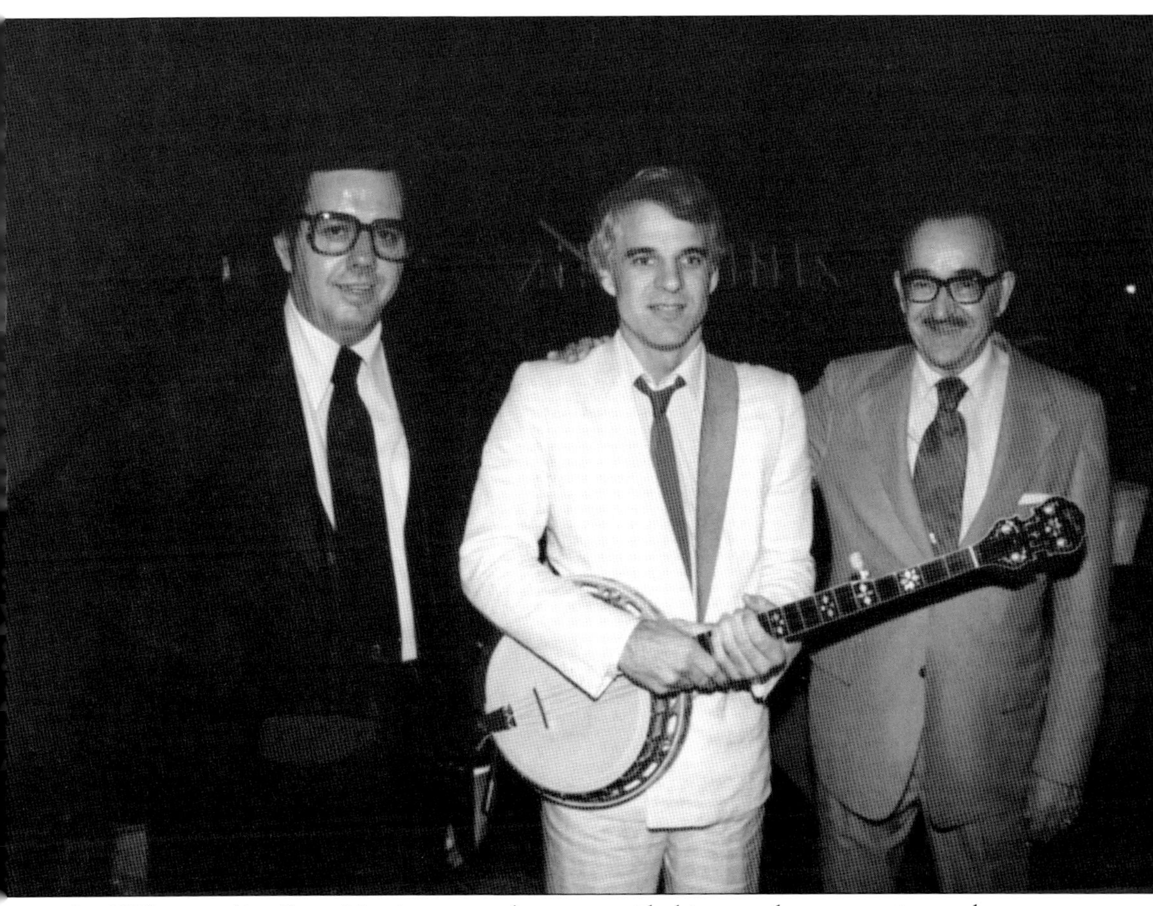

In 1979, comedian Steve Martin was ready to put aside his comedy tour routine and turn to movies. As he toured that year, the Great Allentown Fair was on his list of stops. He arrived at the fair on September 3, 1979, and set a fair record by selling 17,128 tickets for his two performances that day. Martin arrived at the fairgrounds ill, and during his first show, it was clear that he was not feeling well. With only a few hours between shows, Martin was hesitant to return to the stage for the second show that evening. Martin Ritter stepped in and persuaded the performer to return to the stage for the second show. Here, Steve Martin (center) stands with Martin Ritter (right) as he receives some encouragement. A local woman even volunteered to wash Martin's well-known white suit between performances after he had sweated so heavily due to his ailment. Martin's record sales stood for six years before being broken.

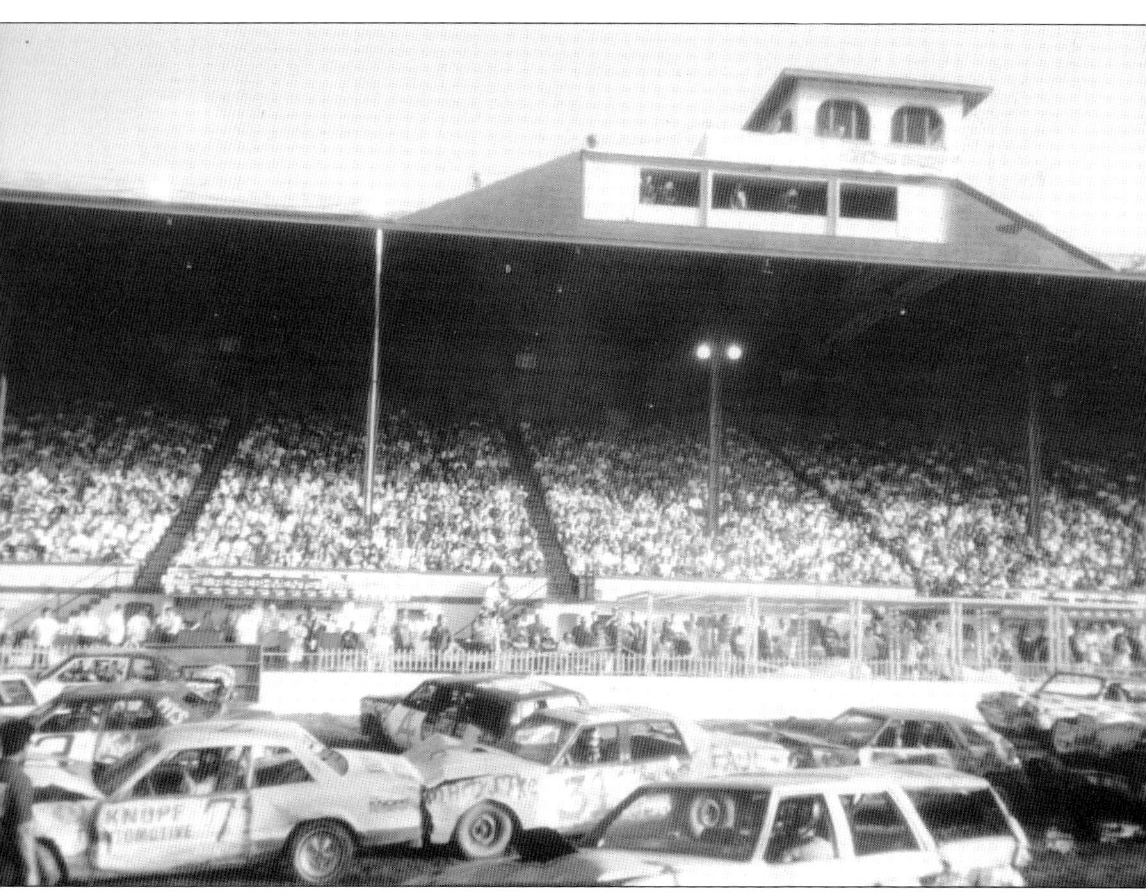

The popular demolition derby first appeared at the fairgrounds racetrack in 1969. Drivers build crowd enthusiasm with themed cars and antics as they crash and bump one another in an effort to remain the last car rolling. Roy Danner Sr., who served on the LCAS board of directors and operated Danner's concession stand, prepped and cleared the track before and after the event using his backhoe to remove the destroyed cars. One year, he found himself in the hospital during the days leading up to the derby. Feeling better, Danner checked himself out of the hospital without waiting for the doctor's release so that he would not miss the derby. As the unofficial end of summer, the Great Allentown Fair leads up to the Labor Day weekend with the derby as the final grandstand event on the last day. (Courtesy of the Danner family.)

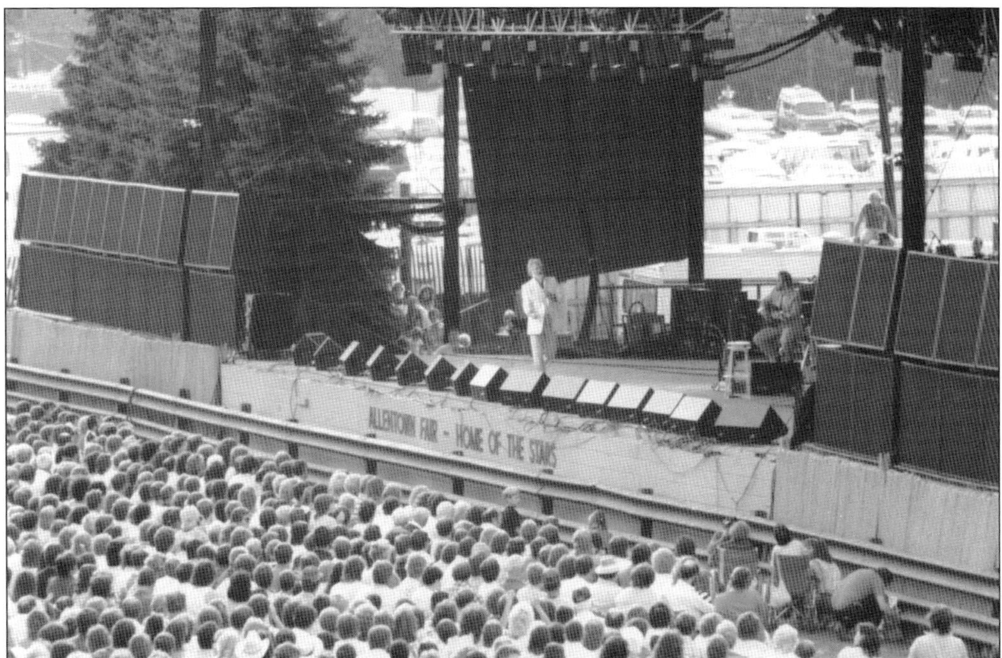

Another star who performed despite being ill was Kenny Rogers in 1985. Rogers had appeared at the fair twice before, but only in 1985 was he the headliner. His show broke the record set by Steve Martin by selling 17,822 tickets for two shows. Rogers brought awareness to world hunger by asking his fans to bring canned goods to donate to the local food bank. (Courtesy of the Danner family.)

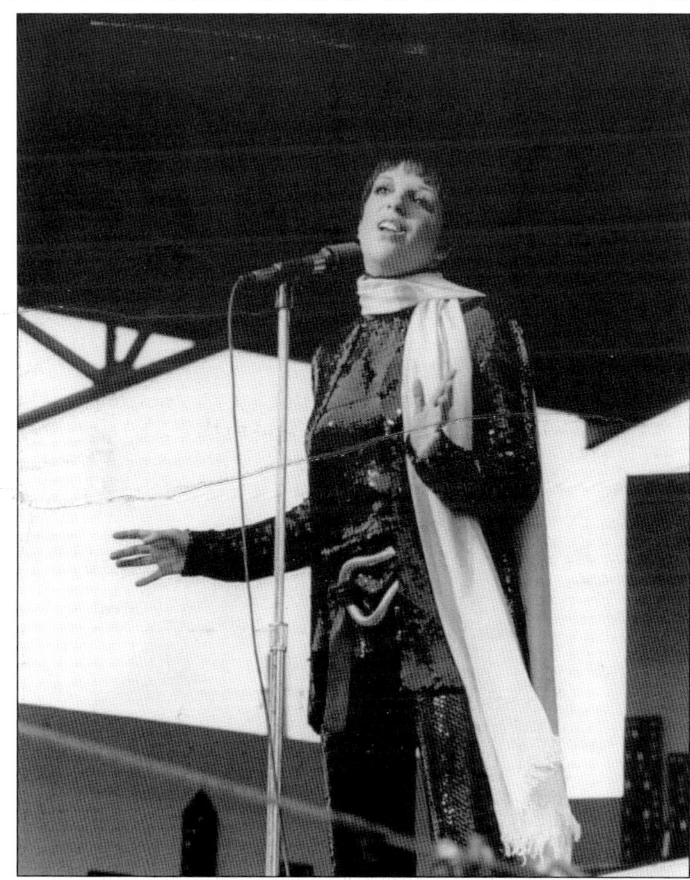

One of the most exciting visitors to the 1974 fair was Liza Minnelli. While at the fair, Minnelli got engaged to Jack Haley Jr. The engagement ring he offered to her that day was made of diamonds and sapphires. Later during her visit, she took the time to stop and watch Richard Nixon's resignation speech on television.

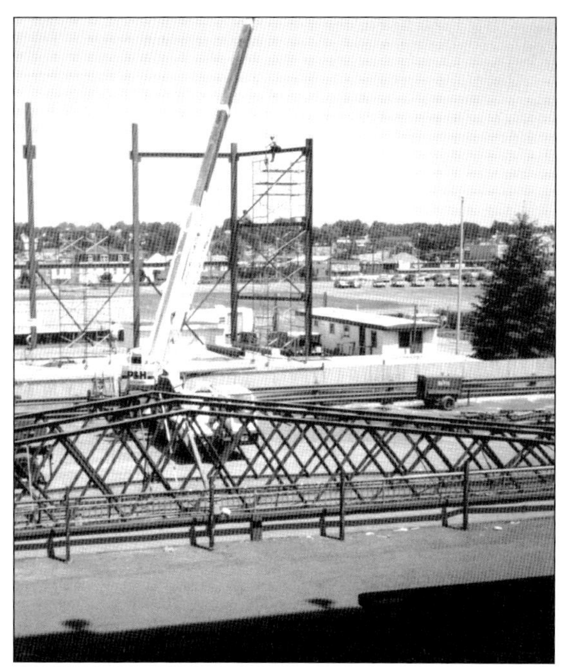

Below, in 1992, fair marketing director Bonnie Brosious (right) stands with Lee Butz (left) of Butz Construction as they look over the raising of the stage roof. Brosious explained that the fair could book more performers if they had higher rafters to accommodate their equipment. When Paula Abdul requested a higher roof to accommodate her rigging needed for aerialist dancers, Butz Construction was brought in to raise the ceiling to a maximum height of 50 feet at the peak. Anything higher would have required variances, and there was no time if they wanted Abdul to perform over the summer. Butz Construction met the deadline, and the show went on. By the time the fair came a few months later, James Taylor utilized the higher rafters to hang his speakers, later commenting that the sound at that stage was the best anywhere.

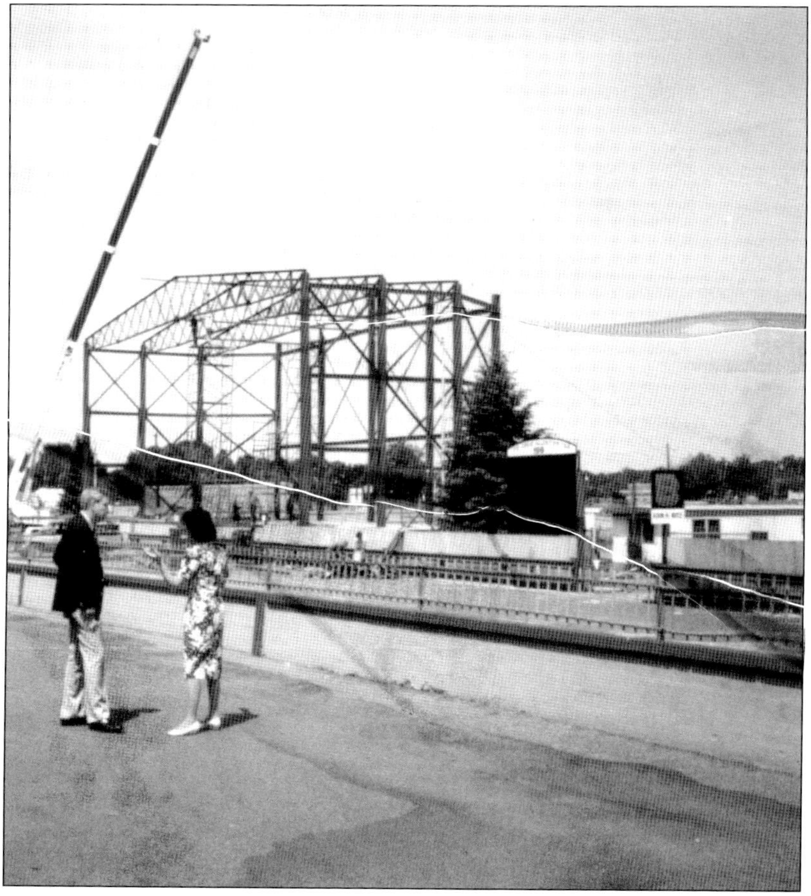

About the Lehigh County Agricultural Society

The Lehigh County Agricultural Society owns and operates the Allentown Fairgrounds and the Great Allentown Fair. Since its founding in 1852, the society has remained a nonprofit organization. The mission of the society is "the improvement and advancement of agriculture, horticulture, livestock, domestic and mechanical arts, and the entertainment of its membership and patrons." The fair serves to entertain and educate both agricultural and nonagricultural communities.

In addition to the annual Great Allentown Fair, the fairgrounds are active throughout the year. The events held year-round support the society's mission and contribute to the ongoing success of the fair. The Agri-Plex, an exhibition hall, hosts expos, community events, and trade shows throughout the year. In addition, the fairgrounds, spanning 46 acres in the city's picturesque west end, is a hub for dining, commerce, and tourism, thanks to its restaurants and the renowned Fairgrounds Farmers Market.

The Lehigh County Agricultural Society is located at 302 North Seventeenth Street, Allentown, Pennsylvania, 18104.